The Ultimate
Supernatural and
Philosophy

Pop Culture and Philosophy®

General Editor: George A. Reisch

VOLUME 1 *Dave Chappelle and Philosophy: When Keeping It Wrong Gets Real* (2021) Edited by Mark Ralkowski

VOLUME 2 *Neon Genesis Evangelion and Philosophy: That Syncing Feeling* (2022) Edited by Christian Cotton and Andrew M. Winters

VOLUME 3 *The Ultimate Supernatural and Philosophy: Saving People, Killing Things, the Family Business* (2022) Edited by Richard Greene

VOLUME 4 *Dark Souls and Philosophy* (2022) Edited by Nicolas Michaud

VOLUME 5 *Pokémon and Philosophy* (2022) Edited by Nicolas Michaud

VOLUME 6 *Queen and Philosophy* (2022) Edited by Jared Kemling and Randall E. Auxier

VOLUME 7 *Punk and Philosophy* (2022) Edited by Richard Greene and Joshua Heter

VOLUME 8 *Better Call Saul and Philosophy* (2022) Edited by Joshua Heter and Brett Coppenger

VOLUME 9 *Asimov's Foundation and Philosophy* (2023) Edited by Joshua Heter and Josef Simpson

VOLUME 10 *Warren Zevon and Philosophy* (2023) Edited by John MacKinnon

For full details of all Pop Culture and Philosophy® books, and all Open Universe® books, visit www.carusbooks.com

Pop Culture and Philosophy®

The Ultimate *Supernatural* and Philosophy

Saving People, Killing Things, the Family Business

Edited by

RICHARD GREENE

OPEN UNIVERSE
Chicago

Volume 3 in the series, Pop Culture and Philosophy®, edited by George A. Reisch

To find out more about Open Universe and Carus Books, visit our website at www.carusbooks.com.

Printed and bound in the United States of America. Printed on acid-free paper.

The Ultimate Supernatural *and Philosophy: Saving People, Killing Things, the Family Business*

ISBN: 978-1-63770-010-5

This book is also available as an e-book (978-1-63770-011-2).

Library of Congress Control Number: 2021941769

For Pippen M. Robison

Contents

Thanks   ix

Part I

"What's done is done. All that matters now,
all that's ever mattered, is that we're together.
So shut up and drink your beer."   1

1. Human, All Too Human
   A.G. HOLDIER   3

2. The Winchesters' Revolt Against the Divine
   Plan
   EMMA STEELE   11

3. Why Do I Have to Be Some Kind of Hero?
   ANDREA ZANIN   21

4. A Muscle Car and a Mythic Quest
   CHERISE HUNTINGFORD   35

Part II

"Every soul here is a monster. This is where they
come to prey upon each other for all eternity."   53

5. Could Hell Be Any Worse than Doc Benton's
   Immortality?
   HEINRIK HELLWIG   55

6. How the Hell Are We Supposed to Kill an Idea?
   NUR BANU SIMSEK   75

Contents

7. More Mothers, Lovers, and Other Monsters
   PATRICIA L. BRACE   85

Part III

"Dude, you were hallucinating sheep on the road."   99

8. Which Brother Is the Good One?
   GERALD BROWNING   101

9. God the Programmer Is Dead
   MICHELLE DEVRIES   111

10. Cas Is Family
    DARCI DOLL   119

11. Why Sacrifice Yourself?
    GERALD BROWNING   135

Part IV

*"There's no higher power; there's no God.
There's just chaos and violence and random,
unpredictable evil that comes out of nowhere."*   147

12. Finally Free
    TRIP MCCROSSIN   149

13. Does God Have the Right to Destroy the
    Universe?
    GALEN A. FORESMAN   169

14. Baby's Identity
    DARCI DOLL   179

15. God Is Good (Chuck Not So Much)
    JOSEPH L. GRAVES JR.   191

The Lore   203

Team Free Will   207

Index   211

Thanks

Working on this project has been a pleasure, in no small part because of the many fine folks who have assisted me along the way. In particular, a debt of gratitude is owed to David Ramsay Steele at Carus Books, the contributors to this volume, and the Department of Political Science and Philosopy at Weber State University. Finally, I'd like to thank those family members, students, friends, and colleagues with whom I've had fruitful and rewarding conversations on various aspects of all things *Supernatural* as it relates to philosophical themes.

Part I

"What's done is done. All that matters now, all that's ever mattered, is that we're together. So shut up and drink your beer."

1
Human, All Too Human

A.G. HOLDIER

When the Winchester brothers first meet Chuck Shurley (and "convince" him that his stories about their adventures are real), he gulps down a glass of liquor and shrugs, saying "Well, there's only one explanation: obviously, I'm a god" ("The Monster at the End of This Book"). Although the boys scoff at the notion, Chuck continues, asking "How else do you explain it? I write things and then they come to life? Yeah, no—I'm definitely a god. A cruel, cruel, capricious god."

With only a couple of hints along the way, Chuck's claim to divinity is eventually confirmed as more than just a joke seven seasons (or one hundred and sixty episodes) later when God reappears and asks the angel Metatron to help write his autobiography ("Don't Call Me Shurley"). As the Scribe of God argues with Chuck about the latter's disappearance (and his apparent reluctance to stand against his sister, who was then threatening to destroy and re-make God's Creation), Metatron pleads with the Almighty, insisting that:

> You're wrong about humanity. They are your greatest creation because they're *better than you are*. Yeah, sure, they're weak and they cheat and steal and destroy and disappoint . . . but they also *give* and *create* and they sing and dance and *love*. And above all, they *never* give up. *But you do.*

In response, Chuck simply clears his throat and turns back to his computer screen. In light of the show's conclusion several seasons later, Metatron's words here are prophetic: humanity in general, and the Winchesters specifically, indeed persist, even managing to eventually defeat Chuck himself. But in this chapter, I want to argue not only that the angel was right, but that his words capture the point of *Supernatural* in its entirety: human beings, despite our flaws, are capable of greatness—perhaps even greatness beyond that of God's.

And to really understand this, we'll need to visit a writer who lived not in Kripke's Hollow, Ohio, at the turn of the 21st century, but in Europe during the late 1800s: the philosopher Friedrich Nietzsche.

Our Father, Who Aren't in Heaven

Although *Supernatural* begins with Sam and Dean hunting monsters like vampires and werewolves, the show quickly introduces more theological elements like demons and angels (and Chuck) as the brothers are revealed to be caught in a divine plot to bring about the end of the world. Having eventually defeated everyone from Satan to the archangel Michael to The Darkness (God's sister) and more in previous seasons, the last chapter of the Winchesters' story sees them finally squaring off against the entity ultimately responsible for the suffering and evil they've challenged throughout the show: God himself.

After learning that Chuck has secretly been manipulating them for the entirety of their lives, pushing them towards a confrontation where one brother is destined to kill the other, Sam and Dean reject this Divine plan and set out to, instead, attack and dethrone God.

In the late nineteenth century, Friedrich Nietzsche told a (very loosely) similar story; in Book Three of his 1882 work *The Gay Science*, Nietzsche tells of a "madman" running through a marketplace yelling:

> God is dead! God remains dead! And we have killed him! How can we console ourselves, the murderers of all murderers! The holiest and the mightiest thing the world has ever possessed has bled to death under our knives: who will wipe this blood from us? With what water could we clean ourselves? What festivals of atonement, what holy games will we have to invent for

ourselves? Is the magnitude of this deed not too great for us? Do we not ourselves have to become gods merely to appear worthy of it?

Ultimately, the madman realizes that his audience doesn't understand, so he throws up his hands and shouts "I come too early! My time is not yet!" and enters the church to instead pray for the dead (though Nietzsche suggests that it is actually *God* for whom the madman prays).

For Nietzsche, the "death of God" is not clearly a *literal* concept or event in history—he certainly did not envision an angelic showdown ending with a nephilim trying to blow up the Almighty—but is rather a *sociological* commentary on how humanity has developed. In *The Gay Science*, for example, Nietzsche considers how art and poetry (and, perhaps, television shows?) can not only give meaning to an individual person's life, but can help define entire cultures and collective ways of living. This is why Nietzsche's madman talks about the burdens and responsibilities that come in the wake of "God's demise": whereas previous cultures might have been defined by religious values or practices, a post-religious culture would need to invent a new sense of meaning for itself.

So, for Nietzsche, the rejection of God entails the rejection of many other things, but this comes as both an exciting challenge and an opportunity: in the absence of divine expectations, people can pursue and enjoy their lives as they desire, free from the restrictions of the culture (and even the deity) who might prevent them from becoming the person that they would otherwise be. Without Chuck around to write the story, the Winchesters (and everyone else) could be free to write their own endings—just as the brothers (especially Dean) desire.

Inherit the Earth

As Nietzsche explains in *The Gay Science*, to experience true freedom is to "no longer be ashamed before oneself," living and expressing oneself fully in each moment:

I want to learn more and more how to see what is necessary in things as what is beautiful in them—thus I will be one of those who

5

make things beautiful. *Amor fati*: let that be my love from now on! I do not want to wage war against ugliness. I do not want to accuse; I do not even want to accuse the accusers. Let looking away be my only negation! And, all in all and on the whole: some day I want only to be a Yes-sayer!

This *amor fati*—"love of fate," as opposed to a love of God— is a matter of a human saying "yes" to their circumstances without obligation, dread, or fear, no matter what those circumstances might be. It is the freedom to choose how you respond to a situation, even (and especially) when that situation seems hopelessly unavoidable.

Consider where the Winchesters find themselves in the final episodes of the series: after failing to prevent God from killing their friends (and watching Castiel sacrifice himself to save Dean's life), Jack and the brothers discover that they are literally the last creatures alive on Earth: Chuck has cleansed the planet to punish the Winchesters for rebelling against his intended story. Nevertheless, the surviving members of "Team Free Will 2.0" persist, poring through their lore library and chasing down whatever thin leads might present themselves in an attempt to still defeat God. When this ultimately brings them to the final confrontation on the lakeshore, Chuck physically beats Sam and Dean to near-death, repeatedly insisting that the brothers give up and "just stay down" ("Inherit the Earth"). Each time, the Winchesters defiantly get to their feet. No matter how bleak their outlook (and how irrelevant their resistance might seem in the face of omnipotence), the brothers stubbornly say "Yes" to their circumstances, not by waging war against God, but by letting Chuck exhaust his own Divine power against them.

Of course, the story quickly reveals what the Winchesters were actually doing: by using his energy to fight them, Chuck had unwittingly fed Jack a super-charged dose of God-power, allowing the young nephilim to withstand (and then absorb) the rest. The series sees its final villain defeated not by being killed or locked away, but by being depowered and sentenced to live out a human life. Moreover, God is not only *beaten*, but *replaced* by Jack (an angel-human hybrid); the world of *Supernatural* ends with a kind of humanity literally *becoming God*.

Carry On

In Section 10 of his book *Ecce Homo* (written in 1888 and published two decades later), Nietzsche calls his sense of *amor fati* his "formula for greatness in a human being," partly because he believed that the person who accepts their circumstances in the right way can be considered great. However, the *right* way for Nietzsche is also connected to his understanding of how your own strength and willpower can bear on *shaping* your circumstances. In the rare, but best-case scenario, Nietzsche says that humanity can give birth to something greater than itself: the *Übermensch* or *overman* who has the strength to create new values for themselves (and, by extension, other people).

Much like his madman in *The Gay Science*, Nietzsche has the title character of *Thus Spake Zarathustra* (published in segments between 1883 and 1885) preach about the ramifications of the death of God, but he begins his first sermon (in Chapter 3 of the prologue) by shouting to a crowd: "*I teach you the overman.* Human being is something that must be overcome. What have you done to overcome him?" In the following pages, Zarathustra explains not only that this overman "is the meaning of the earth . . . and . . . *shall be* the meaning of the earth," but that typical humanity is "a rope fastened between animal and overman—a rope over an abyss." In the absence of God (following his death), one might be tempted to think that nihilistic hopelessness is the only option; against this, Nietzsche says that the best people can offer us a new hope and, in so doing, imbue all of humanity with meaning; as he says, "What is great about human beings is that they are a bridge and not a purpose: what is lovable about human beings is that they are a *crossing over* and a *going under*." Put differently, by precipitating Jack's ascension, the "mud-monkeys" of commonplace humanity can be understood as ultimately valuable in themselves.

Despite its ultimately cosmic scope (spanning multiple timelines, planes of existence, and even dimensions by its end), *Supernatural* repeatedly hones in on the unrepentant humanity of its main characters. Although Sam and Dean have repeatedly cheated death, escaped Hell, Heaven, and elsewhere, defeated scores of monsters far more powerful than themselves, and saved the world on more than one occasion, they nevertheless think of themselves as little more than brothers maintaining the "family business." Even after Jack's ascension, Dean still assumes that the three of them will return home to continue life as normal—despite the fact that Jack is, at that point, literally God.

And let's not forget *how* Jack became God: by following through on a plan originally concocted by none other than Adam himself, the first human being ever created by Chuck ("Unity"). From beginning to end, Jack (as *Supernatural*'s overman) is birthed, taught, and transformed into his ultimately divine state via the mundane "bridges" of his human mother, his human friends, and his human great-great-great-(etc.)-grandfather.

At the end of the road, it's unlikely that Nietzsche was thinking about God's death in the same way as the writers of *Supernatural*—that's to say, he clearly did not think of it as a *literal* death of a literal deity. But this means that we can view the television show as a kind of parable, aesthetically demonstrating familiar Nietzschean ideals of freedom, authenticity, and the power of humanity. The Winchesters' fight to be free of God's schemes is ultimately not that different from the fight to be able to genuinely express yourself and not only discover, but *make* a meaningful existence out of the difficulties of daily life. The fact that Sam and Dean do so alongside the Grim Reaper, the Devil, and the remaining Heavenly Host is just a matter of making exciting television. And, in a similar way, the *amor fati* doesn't mean that nothing bad will ever happen; instead, it's a matter of, like the Winchesters, making the right choice about how to handle the bad when it comes.

Human, All Too Human

This returns us to Metatron's appeal to God (years before Chuck reveals himself as the show's true villain): by pleading with the Almighty to recognize the beauty of humanity's willfulness to continue on, the Scribe of God was appealing to something like Nietzsche's understanding of the nature of human value—we are beautiful, not just for what we are, but for what we continually choose to be (and will one day become). For all our weaknesses—despite being, in Lucifer's words to Gabriel "broken, flawed abortions" ("Hammer of the Gods")—we stubbornly, perpetually carry on. As the erstwhile Trickster put it to his satanic brother: "Damn right, they're flawed: but a lot of them *try* to do better." The freshly divine Jack reiterates this sentiment in the penultimate episode of the show, explaining to Sam and Dean how, going forward, "People won't need to pray to me or to sacrifice to me . . . I learned from you and my mother and Castiel that when people have to be their best, they can be. And that's what to believe in."

So, in a time when spandex-wearing superheroes dazzle movie theaters and television screens with their powers, *Supernatural*'s heroes are just a couple of normal guys driving around in their dad's old car. Notably, the final episode ("Carry On,") features no angels, no demons, no Jack or Chuck, and almost no other named characters beyond Sam and Dean: it is one last hurrah of the Winchester brothers using their father's journal to save some people by hunting some things. After fifteen seasons of magical artifacts, primordial entities, and fateful plotlines surpassing biblical proportions, the story of Sam and Dean Winchester (and, for that matter, Chuck) proudly ends in a profoundly *human* (all-too-human) place.[1]

---

[1] An earlier version of this chapter was originally published in *The Prindle Post* under the title "What Would Nietzsche Think of Sam and Dean Winchester?," available online at <www.prindlepost.org/2020/12/what-would-nietzsche-think-of-sam-and-dean-winchester>.

2
The Winchesters' Revolt Against the Divine Plan

EMMA STEELE

In an epic struggle lasting fifteen seasons, Sam and Dean Winchester repeatedly refuse to accept their destiny. The brothers reject all the roles that are chosen for them, and to the end are a symbol of rebellion and free will. This goes against the typical theme of most shows or movies, especially ones featuring heroes who fight against monsters.

With Marvel or DC superheroes for instance, the good guy must usually accept his role in the battle to ultimately defeat the bad guy. However, in *Supernatural*, the Winchester brothers constantly express doubts about what they're doing, call their destiny into question, or depart from their assigned mission.

In the Season One finale, Sam lets the Yellow-Eyed Demon go (their main mission until that point was to kill him) in favor of saving his family. When the angels make a plan for the brothers to become vessels for Michael and Lucifer, Dean creates "Team Free Will" and they fight against the angelic plan (Season Five, "The Song Remains the Same"). Over the course of the show, the two brothers continually refuse to accept it when one of them dies, preferring instead to make a deal or find a loophole to bring the other brother back. The series culminates in the most emphatic assertion of free will possible—the decision to kill God and never have any divine rule over their lives again.

11

All According to Plan

Think of a million random acts of chance that let John and Mary be born, to meet, to fall in love, to have the two of you. Think of the million random choices that you make, and yet how each and every one of them brings you closer to your destiny. Do you know why that is? Because it's not random. It's not chance. It's a plan that is playing itself out perfectly. Free will's an illusion, Dean.

—MICHAEL, Season Five, "The Song Remains the Same"

There are plenty of times when the Winchesters' fate seems to be sealed, especially with the introduction of the character Chuck. At first it appears that Chuck is a prophet of the Lord, writing down the events in the lives of the Winchesters as or before they occur. However, it's later revealed that Chuck is in fact God himself. When he writes a story, it actually happens of necessity; it can't fail to happen. Chuck has been creating exciting stories for his own entertainment, thereby creating and causing all the events of the Winchesters' lives. (The fact that Chuck is not a very good creative writer adds a nice touch of humor.) This enrages both brothers, especially Dean, who eventually decides to kill Chuck because of this.

CHUCK: Lookit, the . . . the . . . the gathering storm, the gun, the . . . the father killing his own son. This is Abraham and Isaac. This is epic!

DEAN: Wait. What are you saying?

SAM: He's saying he's been playing us. This whole time.

CHUCK: Come on.

SAM: Our entire lives. Mom, Dad . . . everything. This is all you because you wrote it all, right? Because . . . Because what? Because we're your favorite show? Because we're part of your story? (Season Fourteen, "Moriah")

It's a horrible realization for the brothers that their entire lives were predetermined. Defeating Yellow-Eyes, Lucifer, Metatron, Crowley—these supposed victories were all just engineered by Chuck, stories for his entertainment. Weirdly, all the way back in Season Four when we first meet Chuck and think he's merely a prophet, he tells us this in his very first conversation with the Winchesters:

> CHUCK: Well, there's only one explanation. Obviously I'm a god.
>
> SAM: You're not a god.
>
> CHUCK: How else do you explain it? I write things and then they come to life. Yeah, no, I'm definitely a god. A cruel, cruel, capricious god. The things I put you through—the physical beatings alone.
>
> DEAN: Yeah, we're still in one piece.
>
> CHUCK: I killed your father. I burned your mother alive. And then you had to go through the whole horrific deal again with Jessica.
>
> SAM: Chuck . . .
>
> CHUCK: All for what? All for the sake of literary symmetry. I toyed with your lives, your emotions, for . . . entertainment. (Season Four, "The Monster at the End of This Book")

It's entirely possible that at this point in the show, the scriptwriters had not yet decided that Chuck would in fact turn out to be Yahweh, the Almighty Creator of the Universe (and, as it turns out, of myriads of other universes too), or that this God would have a sister with whom he didn't see eye-to-eye. However, in a masterfully successful example of retconning, this small comic-relief side character eventually turns into the most powerful and manipulative being of all time.

In Chuck's first episode, the brothers discover that no matter what they do, no matter what decision or free choice they believe they're making, the prophecies of Chuck/God seem to come true in detail, even when they try to subvert them (in one instance, Dean is told he will have a bacon cheeseburger for lunch, and therefore orders a tofu burger instead. But the waitress makes a mistake and he ends up eating a bacon cheeseburger anyway).

Exactly how God does this is not made clear. We do learn that Sam or Dean sometimes do things that God just doesn't expect, so things can sometimes happen contrary to Chuck's intentions. In the Season Fourteen finale Sam shoots God, and Chuck wasn't able to predict that action ahead of time, or its later negative consequences. When Death moves against God in Season Fifteen, Chuck is unaware of the plan for some time, thus proving him not to be omniscient. In fact, Chuck is very close to the traditional God of the Old Testament—a creator of the universe and an immensely powerful being who occasionally interacts in the world, usually quite impulsively and emotionally, sometimes having regrets and changing his mind, not like the God of the theologians, who can accomplish anything and perfectly foresee everything. Chuck can create and change reality, but can also be surprised or have regrets about things.

The fact that bigger powers are at play in the universe doesn't in itself negate the possibility of free will. There are many times when Zachariah, Chuck, Loki, and many others have set great events in motion, and the brothers are powerless to stop it. But being powerless doesn't mean you lose the ability to think for yourself or make decisions, using your own will.

Compatibilism

In the mind there is no absolute or free will, but the mind is determined to this or that volition by a cause, which is also determined by another cause, and this again by another, and so on ad infinitum.

—BENEDICT SPINOZA, *Ethics*, p. 76

The kind of "free will" referred to in the *Supernatural* scripts is not quite the same as the issue of free will and determinism most often discussed by philosophers. You might think that if someone secretly interferes in your life to make it come out a certain way, this takes away your free will, but this is not the concern of most philosophers who talk about free will. When philosophers discuss free will, they're talking about the ability to choose individual actions.

In philosophy, the fundamental threat to free will is determinism. This is the idea that the precise state of the universe at any one moment is the only possible outcome, given the precise state of the universe at the previous moment and the laws of nature that are in place. According to this view, there are no loose joints in the chain of cause and effect. The precise state of the universe right now is the only possible outcome of the precise state of the universe a billion years ago. Rigid causal laws secure each successive outcome.

Some philosophers take the view that determinism is compatible with free will—a theory known as compatibilism. The argument is that no one is stopping you exercising your freedom of choice, so it can't matter to you that causal necessity along with the laws of nature ensure that only one outcome is possible. Compatibilism is not as popular as it used to be, partly because quantum physics tells us that the world just is not deterministic; there is genuine randomness, and "what happens next" is not strictly determined, but only made somewhat probable, by "what just happened." This issue of strict physical determinism is not directly covered in *Supernatural*, only indirectly alluded to.

Although free will is sometimes used colloquially to mean the freedom to do whatever you like, the philosophical term is more strict—free will means the power of an individual to make conscious choices purely of their own volition. This is freedom of decision, not necessarily freedom of action. When Sam and Dean try and fail to kill Lucifer in "Abandon All Hope" (Season Five), the fact that they failed doesn't negate the free choice they made in deciding to kill him. Whereas when Sam was possessed by Lucifer later on, he truly did not have any free will anymore—meaning, in this case, that he could not make independent choices.

Many philosophers believe that determinism and free will can coexist. The fact that greater powers design the happenings of the universe doesn't necessarily nullify the existence of free will. Even if the ultimate destiny is decided, humans can potentially still make real free decisions within that.

For instance, when Zachariah and the angels insist that Sam and Dean fulfill their roles in becoming angel vessels so that the prophesied end of days can begin, Sam asks Dean why they should continue resisting them:

SAM: I saw your eyes. You were totally rockin' the "yes" back there. So, what changed your mind?

DEAN: Honestly? The damnedest thing. I mean, the world's ending. The walls are coming down on us, and I look over to you and all I can think about is, "This stupid son of a bitch brought me here." I just didn't want to let you down. I don't know if it's being a big brother or what, but to me, you've always been this snot-nosed kid that I've had to keep on the straight and narrow. I think we both know that that's not you anymore. I mean, hell, if you're grown-up enough to find faith in me . . . the least I can do is return the favor. So screw destiny, right in the face. I say we take the fight to them, and do it our way.

SAM: Sounds good. (Season Five, "Point of No Return")

Dean completely disregards the bigger plan, even when it comes to the end of the world. It's not about how the story ends; what's important to Dean is his relationship to his brother and doing what's right in the moment. As we learned with Anna and Castiel in Season Four, most angels don't naturally have free will and it's very difficult for them to develop it. To the angels, with no free will, all that matters is the end result. But to Dean, living up to the ideals of being a good brother is more important, regardless of the consequences. The angels eventually get their destined ending that they wanted (Lucifer fighting Michael in human body vessels), but because of Dean's refusal, he had real impact on how the story played out, and the angels had to adjust their original plan. There is free will in the details!

In the real world (yes, that one) there are no gods or other supernatural powers, but it might conceivably be the case that ultimate outcomes are predetermined, whereas there is some wiggle room for individual human choices. However, that possibility is challenged by chaos theory. Chaos theory means that tiny differences at one point in time can bring about vast differences in later outcomes. Chaos theory is itself entirely compatible with determinism, but if combined with some indeterminacy, it could mean that today's wiggle room is tomorrow's apocalypse.

The Will to Power

If humans do have the power to change the course of events, perhaps there is not one ultimate plan, but in fact multiple forces and plans that are continuously in conflict with one another. This was the view of Friedrich Nietzsche

(1844–1900). In his treatise *Beyond Good and Evil*, Nietzsche explains that free will in the traditional sense does not exist, but that instead, there is just "Will" in itself, and in fact there are many "Wills" in the universe, which are constantly striving and competing against one another. These are the power centers that exist outside of human beings, but are the greater forces that fundamentally exist everywhere. It's probably as close to the metaphysical version of "survival of the fittest" as we can get.

> The world itself is the will to power—and nothing besides!
>
> —FRIEDRICH NIETZSCHE, *The Will to Power*

The world of *Supernatural* can easily be seen as an allegory for many of Nietzsche's ideas. The angels, the demons, Chuck/God, and the Winchesters are all competing forces in the universe. They all struggle for power constantly.

When God disappears from Heaven, the angels try to gain control and fill the power vacuum. Lucifer and Crowley compete over control of Hell, and Rowena later usurps both of them. In the last season Death makes a final power play against God, to try and take over in his stead. The Winchesters take turns struggling against these other powers, or joining them as the situation demands. According to Nietzsche, these powers will continue to be in conflict with one another until the greatest and most powerful emerges. This is not only inevitable but a desirable result.

> What is good?—Whatever augments the feeling of power, the will to power, power itself, in man.
> What is evil?—Whatever springs from weakness.
> What is happiness?—The feeling that power increases—that resistance is overcome.
> Not contentment, but more power; not peace at any price, but war; not virtue, but efficiency. (Friedrich Nietzsche, *The Antichrist*)

Supernatural plays with Nietzschian ideas but in the end rejects them, and upholds an ideal which is very averse to what Nietzsche stood for. The Winchesters are usually the weakest of all these powers in the universe, and still they are ones that ultimately defeat the angels, the demons, and God himself.

They do all this not by becoming more powerful themselves, or ascending to any higher level of humanity, but instead by remaining true to exactly how they always were, with every human vice and weakness. It is their faith in each other, and their determination to keep resisting that ultimately allow them to win. No matter how great the power or how persuasive the argument, they continue to resist simply for the sake of resisting.

> **DEAN:** Just when we thought we had a choice. You know, whenever we thought we had free will. We were just rats in a maze. Sure, we could go left. Sure, we could go right. But we were still in the damn maze. Just makes you think, if all of it . . . you know, everything that we've done . . . What did it even mean?
>
> **SAM:** It meant a lot. We still saved people.
>
> **DEAN:** Yeah, but what for? You know? Just so he could throw another End of the World at us and then sit back and chug popcorn? . . .
>
> **SAM:** Yeah, well, what's one more apocalypse, right? But, seriously, if we win . . . When we win this, God's gone. Hm. There's no one to screw with us. There's no more maze. It's just us. And we're free.
>
> **DEAN:** So, you and me versus every soul in Hell? I like those odds.
>
> **SAM:** Yeah, me too. (Season Fifteen, "Back and to the Future")

The overall message is a rousing endorsement of humanity and individual will, triumphing over all greater powers in the universe. Not only do they kill God, they create a new and better God, which in turn allows for a reformation of the structure of Heaven as well. When Nietzsche famously said that God is dead, he meant that the Christian influence on society and its morals was now fallen and corrupted, too broken to repair. Nietzsche was concerned with creating a new way of living, stronger and more pure, free of corruption. But in *Supernat-ural*, the death of God is not inadvertent—they actively try to get rid of him. Although Chuck is an actual character in the show, the death of God in *Supernatural* is also a symbol of the rejection of destiny in favor of free will.

The General Will

TESSA: I just think, whatever's gonna happen's gonna happen. It's out of my control, it's fate.

DEAN: Huh. Well, that's crap. You always have a choice. You can either roll over and die or you can keep fighting, no matter what.

—Season Two, "In My Time of Dying"

If there's one philosopher that *Supernatural* champions, it is not Nietzsche but Jean-Jacques Rousseau (1712–1778). Not only did Rousseau believe that free will exists, and is the only thing that sets apart humans from animals, but he also invented the theory of the General Will, the will of a society, which an individual may or may not choose to go along with. Rousseau's point which he laid out in *The Social Contract*, was that the most ideal world to live in is one in which the General Will of a society and a person's individual free will are one and the same. He is quick to point out that this is an ideal which has almost always failed in practice, due to corrupt governments and too much authoritarian power.

Rousseau thought that free will should be respected, and that an individual's free will was the strongest type of will, and should be the foundation of everything. His ideal closely resembled that of the classical Greek city-states, or the contemporary government in his hometown of Geneva, Switzerland.

Three wills essentially different . . . the particular will of the individual, which tends only to his private advantage: secondly, that will is common to him as a magistrate, tending solely to the advantage of the prince; being general with respect to the government, and particular with regard to the state, of which the government is only a part: and in the third place, the will of the people, or the sovereign will, which is general as well with regard to the state considered as a whole . . . (Rousseau, *The Social Contract*)

The respect Rousseau had for individual free will goes along with his conviction that human nature is fundamentally good. The idea of the "noble savage" is often connected to Rousseau, even though he never used that phrase. He did, however, believe that the natural state of man is to be highly admired, and "civil society" so often corrupts and controls the pure humanity of a person.

Dean Winchester is a strong example of Rousseau's ideal man. He is shown clearly to give in to base and primitive impulses routinely, eating delicious burgers whenever he likes, having sex with many women on the spur of a moment, fully embracing killing monsters, and enjoying the Hunter lifestyle. Free will is incredibly important to Dean, and he chooses it many times above all else, no matter the consequences.

By creating a new God and a new Heaven, Sam and Dean establish a new structure of the universe which is much more reflective of their own individual will. Dean is free to Hunt, Sam is free to settle down and start a family, and once they die, instead of being locked in individual cells of illusion, all human beings are together and happy in Heaven. Since the systems in place did not reflect the individual will of the Winchesters at first, Dean and Sam do everything they can to break the chains and destroy them.

The show's ultimate story is one of human individuality triumphing over the forces of fate. Over the course of the seasons it treads a line between compatibilism and a full-on rejection of determinism. Sometimes it really does seem that the Winchesters have had their entire life written out by Chuck, and their deaths written in the pages of Death's books. And other times it seems clear that the powerful forces try to control Sam and Dean, but they use their free will to make choices and struggle against the destiny laid out for them.

The brothers succeed not because they fulfill a destiny or gain special powers, but because they stubbornly insist on forging their own path and being loyal only to each other. Whether free will exists in the real world or not, in the *Supernatural* universe the Winchesters insist that it does.

3
Why Do I Have to Be Some Kind of Hero?

Andrea Zanin

The Hell Gate opens. A torrent of orange and grey smoke vomits chaos from a maw so black that night recoils. Catastrophe is fetid in the air. Long, languished tentacles reach out from the soul of the abyss in search of a host. Putrid, pulsating and hungry, a vaporous miasma of decay chokes water, bird, sky and tree, and the Earth balks as a pandemonium assaults her essence. It's pretty dire. Someone's got to save the world.

Bobby, Ellen, and Sam do the only thing they can—wedge their shoulders against the black gates and push like it's 1999. Where's Dean? Over in the corner, getting a lesson on the dangers of playing with "daddy's guns" from ol' Yellow Eyes. It's a short lesson. A blast of kinetic energy sends Dean hurtling through the air and into a gravestone, headfirst. Luckily, he is hard-headed and although bloody, stunned (and still ruggedly handsome) remains conscious. Providence shows up and as Sam turns to throw some more muscle into Hell's gate, he catches a glimpse of his wrecked brother—hunched, pained and about to be killed by a stalking demon with eyes the colour of sparkling yolk.

The fate of the planet collapses to a "split second": close the Hell Gate to stop creatures from the nether emerging into the world to destroy life as we know it, or help his brother. He helps his brother. And then John Winchester claws his way through the billowing torrent of pulsating chaos and out of Hell (because of course he does) and gets Yellow Eyes in a headlock, allowing Dean to grab the Colt and enact the vengeance his family has been dreaming of since Mary burnt on the ceiling all those years ago. Obliterated by the bullet, the demise of the yellow-eyed demon seems to weaken hell for a millisecond; long enough for Bobby and Ellen to close the Hell Gate. Phew! All is well.

Except it's not. Remember a few minutes ago, back before the abyss opened and pulsating pandemonium threatened Earth . . . when Dean sacrificed his soul at the crossroads to save Sam? Yes, that. It's only Season Two ("All Hell Breaks Loose: Part 2") and the full-blown "*Supernatural* sceptic" who knows *nothing is ever well,* is still in the making; so, you're forgiven for thinking that "happily ever after" is a thing and that Dean might somehow be relinquished from his deal. Nope. No relinquishing. The hell hounds will eat his ass in Season Three ("No Rest for the Wicked"). Okay sure, Dean gets out of Hell and gives Sam a chance to repay the favor a couple of season endings down the line (the mark of Cain and all that) but being possessed by a demon and releasing The Darkness into the world ain't no fairy tale, even if to save Dean. The "brother's keeper" pendulum swings back and forth for fifteen seasons, and it's this game of: "now *you're* it, now YOU Dean . . . now you Sam, okay—my turn now" that makes *Supernatural* so addictive. Sure, there are crazy-cool monsters, horror, layer upon layer of irony, satire, blood, guts, murder, death, humour (Scooby freakin' Doo) and an all-out war against destiny (and so on) but it's the brothers; it's Dean and Sam—the sibling spats, rivalry and hilarity, and also the violence, heartache and trauma—that keep us hooked. We want what they have; unconditional, unyielding love. Oh, *plus* they're super-hot.

Whilst Season Two's Hell Gate has been thwarted (this time), it always lurks—a metaphysical presence, an existential metaphor (is there life after death?) and a reminder that the Winchester boys are in the family business: they Hunt things, save people and one another. They bear the burden of responsibility as brothers (bonded) because they're stronger together than apart, so the universe seems to be telling them.

That line from Michael Bay's *Bad Boys* film, "We ride together, we die together. Bad Boys for life"—that's Dean and

Sam; with Dean the Mike Lowrey in the *Bad Boys* duo (his fast cars and booty calls) and Marcus Burnett 'the Sam' (wife, family, health-and-safety allegiance). The hedonist and the eudaemonist, respectively; the first placing the highest of value on the pursuit of pleasure and the latter tending towards "right" or moral actions to produce happiness. Funnily, Dean and Mike are recreational eudaemonists when they go and save the world and America and all that (people above pleasure, right!?)—even if it's not the saviour thing that stokes their fires, or is it?

Perforating Eric Kripke's series with unavoidable poignancy is the question: why do the Winchester brothers do what they do? *Supernatural* questions the motives of its protagonists—placing Dean and Sam in the most excruciating of situations where they have to choose to sacrifice themselves, one another and even others, for the greater good; for the good of community, society . . . *for the survival of the world.* For the brotherhood of mankind. In so doing, a terrifying light is shone on the notion of "moral responsibility" and what that looks like in the world of the Winchesters; how deserving of praise, blame, reward or punishment they might be in accordance with their moral obligations.

Yet the question of "how deserving?" cannot be answered until we have some sort of understanding of the moral framework within which the brothers operate; judgment (moral deservedness) is dependent on whether Dean and Sam are morally obligated in the first place. Philosophy can help us out here and *there is a guy* who deals in morality . . .Fyodor Mikhailovich Dostoevsky. He was a Russian novelist, philosopher, writer, essayist and journalist, and was most prolific in the latter half of the nineteenth century. One of his most famous works is bazillion-page *The Karamazov Brothers*, which is an exploration of life's most ball-breaking questions: is there a God, do I have free will and am I responsible for my fellow man? Basically, what's the meaning of life?

Thinking about *Supernatural* through the lens of Dostoevsky adds another layer of depth to fifteen seasons of philosophical wrestling, whereby Dean and Sam perpetually find themselves embroiled in some or other form of personal/existential crisis (much like the Karamazovs) rooted in what appears to be a moral responsibility to save the world—as Dean puts it: "Why is it my job to save these people? Why do I have to be some kind of hero?" ("What Is and What Should Never Be"). *Why indeed?* Dostoevsky enables us to go deeper than Dean and Sam's battle with God's will and their own; he allows us to dig into the psychology of brotherhood and how that sets up the construct for morality in the world of Winchester.

Through These Fields of Destruction

In order to revel in Dostoevsky's philosophical musings in relation to the world *à la* Dean and Sam, we've got to understand his tome; so, here's *The Karamazov Brothers* in a very neat little nutshell:

There were once four brothers; Ivan and Alyosha born of the same mother, Dmitri of another mother and Smerdyakov of yet another. All shared the Karamazov bloodline through their father Fyodor who, suffice to say, was quite the playa. The book is set in a small town in Russia, and tells the story of a brutal murder—the murder of Fyodor Karamazov himself. Committed by one of his sons . . . but which one? *Don't guess!* Let's play a little character Clue first.

The eldest Karamazov brother, Dmitri, is described as a "sensualist" because of his pleasure-seeking spendthrift ways. He's a sex, drugs and rock n' roll kinda dude who's dominated by his passions and base human desires. Remember "Houses of the Holy" back in Season Two? It starts out in a motel (naturally) . . . Dean's hanging out on a vibrating bed, to the backdrop of a rock song and naked girl silhouette; Sam quips, "You're like one of those rats that pushes the pleasure button instead of the food button, until it dies"— *this is Dmitri*, who, like Dean in virtually every episode, manages to offend practically everyone. It would not be difficult to imagine Dmitri careening down the road in Dean's black Chevy Impala singing Bon Jovi's "Dead or Alive" in a non-socially awkward last day on Earth ("No Rest for the Wicked").

Dmitri's a soldier (serving in the Russian military) and although his fight is with flesh and blood rather than the dark forces of the supernatural realm, he's at war with his own nature. Dostoevsky describes Dmitri as headstrong, reckless and self-destructive, and if you had to play Franken-

stein and tack on an arm or leg of atheist Ivan, the Karamazov brother-combo (DmiVan for short—a bit clunky but you
get the point) would be a sensualist/atheist with a soft spot
for beer and women . . . so, a Russian Dean Winchester.
Dean's faithlessness emerges early on, when he tells Sam,
"There's no higher power, there's no God. There's just chaos
and violence and random, unpredictable evil that comes out
of nowhere. It rips you to shreds" ("Houses of the Holy")—
this is Ivan. Whilst Dmitri's preoccupied with "getting some"
Ivan's severe intellect is at war with his brother Alyosha's
unwavering faith in God and immortality.

Alyosha is Dostoevsky's self-proclaimed hero. He is handsome, graceful, moderately tall with hair of dark brown and
dark grey shining eyes, and gravitates to the character of a
loving God; devoting himself to doing good. Like Sam Winchester, Alyosha's strength is an easy morality rooted in spirituality. Sure, Sam drank demon blood and also lost his soul
(a blip in the radar of good intention) but he does not have
the same sensualist tendencies as his older brother; he looks
after his body, is less interested in frisky women and admits
to a confounded Dean that he prays—he prays *every day* (in
fact) and has done so for a long time ("Houses of the Holy").
He readily believes in angels and the possibility of supernatural healing ("Houses of the Holy" and "Faith").

Whilst Dean is a hardass like dad John (life has required
this of him), Sam seems to have the faith of his mother Mary
(providence, *again)*, who prayed just like Sam does. Sofya,
Ivan and Alyosha's mother, was a woman of faith; she was
unloved for much of her life (even in her marriage to Fyodor,
who had orgies at his house in front of Sofya) and suffered
as a consequence. Her faith saved her (not from physical
death but in life eternal). Sofya's faith inspires Alyosha to a
monastic life whilst Ivan is jaded by the severity of his
mother's suffering and rejects this so-called world of God.
Mary Winchester suffered in her own way—the life of a
Hunter is tough; and she told her boys every night as they
lay down to sleep, that angels were watching over them
("What Is and What Should Never Be"). Alyosha, like Sam
(and presumably Mary), lacks the nihilistic tendencies of
Dmitri (who is much more a 'Karamazov' in this sense—like
his father) and although deeply intelligent (as Ivan),

Alyosha's philosophical mind is no obstacle to belief in the supernatural.

As for Smerdyakov; he's just an asshole—a "trickster." Loki incarnate. We can only liken him to the Winchesters' rogue half-brother Adam in so far as he throws a spanner in the Winchester-works by revealing dad John to be a liar and perhaps a little unfair—thrusting Hunting on Dean and Sam from the womb; not their precious half-brother, though. But Adam's a good kid. Smerdyakov is not; he's unfriendly, mistrustful, was fond of hanging cats in his youth and also, killed his dad. Yup, you heard it: Smeryakov murdered his own father. Patricide alert! It's true that Fyodor wasn't a great dad at all, forgetting the existence of all four of his sons in pursuit of pleasure but still; *murder's pretty final* (unless you're a Winchester). And it gets dirtier . . . Dmitri is arrested and also convicted for the crime of his brother but not before Smerdyakov confesses to killing Ivan and hangs himself, leaving Ivan with the moral responsibility (or burden, if you like) of saving his brother's life.

As Dostoevsky builds up to the climax of the murder and proceeding whodunit, he explores the existence of God, the concept of morality, and moral responsibility to our fellow man through the relationships and interactions of the Karamazov brothers—whose love for one another is all the things of brotherhood; unyielding, unconditional, passionate, messy, confusing, painful, tragic and even torturous. Sound familiar?

As a Battle Raged High

Dean claims to have no faith and so, early on, his actions and character allude to a humanistic philosophy, which is an approach to life based on reason and our common humanity; recognizing that moral values are properly founded on human nature and experience alone. There's no room for God in humanist philosophy, only man. Of course, Dean would definitely "pooh-pooh" philosophy but *hypothetically* speaking, could this work?

The answer is no. It can't work. The problem with Humanism when applied in this context is that it excludes God and the supernatural, which throws the whole thing under a bit of a bus. *Supernatural* is fundamentally rooted in the supernatural (event to the detail of its title) and Dean, whilst he proclaims no belief in God—atheism if you will, does clearly believe in the existence of the supernatural; if only the evil parts. Philosophically, it's a bit awkward. In "Faith," Sam challenges the logic (or lack thereof) of Dean's anti-God position, asking him; "How can you be a skeptic with the things we see every day? If you know evil's out there, how can you not believe good's out there, too?" (Assuming God and good are one and the same, at this point in the show at least.) Ultimately, Kripke and the gang do not allow Dean to hold this position; much like Dostoevsky in *The Karamazov Brothers*. The book might present both existential arguments (pro- and anti- God) with empathy and clarity but the hero is always Alyosha—the man of faith.

Kripke forces Dean's hand. He meets God face-to-face ("Don't Call Me Shurley") and becomes BFFs with Castiel— angel of the Lord, also responsible for saving Dean from hell ("Lazarus Rising"). But even before then, Dean was wavering. In "Faith" he tells Layla (who is dying), "I'm not much of the praying type but I am going to pray for you" and in "Houses of the Holy" he admits a higher power, ". . . maybe I could be saved" (as "Knocking on Heaven's Door" plays in the background) after seeing the episode's badass murder guy (whom Sam was supposed to kill) die in a car; divine retribution or "God's will" as Dean puts it. *Also*, saved from what? Himself, 'the life'?

After Chuck, Castiel, angel wars, Lucifer, and all that stuff, what emerges in Dean is a bit of a philosophical mess: a belief in God but a lack of faith in Him; and a war with Chuck where Dean and Sam (and other members of Team Free Will) fight to forge their own destiny—the right to a path *other* than that which appears to be preordained. What's the most interesting in the midst of this 'screw you' to God (and resulting existential mindfuck—God is real but also bad and killable?) is the fact that Dean and Sam continue to save lives, whether they believe in God, his character, destiny or free will, or a strange conglomeration that makes *Supernatural* either pure genius (a new philosophy in the making) or total trash. They even get to go to Heaven (in spite of aiding and abetting the decimation—or *reformation*—of Chuck)! But here's the question: if the boys have decided to middle-finger destiny and go wherever the story takes them ("Inherit the Earth"), *why do they do it* (continue Hunting)? There has to be *something else* that drives them, and ultimately (also ironically) this *something else* is the brotherhood that is rooted in the Christian ethic of community as described by Dostoevsky.

You Did Not Desert Me

In *The Karamazov Brothers*, Dostoevsky argues for the imperative of moral responsibility, based on a divinely inspired moral code. Father Zossima (a Bobby Singer type figure) is a spiritual mentor to Alyosha—a guide in matters of life and faith; it is through this character that Dostoevsky articulates his philosophy; that we are all responsible to all for all. Father Zossima explains that the transformation of the world is reliant on brotherly love, and until you have become really, in actual fact, a brother to everyone, brotherhood will not come to pass. So, what exactly is this "brotherhood" that the world needs in order to survive?

Father Zossima looks to the person of Jesus (the sacrificial lamb in Christian doctrine) for the answer, which is self-sacrifice. Brotherhood is to deny your self in service of humanity, like Tony Stark in *Avengers Endgame* (it took him some time but he got there eventually!). Thus, Father Zossima calls on Alyosha to make himself, as a human being and a man of faith, responsible for everything and for all men even in face of evil; he tells him:

> If all men abandon you and even drive you away by force, then when you are left alone fall on the earth and kiss it, water it with your tears and it will bring forth fruit even though no one has seen or heard you in your solitude. Believe to the end, even if all men went astray and you were left the only one faithful; bring your offering even then and praise God in your loneliness. And if the two of you are gathered together—then there is a whole world, a world of living love. Embrace each other tenderly and praise God, if only in your two His truth has been fulfilled.

Dean and Sam Winchester may not be praising God but they sure as heck seem to be applying His version of moral responsibility (at least, Dostoevsky's biblical version rather than Chuck Shurley and Kripke's bastardized version). It's such a complex, interesting irony. We see, again and again, Dean and Sam giving up their lives—their dreams and desires for family and normalcy—to save humankind. Dean might live a sensualist lifestyle of fries, pies, speed, and sex but is this what he really wants?

In "What Is and What Should Never Be," Dean is captured by a djinn and exposed to an alternate reality, where Mary is alive (John dead), and Sam and Jess are engaged and happy. It's not a perfect version of life (Dean still drinks too much, offends, and upsets) but it's normal, and Sammy is safe. *But* all the people Dean and Sam have ever saved are dead. Dean is offered happiness (an escape, really, because the djinn's version of life is not real) but he chooses his "real" life, and the point is made: although Dean is driven by a desperate need to see his brother alive and well, he is also driven to save lives; to keep fighting the fight. When Dean asks, "Why's it our job to save everyone? Haven't we done enough?" Sam reminds him that there are bad things (nightmares) out there and if they don't save people, no-one will.

In Season Six we see Dean living an "Apple Pie Life" with the Braedens (Lisa and her son Ben); he finds love and happiness (albeit without Sammy) but when responsibility calls; when Sam turns out not to be dead (albeit without a soul) and the family business takes an almighty bite out of his squidgy apple pie, Dean can't ignore it. His moral compass does not allow him to stand by and let people, his community, get hurt. Sam says to Dean (after he dashes across the road to save his neighbours): "You just went; you didn't hesitate—because you care. That's who you are," also alluded to in "The Mentalists" when the museum guide says to Dean, "Sometimes one's true gift is taking care of others."

Dean chooses to go back to Hunting and Castiel wipes Lisa's memories, erasing her time with Dean to save her the pain of loss ("Let It Bleed"). *Dean* remembers, though. He cannot erase the pain. Similarly, Sam gives up his life with Amelia (twice—"Citizen Fang" and "Torn and Frayed"), who he loved and lived with whilst Dean was in purgatory. He gives up normalcy. He chooses Hunting.

Always, we're left with Dean and Sam, pitted against the forces of darkness. They have some allies but it always seems to come down to the two of them, doesn't it? Like Father Zossima says, *even if it's only two of you . . .*

But It's Written in the Starlight

It's the Winchester brothers' love for one another that enables them to love people; to save the world. Without the core foundation of brotherly love that motivates so many of their decisions and the attitude of self-sacrifice, there would be monsters in everyone's closet. It starts at home.

One of the most poignant episodes in the *Supernatural* mythology is "Bad Boys," where we gain insight into Dean's motivations, and realize that his desire to protect is not simply because his dad told him to. In the episode, Dean is busted for stealing peanut butter and bread (JW's on a mission and the boys have been left to their own devices) so that he and Sammy don't go hungry. He's sent to a boys' home run by a guy called Sonny. We see Dean telling him to stand up to bullies; advising and protecting as an older brother would—but he is not this kid's older brother and yet he feels responsible for his wellbeing regardless. For two months in his youth, Dean lives a normal life—falls in love, is cared for (by Sonny, who becomes like a father figure to Dean), stays in one place long enough to become a wrestling champ. When JW inevitably comes to pick up his son, Dean has a decision to make; stay or go.

He's dressed for prom, has a cool girlfriend and a "dad" who cares but as he looks out of his room at Sonny's and sees Sammy peering out the car window, the choice is clear: Dean chooses his family, his little brother. And it's in this episode perhaps more than any other that we realise what Dean has given up and that the choices he has made have been purposeful: he chooses responsibility, and it is incited by his love for his brother. Dean's choice in "Bad Boys" is rooted in his blood tie to Sam but the 'brotherhood' that Father Zossima is referring to in *The Karamazov Brothers* is more than family, it's an ethic that binds a community of people linked by a common interest—humanity. It has an almost religious connotation; denoting friendship, loyalty, love, respect and sacrifice. A brotherhood of man; working for the whole, acting for the future. Dostoevsky uses the relationships between the four brothers—Dmitri, Ivan, Alyosha and Smerdyakov—to explain "brotherhood" as love in action. Dean could have left Sam at sixteen years old; he says earlier in the episode when taking about his dream of being a mechanic that part of the appeal is that, "When you're done they leave and you're not responsible for them anymore"—he's talking about cars but the subtext is obvious; responsibility is hard. He chooses it anyway. Dean might be born into Hunting but he is no martyr to destiny (whether it exists or not) because in that moment (and others), the choice is always his. He chooses the life because he is his brother's keeper. Not just Sam's keeper but the keeper of his brothers and sisters in humanity. By choice.

In *The Karamazov Brothers*, there is an easy love between half-brothers Dmitri and Alyosha (the pair who are the most obviously like Dean and Sam). Dmitri refers to Alyosha as his dear little brother, an angel; whom he loves more than anyone in the world. The bond invokes a physical reaction in Dmitri: "Why have I been longing for you? Why have I been thirsting for you all these days, and just now? . . . Because it's only you I can tell everything; because I must, because I need you . . ."

The spirit of this brotherly longing smacks of Dean and Sam's "Don't die. I need you. I can't do this without you, brother" speeches, which are always heart-wrenching. Like Sam's speech to Dean in "All Hell Breaks Loose Part 2": "And what do you think my job is? You saved my life over and over. I mean, you sacrificed everything for me—don't you think I'd do the same for you? You're my big brother. There's nothing I wouldn't do for you." However, amidst all this lovey-dovey brother stuff is mess and complexity.

A few resurrections after the crossroads rescue, Dean allows Gadriel to possess Sam to keep him alive after he killed Kevin and Sam calls Dean out, saying, "You didn't save me for me; you saved me for you; because you don't want to be alone. You can't stand the thought of being alone...you're willing to do the sacrificing as long as you're not the one being hurt" ("The Purge"). Here, Sam accused Dean of being selfish; what's crazy about this tag-team saving thing is that Dean, who fights so hard to protect Sam, takes away his brother's agency (his right to choose—*the exact thing he's fighting God to keep*) when he keeps resurrecting him.

Whilst Alyosha and Dmitri's relationship is natural, Alyosha has to work harder to be brothers with Ivan (the faithless part of Dean that Sam also finds more difficult to relate to). Ivan can't relate to Alyosha's ready faith but he admittedly loves Alyosha regardless, and Alyosha's protectiveness over his older brother emerges when he defends him emphatically in the face of his father Fyodor, telling him not to be ill-tempered with Ivan and to stop attacking him. But it's Ivan's love for his older brother Dmitri that is the greatest test in Dostoevsky's novel; where brotherhood is truly put through its paces. Alyosha believes to his core that Dmitri did not murder their father, in spite of overwhelming evidence to suggest otherwise. Ivan is not sure. But when Smerdyakov confesses, Ivan knows the truth. However, Smerdyakov kills himself leaving Ivan *the only one* to know the truth.

He's now faced with a choice: to bring this confession to light (that his epileptic half-brother, who had suffered a seizure and was lying in bed, with witnesses and a Doctor's note, killed Fyodor) the improbability of which (albeit the truth) will render him a lunatic in the eyes of the world, or to keep his mouth shut. Not only that but Smerdyakov implicates him in the murder by virtue of omission—saying that Ivan is complicit as subconsciously he knew what Smerdyakov was going to do and did nothing to stop him. And then the devil goes and pays him a visit (much like the Yellow-Eyed Demon blaming Sam and Dean for Mary's death) and the existential ramifications of the existence of the supernatural plus the pressure of revealing the truth about Fyodor's murder *plus* his own guilt and role in the crime . . . the mental turmoil makes Ivan ill.

Alyosha recognises that Ivan will either rise up in the light of truth, or he'll perish in hate. Ivan tells the truth. At great cost to himself. He does what he believes to be the right thing and he suffers for it. *This* is brotherhood in action. Self-sacrifice. In spite of the fact that Ivan does not love Dmitri in the same way that he does Alyosha, he does feel a moral responsibility for his brother. Whist Dean and Sam might not love their neighbors as they love one another, they feel a moral responsibility for humankind.

Every Man Has to Die

It's not just about the brothers (*Supernatural* is a mythological beast) and yet it's all about them. Isn't it? The love between Dean and Sam (Dmitri and Alyosha, Ivan and Dmitri) exemplifies brotherhood and what it means to love others. It might be easy to say that Dean and Sam save everyone because ultimately that's how they keep one another alive . . . and perhaps, even, it starts this way. In "Houses of the Holy," Sam says: "There's so much evil out there in the world Dean, I feel like I could drown in it"—and he does almost drown at one point (drinking demon blood and all that). Dean's always there to pull Sam out of the pit and into the light.

After the death of Father Zossima, Alyosha, almost drowns, too; deviating from a diet of holy bread and allowing his appetite to wander into the realms of vodka and sausage (not quite demon blood but he'd have been in trouble for sure!) but in the depths of despair, "Suddenly the image of Dmitri rose before his mind...it reminded him of something that must not be put off for a moment, some duty . . ."—a quick mental detox, like the kind Dean gives Sam to get him off the demon juice in "When the Levee Breaks." But what happens over the course of fifteen seasons of *Supernatural* is that the motivation to save the world because it protects the brotherhood of Dean and Sam becomes bigger. When Sam's about to sacrifice himself in "No Rest for the Wicked," he reminds Dean; "This isn't just about saving you Dean. It's about saving everyone." And when Dean's explaining why he and Sam are Hunters, a life their mother never ever wanted for her boys, he tells Mary (newly resurrected): "Sam and me, saving people and Hunting things; this is our life. I think we make the world a better place. I know that we do . . ." ("Keep Calm and Carry On").

In the end, the brothers' love transcends selfishness—and *need*. Dean paves the way for Sam to lead, standing aside to let his little brother drive the fight, "You show those sons of bitches who's boss. You Got this" ("Who We Are"). In the very *very* end Sam lets Dean go and Dean allows himself to be let go—no crossroads or takebacks. This is love. Enlightenment, even. And perhaps the best answer to the question of moral deservedness is the Heaven the boys (and the Impala) find themselves in. It was a tough ride but no one said it would be easy.

Father Zossima tells Alyosha, "I am sorry I can say nothing more consoling to you, for love in action is a harsh and dreadful thing compared with love in dreams . . . active love is labor and fortitude"—ain't it the truth?, Bobby Singer would say. Something else he might say is, "You done well, boys; *you done well.*"

4

A Muscle Car and a Mythic Quest

CHERISE HUNTINGFORD

Myths are things that never happened but always are.

—SALUSTIUS, Roman mystic and historian

Some kind of monster, some kind of monster,
Some kind of monster, this monster lives.

—Metallica, "Some Kind of Monster"

Supernatural has strip-mined the ore—or lore—of urban legends, folklore, and fairy tales to irreverent (but successful) excess. Vamps, were-women, wraiths, djinns, and a Babel-esque tower of bastardized Biblical cast members . . . the brothers Winchester have Hunted the length of the freakshow food chain.

The "Monster of the Week" formula has held strong for fifteen seasons. And fifteen freakin' years. Supernatural is an empire of penny-dreadful pastiche, and clearly, we dig it. The pulpy tales are in no way high art, or high drama— instead they're more Halloween candy; and just as redolent of our childhoods. But regardless of the shtick, and no matter how seemingly untethered to the sophistication of reality, these myths that span centuries and continents are all intrinsically rooted in anthropology—our shared psychic landscape. (Who woulda thunk it? . . . Supernatural goes deep.)

Cherise Huntingford

On a Steel Horse I Ride

Cause I'm a cowboy
On a steel horse I ride
I'm wanted (wanted), dead or alive.

—*Bon Jovi,* "Wanted Dead or Alive"

"Mythic imagination can break the spell of time and open us to a level of life that remains timeless", writes Michael Meade, in *The Genius Myth*. Entertainment has little to do with it: *extraction* and *distillation* are myth's primary functions. They extract the essence of human truths from the confines of the temporal—a construct hinged on manmade notions such as the past, the future, and even progression of the upright species itself. The final distillate is simple and unambiguous: people do not change, and there are consistent internal themes which guide the hand. (If you doubt, just take a look at history.)

These revelations are pretty dismal. So why do myths and legends abide as fireside pastimes? Why do we perceive them as entertainment rather than didactic? And given their morbid, even *grotesque* plots, why do we feel obliged to pass them on as cultural legacy?

Part of it is in the mechanics. Because we expect oral tales to blur the lines between banal and the supernatural, our automatic suspension of disbelief makes us process the narrative more deeply. We consume without judgement—nothing need make sense in these weird, wonderful and deliciously antisocial storyscapes. And we absorb their encoded messages in titilated oblivion. Myths hold court with our most primitive of selves and in turn, we feel a strange, unarticulated connection to them.

In *Supernatural* the near-esoteric power of storytelling is afforded great significance in the character of Chuck Shurley, an average Joe who writes Sam and Dean's misadventures into existence, and who later turns out to be the Grand Architect himself. (He describes his flashes of inspiration as blinding headaches, which lead to the creation of the *Supernatural* universe—not unlike the Greek tale of Athena sprouting from the cleaved skull of god Zeus. Zeus makes a cameo in "Remember the Titans" (Season Eight)—he's less impressive without the toga.)

In its very structure, the show builds upon age-old story-telling motifs that pull us in. Mythology, like *Supernatural*, tends to recycle plotlines, and figures recur under only vaguely different description. The reason is not so much lack of imagination as it is basing narratives on typical human behavior, or, archetypal behavior.

An archetype refers to *a symbol or motif reanimated time and again in literature, art and mythology*. Psychoanalyst Carl Jung describes it as an ancient mental image, one inherited from our earliest ancestors.

Compelled by our own condition—natural narcissists—we as the audience are held captive by that with which we identify. In short, archetypes produce a kind of subconscious resonance.

The concept of the Mythic Hero Archetype was first developed by Lord Raglan in his 1936 book, *The Hero: A Study in Tradition, Myth, and Drama*. It's a rubric of common traits he claimed are shared by many heroes in various cultures, myths, and religions across history and throughout the world. Raglan argued that the higher the score, the more likely the figure is mythical, and thus, archetypal.

Wittingly or not, *Supernatural*'s creators set one particular archetype—the most famous of all—as the central figure of the show.

The Mythic Hero

It seems so obvious—but the reason we're drawn to the dusty old fables *Supernatural* proffers . . . so much so we'll dedicate our lives to 320 episodes choked with the stuff, is that every mad, bad situation is ultimately resolved, in the person of the hero; the effect is deeply comforting, if not palliative. He represents triumph over adversity, transcendence, and according to mythological formula, *freedom*. The mythic hero is, in short, the American Dream.

Supernatural simply takes this metaphor to its natural conclusion—loaded with guns, brewskis, and a muscle car. And in the typical excess of all things American, a two-for-one special on the deal: a pair of chisel-chinned contemporary cowboys, Sam and Dean.

An interesting quality of archetypes is that, while they hold sway over our perceptions and behavior, we're not

directly conscious of them—we only experience archetypes
when they're incarnated. As Mark Vernon notes: "Buddhists
tend not to have visions of Jesus, and Christians tend not to
have visions of Siddhartha Gautama." We relate to archetypes via the cultural images available to us.

And so—*the Cowboy*.

The legendary image of the Cowboy is one that striates
the history of America. The popular notion of a cowboy is actually closer to the original Texas ranger than frontier track-
ers and shooters, or herd riders. Pop culture seems to have
merged these figures in the collective consciousness, to create a mythic, somewhat historically inaccurate, figure of
reckless heroism. As such, the Lone Ranger lawman manifests in various iterations, but the basic premise—and the
basic truth—is that he was a byproduct of a world where
hard tasks were outsourced to those who existed on the pe-
riphery of civilization. Rangers appeared to be imbued with
a preternatural intuition and skill set that could really only
be gained through regular communion with their natural
surroundings, and immersion in tribal ways.

Cowboys, or *rangers*, did for common folk what could
not—or would not—be done. And this archetype, synony-
mous with the mythic hero, is one we are especially respon-
sive to—because it betrays a deep desire.

A Wicked Witch, a Key, a Quest?
Let's Do This.

I've been runnin' down this dusty road.
Wheel in the sky keeps on turnin'.
I don't know where I'll be tomorrow.
Wheel in the sky keeps on turnin'.

—Journey, "Wheel in the Sky"

Supernatural is a western—a western that routinely veers
off the dirt path into dark frontiers. At its heart, it's a western because, as philosopher Peter French writes in *Cowboy
Metaphysics*, the archetypal cowboy "risks his life and confronts death on a daily basis"—a matter of regular occur-
rence for *Supernatural*'s protagonists.

The series is a western in terms of its environs, too. The insta-suburbs stamped into the graveyard prairies, blighted industrial towns and ancient farmhouses in the Styx . . . each episode's backdrop is not dissimilar to the feel of a Sergio Leone mise en scène. The result is a restlessness, a gnawing emptiness; the prerequisite, it so happens, for a mythic quest.

The lineage of the mysterious stranger who walks into town, takes out the garbage, and disappears into the dust, can be traced all the way back to Odysseus, the legendary Greek hero most famous for his decade-long journey, or *odyssey*, through elaborate netherworlds. Ultimately, the Grecian swashbuckler makes his way back to wife and son, and reinstates his position as rightful king of Ithaca, but the meat of the tale has always been the journey, not his triumphant homecoming.

In 1949 Joseph Campbell penned a seminal work for the field of mythology: *The Hero with a Thousand Faces*. The book built on the ideas of German anthropologist Adolf Bastian, who first proposed that myths from all corners of the map seem to be pulled from the same pool of "elementary ideas." Jung fleshed out the hypothesis in psychoanalytic terms, describing the elementary ideas as "archetypes," and propounding the notion of a *collective unconscious*. Vladimir Propp, renowned folklorist researcher and structuralist, would go on to explore the monogenesis of myths, arguing that the remarkable congruity found between fairytales of all cultures points at the uniform disposition of the human mind.

The characteristics of the archetypal hero story are outlined as such:

1. **Born under unusual circumstances**

2. **Leaves family to live with others**

3. **Experiences a traumatic event that leads to a quest**

4. **Has a special weapon**

5. **Receives supernatural help**

6. **Proves himself by performing feats**

7. **Descends into a hell-like area and suffers wounding from an encounter with evil**

8. Experiences atonement with his father

9. Receives a reward, often after death

The concept of the Quest, specifically, correlates with a real-world existential process, and Jung assigns prominence to its power to reintegrate the dark and light aspects of human essence, termed "individuation"—a favorite *Supernatural* motif as the cowboy brothers ping pong alliance between Heaven and Hades.

In fact, by design or default, *all* of the archetypal hero characteristics are unmistakable in the Sam and Dean saga.

1. As an infant, Sam is cursed with demon blood.

2. He leaves his father and brother to pursue a "normal" life.

3. His girlfriend, Jessica, is then roasted Azazel-style; the catalytic event leading to Sam joining Dean to form the demon-Hunting duo.

4. The Colt, Ruby's Knife, Angel Blades . . . It could even be argued that Dean's beloved Chevy Impala acts as a weapon—as alluded to in the fifth season's finale, "Swan Song." (In this same season, Dean briefly becomes a weapon himself, the vessel for archangel Michael).

5. Help does indeed come from above, and below, albeit with ambiguous intentions: Angels Castiel, Balthazar, Gabriel; demons Ruby, Crowley, Meg; the vengeful spirit of Bobby, the nephilim Jack, among many others.

6. Sam and Dean are tested by various entities, and in different ways; most explicitly in "Trial and Error" where they must complete three trials set by God in order to close the gates of Hell.

7. Both brothers endure trips to the Fiery Pit.

8. In "Lebanon," Sam and Dean's father, John, is summoned from the past. The episode acts as a bittersweet closure for the troubled relationship between the brothers and John, where he expresses his pride for the Hunter Dean has grown into, and exchanges apologies with Sam for long ago arguments.

9. The reward, is of course, Heaven. A Heaven where Dean
   gets to ride the Impala, and Sam joins him after a full life
   of raising a family.

While the quest is referred to as a specific stage in the hero story, all of the above characteristics taken together describe an odyssey, or spiritual journey. The *road trip*, a touchstone of American culture, referential of the land's wide-open spaces, metaphor for freedom and opportunity, is where *Supernatural* begins, and where it ends. Sam and Dean's encounters with otherworldly forces are bracketed by long car rides through the Midwest, during which we are passengers to the most revelatory of conversations between the siblings. Demonic phenomena are also triangulated on road maps. And it's no coincidence that the brothers' devil-fighting armory and talismanic family heirloom is a mode of transport.

This peripatetic theme is what sets the show apart from its most direct predecessor. For contemporary generations, a memorable source of Hunting expeditions through the unbelievable is *The X-Files*. *Supernatural* picks up the thread, but only as far as plundering that collective pool of primeval bogeymen. Sam and Dean's story instead wrests the hero-journey from Vancouver and government protocol, out onto the open road—governed only by Lone Ranger code.

And this time, Scully's skepticism is replaced with two believers; the potency of the plural a key component in the hero's journey—a profound existential impetus. Like Mulder, the brothers are impelled by the search for something consistently undefined, or little understood, throughout the seasons—analogous to the Jungian spiritual quest that only achieves resolution in the act itself . . . even if it takes fifteen years (or seasons) to get there.

It's the essential listlessness of the cowboy-Hunter duo, coupled with that matter-of-fact acceptance of the metaphysical—the knowledge that, as Stephen King says, "there are other worlds than these," which sets them up as *Other*. And it's this Otherness, or separateness, that determines the Mythic Hero, and preordains his Quest.

Driver Picks the Music

I ain't tellin' no lie.
Mine's a tale that can't be told.
My freedom I hold dear.
How years ago in days of old.
When magic filled the air

　　—Led Zeppelin, "Ramble On"

America, by virtue of its sheer grandiosity of size and cultural dissemination, is thick with myth. Historian Hampton Sides describes the Land of Liberty as "such a glorious mess of contradiction, such a crazy quilt of competing themes, such a fecund mishmash of people and ideas"—and yet, at the same time, there's a singular brand of mythology that characterizes the country for both anyone who is and isn't American: *Americana*. Americana describes that unique nostalgia for a time when small town life was The Dream, and the Stars'n'Stripes was a sacramental totem.

The epoch is gone with the gunslingers, but there's a faded fetishism to the moment that lives on in the pit stops of the cross-country road trip: diners, motels, ghost towns, freak rock formations, and Route 66. *Supernatural* regularly pays homage to these sightseer attractions (with a spectral twist, or as simple backdrop). In fact, even the most emotive score of the show, one that features in "Swan Song," is entitled "Americana."

Nostalgia is the easiest way to hack into the heart of an audience; we feel a preverbal connection with the subject matter—much like we identify unconsciously with archetypes. The Ancient Greek word *nostimon* is the etymon, or forebear, of 'nostalgia'. Ironically, it first appears in Homer's *Odyssey*, to describe how Odysseus yearns for his "day of return"—or *nostimon emar*.

The homesick hero eventually returns to halcyon days; but you don't need to read the tale to know that Troy isn't quite how he left it.

With modern research into the unreliability of memory, nostalgia is more accurately a term for pathological longing for a place impossible to reach. Linda Hutcheon summarizes the lie of nostalgia in poetic frankness: it "exiles us from the present as it brings the imagined past near."

It's possible that the era of Americana is only experienced in rose-tinted retrospect. More *wistful ideal* than actuality. The product of this disparity is personified in Sam and Dean, with their characters a juxtaposition between ode to America—and a spirit jonesing for something other than white picket fences.

Show creator Eric Kripke has long mentioned Jack Kerouac's *On the Road*, the famous novel about rebellion against middle class materialism, as inspiration behind *Supernatural*. For one of that novel's protagonists, cowboys recur as a motif that epitomizes the mystique and expanse of the Midwest, an allegory befitting the connection between individuation, the hero journey or *mythic quest*, and freedom. The rebel mindset in *On the Road* is an integral parallel with the show because both the minutiae and greater myth-arc of *Supernatural* serve as metaphor for *an alternative to perceiving the world* . . . within the packaged irony of All-American archetype.

Kerouac's book became a heavy influence on the Beat Generation—a 1950s literary movement that questioned American culture and values in a post-war age; their aim a liberation from the rules and ideas governing the spectrum of life—everything from spirituality and ecology to aesthetics, drug use and sex. The movement would eventually go on to inspire shifting attitudes in music, art, and the emergence of an underground counterculture.

For the *Supernatural* superfan, the Beat philosophy of anti-materialism and soul searching most notably influenced the hard rock genre that is the show's biggest hook. If you don't come for the music, it's usually the reason you stay—long after you can't justify another Sam/Dean/Castiel resurrection. And of course, it's in the car—on the road—where Dean cranks up the Zepp, Styx, and Leppard anthems; symbolic synchronicity at its loudest.

You know what humanity's greatest creation has been? Music. That and nacho cheese. Even I couldn't have dreamt up that deliciousness. (Chuck, "Don't Call Me Shurley")

The origins of *Supernatural* are revealed best in the sound-track. The gritty riffs that play at dissonance; the cocky, rebellious drum solos; the moody ballads that stretch and distort into Plant's yowls and Axel's unearthly pitch—the breadth of despair and anger so visceral in the vault of Dean's tape deck that little else more succinctly captures the essence of Beat Generation discontent.

This cultural and emotional displacement is repeated as much in Dean's love for a music before his time as it is in the Lone Ranger hero archetype. And to quote Aerosmith, it's more than just about *livin' on the edge*. The most poignant shared quality between the series's characters and old-world guns-for-hire is that this renegade lifestyle, as French argues, both requires and engenders a set of virtues alternative to "civilized" culture: displaced and "Other," Sam and Dean stand in stark contrast to the typically suburban playgrounds of their adversaries, as well as the local straight-laced rationalism of the people they save.

> C'mon, we Hunt monsters! What the hell? I mean, normal people, they see a monster and they run. But not us, no, no, no, we . . . we search out things that want to kill us! Yeah, huh? Or eat us! You know who does that? Crazy people! (Dean, "Yellow Fever")

Ultimately, it's the awareness of their own alienation—made literal in Sam's demon blood, and Dean's Mark of Cain—that's key to finding freedom from their dissatisfaction.

One Thing I've Learned—Heroes Aren't Perfect

For nonconformity the world whips you with its displeasure.

—RALPH WALDO EMERSON

Georg Hegel (1770–1831) mapped an entire philosophy on the experience of alienation. He explained that our consciousness is alienated from itself; in other words, it fails to understand its own true nature. And yet, this does not mean it cannot achieve that understanding. According to Hegel, the process of developing absolute knowledge would allow consciousness to know its authentic self. Viewed in this way, alienation is not problematic, but merely *the start of a process of self-discovery*. The beginning of the Quest.

In everyday life, alienation manifests in various ways. Social institutions—bureaucratized government, political parties, mega corporations, national religious organizations—all of these are disengaged, depersonalized monoliths of power. Their inner workings seem deliberately arcane, and we have little say (if any) in the level of control they exert upon our lives. We exist in alienation from them, all the while remaining subjugate to them. (In *The X-Files*, the "Smoking Man" stands as fug-swathed cipher for the abstract menace of government authority, and Mulder eventually goes into hiding from the entity. Sam and Dean, on the other hand, perpetually buck the system; their credit card stash and pseudonyms are a running joke . . . their cocky attitude and brazen impersonations of law enforcement effectively strips the institution of its dominance.)

On a more intimate level, we are alienated from loved ones—in fact, the poison of feeling misunderstood infects most interpersonal relationships. Jean-Paul Sartre's play *No Exit* bore the famous line "Hell is other people"—our freedom to simply *be* will always be threatened, because of others' gaze. We are forever under judgment's surveillance, and so we contort the expression of self in response. The internal discordance breeds resentment for others, and hostility bristles between parents and children, between colleagues, between lovers, between friends, between siblings. It is this type of conflict-inducing alienation that is the chink in the Winchesters' armor; and a recurrent theme in *Supernatural*—beginning with Sam's fraught relationship with his father, and persisting between the brothers, mostly in undertones.

Still, Hegel explains, alienation isn't a bad thing—if you take its cue. In legends, mythology and fairytales, separateness from the ordinary world is what determines the hero. And it's what sharpens sensitivity to *The Call to Adventure* (the Quest) as Campbell writes in *The Hero with a Thousand Faces*. If you're immersed in the mundane, enamored of its comforts and familiarity, you are likely to view that invitation onto the open road with fear. You are likely to refuse. This corresponds with real-world psychology; the general fear of the unknown—and a preference for *the devil you know*. Thus, the stronger your sense of alienation, the more readily you embark on the Quest.

Ironically, Hegel seems to eschew the need for a hero. His antidote to the original problem of feeling disconnected from our true nature is to discard such constructs as "subjects" and "objects," "slaves" and "owners," and instead embrace a mutual dependency in societies. For Hegel, our true nature is one that reaches its fullness in collaboration with others. Being "Other" is a product of faulty thinking. To be an outlier is to go against nature.

There are other philosophers who disagree.

Søren Kierkegaard writes that cultivating one's unique-ness is like "riding a wild stallion", while conforming is like "falling asleep on a moving hay wagon." One is significantly riskier; although the other implies a kind of existential stupor, a lethargy of will. Read this way, the latter condition is cer-tainly an affront to pride. And yet, so few heroes are among us. Sam and Dean are anomalies amid their peers. The 'mythic hero' is mythic because he is exceptional, rarefied. The desire to conform may be a force more powerful than the discomfort of alienation.

In *The Sickness unto Death* Kierkegaard writes,

> Surrounded by hordes of people, busy with all sorts of secular mat-ters, more and more shrewd about the ways of the world—such a person forgets himself, forgets his name divinely understood, does not dare to believe in himself, finds it too risky to be himself, far easier and safer to be like the others, to become a copy, a number, *part of* the crowd.

Unlike Hegel, Kierkegaard believes that to function as a cog in the wheel, towards some abstract ideal, with group cohe-sion as both means and end, is precisely what stymies self-discovery. Alienation is both precursor and continual proof of being an agent for change. The Lone Ranger incarnate.

Sartre, commonly considered the father of existentialist philosophy, emphasizes the importance of the individual versus the group: "We ourselves are responsible for our world and our choice. But when we refuse this responsibility, 'alienation' happens." The experience of alienation, discontent, is a circuitous route—unless you veer off the well-worn roads.

Once you're on the Hero Journey, however, that struggle against the ease of conformity—all the golden calves of convention we're brought up to aspire to—is never really won:

> Your happiness, for all those people's lives? No contest. Right? But why? Why is it my job to save these people? Why do I have to be some kind of hero? What about us, huh? . . . Why do we have to sacrifice everything, Dad?" (Dean, "What Is, and What Should Never Be")

The Quest incurs sacrifice. The killing off of desire. In myths, the monsters are ganked. In real life, you must kill your Self. Castiel sums up the ultimatum: *What would you rather have: peace . . . or freedom?"* (Castiel, "Swan Song").

Sartre goes on to define freedom: "We are free because we are not a self . . . but a presence to-self. This implies that we are 'other' to ourselves." For Sartre, the moment you acknowledge the distinction, the distance, between Self and 'true nature'—as Hegel puts it—is when you achieve absolute knowledge, the death of ego, and true freedom.

With Chuck Not Writing Our Story Anymore . . .

Once I rose above the noise and confusion
Just to get a glimpse beyond this illusion.

—Kansas, "Carry On Wayward Son"

The thing about stories is that some are true and some are not. The wildest ones are often the ones that are truer than truth.

The term "myth" has become a synonym for "lie" but a myth can convey more truth than the surface of facts. It communicates deeply ingrained beliefs, values and conceptual ideas through its tropes and symbols. It reveals our genealogy of forever fears and desires. Mythology is anthropology—the study of that which makes us human—encoded.

But then there are the stories, not passed down at the hearth, but conjured inside our own heads; the stories we tell ourselves about ourselves. These are the tales too often untrue. The false constructions of Self.

In *Supernatural*, Chuck Shurley masquerades as a nebbish-writer-turned-prophet—eventually revealing himself to be God, a supercharged narcissist who revels in creating twisted plots and killing off characters for his own enjoyment. Shurley is the 'unreliable narrator' for Sam and Dean's story. Campbell would've called him the Trickster—the detached manipulator preventing the brothers from seeing beyond the stage curtain.

Chuck is not unlike mega corporations—inhuman sources of power which, by function and design, alienate their playthings. He is also not unlike the Ego; the gatekeeper of consciousness. More than anything, the master of the *Supernatural* multiverse represents the point at which we become tired of the lies. Chuck's revelation of his true self coincides with his cowboy adversaries' ennui with the game. In the same way, embarking on the Quest, in the cognitive sense, will eventually lead to a confrontation with narrative versus authenticity. The point at which you might gain Hegel's "absolute knowledge" in exchange for old delusions. At the psychological level, identity narratives feel safer, but they keep you stuck in a loop where even if nothing gets worse, it doesn't get better, either—

> You know, eternal suffering sounds good on paper, but as a viewing experience, it's just kind of . . . eh. So we're done. I'm canceling your show. (Chuck, "Inherit the Earth")

Playing fast and loose with Judeo-Christian myth was always a risk for *Supernatural*, but only such disregard for theological accuracy could serve the bigger point of the show; a kind of lowbrow *Paradise Lost* where the notion of good versus evil is never a clear division, and the mainstream idea of "God" is criticized.

Of course, a plotline with two full-throttle American hero archetypes would be remiss to neglect the stinging whip of the Bible Belt. Christianity is as much a part of Americana as Stetsons and Pepsi. *Supernatural* smirks at the commercialized spirituality that has been found wanting, along with all the other cultural trappings, and provides an uncomplicated solution—get the hell outta Dodge and drive.

> You never get tired of the rat race? Never get the urge to just . . . bugger off and howl at the moon? (Crowley, "Do You Believe in Miracles?")

It's about embracing alienation and leaving old identities behind. Traveling stretches of distance to those sacred spiritual wellsprings of long-ago civilizations, the likes of which we have largely lost to colonization.

I See Light at the End of This Tunnel . . . And If You Come with Me, I Can Take You to It

> Boy, don't you worry, you'll find yourself.
> Follow your heart and nothing else.
>
> —Lynyrd Skynyrd, "Simple Man"

Philosophers and historians have written at length about the initiation rites of indigenous and ancient peoples. These rites often involve a physical separation from the community, during which point the youth is brought into contact with its subconscious, or "shadow," where they must overcome its terror and integrate its vital power.

The western analogue to this ritual is Jungian individuation, that merging of personal, and collective archetypal unconscious with conscious awareness. In other words, the Hegelian journey of self-discovery.

Supernatural's version of this marriage of light and dark is straight out of Jung's handbook. Chuck's sister, Amara, is also known as "The Darkness"—a powerful primordial entity who has existed since before the birth of creation alongside God. She describes her relationship to Chuck as being his "twin"; the alternate side of one coin. Further descriptions of her include "ancient," "mysterious," and mythic—all fitting language for the subterranean pull of the subconscious. At one point, she is exiled from Earth—*alienation*—eventually being freed and coming to live in harmony with (and within) the new God, Jack—*individuation*.

Traditionally, Native Americans traveled the distance to individuation, or initiation (their "vision quests"), via peyote or ayahuasca—psychedelics which many claim open a portal to a dimension of cosmic knowledge. Individuals outside of these indigenous circles utilize the same ego-dissolving techniques, too, alone or guided by shamans towards a greater consciousness. The experience is often recounted as transformative. This is the *hero journey*.

Of course, psychedelia isn't the prerequisite; however you get there, the goal is to access the archetype.

Beneath the flannel shirts and boots—and even beyond that black steed Chevy Impala—the cowboy archetype is at its core the universal hero. And beneath the *hero*, there is something less tangible, and yet more potent . . . and within reach.

Jung explains that an archetype is not a particular entity, but rather a pattern of thought "built up slowly over millennia . . . that allows people to respond instinctually to types of experience." Archetypes predate humankind itself, but they are also active and vital, in that they have strong influence over our lives. Archetypes are that "collective unconscious" which Jung describes, and thus, within us all.

After fifteen years, the Winchesters are as familiar as brothers to us. Ever since the Woman in White, the Wendigo, they have offered us a brand of hero that is reluctant, imperfect, *and just like us*.

We have tuned in this long not because of that Monster of the Week shtick, but because the main characters are so damn likeable, relatable.

Dean was wrong. It's not just him and Sam who are different—the "crazy people"; we are all the crazy ones, alienated from the perceived normalcy of contentment in the material, the safety under external loci of control . . . whether we know it or not.

Jung writes, "Individuation does not shut one out from the world, but gathers the world to oneself." The psychoanalyst explains that bringing the unconscious unknown into the light of consciousness enables the individual to become more whole and complex, and in doing so, he becomes distinct from the societal norm—the norm a kind of half-waking state; the stupor maintained by consistently surrendering power over to separate entities. And yet, Jung emphasizes that the enlightened individual does not become separate from society. Instead, he is increasingly made aware of his connectedness with humanity through the experience of self-acceptance. Jung effectively unites Hegel and Kierkegaard: Separation from societal structures is imperative; but from that severance comes clarity, and empathy.

Those tribal rites of passage where the dark half of self is confronted contain one final step—after departure and initiation, comes reintegration with the community. The spiritual gifts received on the quest are brought back to enrich the tribe.

The final episode of *Supernatural* opens with a discordant montage of domesticity. Sam and Dean are savoring the low-key life of no drama—to the soundtrack of an old country Waylon Jennings cover. It clashes with what we're used to, and we know the scene betrays an edge of irony.

And the edge comes quickly—no hellfire fireworks, no resurrections. Dean is gone, Sam is left behind, looking at the utterly ordinary, beloved ephemera of a life lost, while Dire Straits laments baptisms of fire.

The hero story isn't always spectacular. Sometimes it's those normal life moments that require you to be heroic. To summon the archetype you've read about, watched and imagined, from your earliest years.

Campbell argues that myths were never entertainment. Nor were they merely a grim commentary on the unchanging habits of humanity. He contends that the purpose of mythology and its heroes is to guide every day, fearful people. To inspire us. They help us embrace adventures and trials, and gain the wisdom that enables us to contribute something to society.

Campbell illustrates his point in the language of legends,

We have not even to risk the adventure alone, for the heroes of all time have gone before us. The labyrinth is thoroughly known; we have only to follow the thread of the hero path. And where we had thought to slay another, we shall slay ourselves. And where we had thought to travel outward, we shall come to the center of our own existence. And where we had thought to be alone, we shall be with all the world.

The Cowboy repeats in countless cultures. He is the White Knight, Beowulf, Horus, Odysseus. Each of these heroes possess the willingness to die a death—and to ride the wide expanses where there are no recognizable landmarks. And on this road their shared dharma is to encounter the beasts, the sublime . . . the *supernatural*. And to return with an epic freakin' tale.

What are you gonna do, Dean?
I'm gonna go for a drive.

Part II

*"Every soul here
is a monster.
This is where they
come to prey
upon each other for
all eternity."*

5
Could Hell Be Any Worse than Doc Benton's Immortality?

HEINRIK HELLWIG

Suppose I told you that I knew the formula for how human beings could live forever. By regularly replacing old organs and fluids with new ones, a person could keep their body young and strong for years and years.

I explain to you that I know the medical science and all the right replacement procedures that could add hundreds of years to your life. You could still die—say, in an accident, or from some terminal disease. But as long as these things don't happen and you keep replacing body parts, you could effectively live forever. Would you choose to do it? And would it even be desirable to live forever?

In Season Three of *Supernatural*, Dean and Sam Winchester are in the situation I just described. In the episode "Time Is on My Side," Dean can learn the secret to living forever from Doc Benton, a brilliant, evil doctor and serial killer from the early nineteenth century. Dean chooses not to live forever. Yet Dean's reasons for turning down immortality are different from the standard accounts, and on that score, *Supernatural* potentially teaches us something new about the philosophy of immortality—namely, that we should not want to live forever if we have to damage, maim, or replace much of our bodies. We risk losing an important part of our humanity if we alter our bodies to the point that we no longer recognize ourselves.

Dean's Dilemma

In the episode "Time Is on My Side," Dean has three weeks before he goes to Hell according to his deal with the Crossroads demon. Dean believes that the only way out of the deal is to find the Colt revolver that will kill the demon who holds his contract, but Sam has a different idea. A recent string of assaults and organ thefts in Erie, Pennsylvania leads Sam to Doc Benton.

In 1816 Benton quit his medical practice to pursue his obsession of discovering how to live forever. Benton would kill or drug people and harvest their organs to upgrade or replace his own. It worked. Dean and Sam are familiar with Benton. When they were young their father, John Winchester, told them he killed Benton by removing his heart. Sam guesses that Benton "must have plugged in a new one," is alive, and the one responsible for the assaults. Sam's idea is to track down Doc Benton to help save Dean. Since Dean must die to go to Hell, Sam reckons that Dean can avoid Hell if they find out from Benton how to *not* die.

Once Sam and Dean capture Doc Benton, we see that Benton is horribly disfigured. One of Benton's eyes needs replacing because it has a cataract. Although Benton's body is robust—he is not hurt by Dean's gunshots—Benton's face is held together by numerous sutures from decades of opening up his own body. Earlier in the episode Dean was unable to find the Colt, so Dean is now faced with a choice: Dean could either learn from Doc Benton how to extend his life and buy more time, or he could go to Hell. Dean decides against life extension. As Benton lays strapped on his operating table pleading that he can help, Dean explains his choice to Sam:

> SAM: Don't you want to live?
>
> DEAN: No. What he is isn't living. Look, this is simple to me: . . . human, not human. You see, what the Doc is, is a freakin' monster. I can't do it. I would rather go to Hell. (Season Three, episode 15, "Time Is on My Side")

Dean's explanation is extraordinary. Typically, people believe that death is the worst thing that can happen to a human being in a mortal life. Not only does Dean reject this idea, but by choosing death and Hell, Dean rejects the idea that Hell is the worst possible thing that could happen to a human being at all! Nothing is worse than Hell. As the demon Meg Masters describes it in Season Two of *Supernatural*, "Hell is like, well, it's like Hell—even for demons. It's a prison made of bone and flesh and blood and fear" ("Born Under a Bad Sign"). For Dean however, at least one outcome is as bad as Hell. For Dean, it would be just as bad to live forever if living forever means resembling Doc Benton.

Breaking Down Dean's Argument against Immortality

What is Dean really saying? To figure it out, we must know what *kind* of immortality Dean is talking about in the first place.

In his book *Death, Immortality, and Meaning in Life*, John Martin Fischer explains that there's a difference between *true immortals* and *medical immortals*. A medical immortal is someone who is not vulnerable to death "by "natural causes," such as biological aging, disease, or catastrophic... biological events like heart attacks and strokes" (Steven Cave). Such invulnerability is achieved through medical means—perhaps by taking drugs that repair wear and tear of our cells, or through blood transfusions (replacing old blood with new blood), or by restricting diet and taking lots of vitamin and growth hormone supplements. Although medical immortals do not die from natural causes, they can die in other ways—such as being hit by a bus or blown to bits in a missile attack.

True immortals are different. Fischer describes a true immortal as someone "who is not vulnerable to death in *any* way." So, a true immortal does not die of age-related disease because they might not age whatsoever. True immortals could also survive the bus or the missile attack or a pratfall off a cliff—perhaps because they have extraordinary healing powers, or they can be put back together or recovered somehow. There are no true immortals in the *Supernatural* universe—even The Darkness can be killed, though only by God—but true immortals are the subject of some great science fiction. One of the best examples is Henry Rollins's character, Jack, in the horror comedy movie *He Never Died* (2015), directed by Jason Krawczyk.

When Dean says he would rather go to Hell, he's talking about medical immortality. Doc Benton is not a true immortal. Doc Benton is a medical immortal. The Doc has added hundreds of years to his life by relying on medical science, albeit "weird" science (Sam calls it that)—self-surgery and organ replacement experiments. We know that Doc Benton is not a true immortal from the organ replacement alone: his body does not heal all by itself. We also know that Doc Benton can die because he does die in the episode. After Dean rejects the Doc's offer, Dean and Sam knock out Doc Benton with chloroform, lock him in a refrigerator, and bury him alive with the lab book that contains the formula for immortality.

Dean is considering whether Doc Benton's version of medical immortality would be desirable. Would I want to live forever in an embodied state which requires constant body modification? That's the question for Dean. It is possible to believe, as Plato did and many organized religions do, including Christianity, that living forever in any embodied state is undesirable while an afterlife might be desirable. Conversely, it is possible to believe that living forever in any embodied state would be better than an afterlife. What should we believe? That's a different question which Dean does not consider, and the answer depends entirely on what we think the afterlife is like. (In lines 40e–41c of Plato's *Apology*, Socrates says he looks forward to meeting famous people in the afterlife—great poets such as Hesiod and Homer, and kings like Odysseus and Sisyphus. To meet these souls, to talk and spend time with them, is desirable according to Socrates.) The choice for Dean is between living in a particular kind of embodied state and living in the worst possible disembodied state, Hell. But in choosing Hell over Doc Benton's variety of medical immortality and calling Doc a "freakin' monster," again, what is Dean really saying?

Two Ways of Understanding Dean

Dean's argument can be interpreted in two ways. On the one hand, Dean could be saying that medical immortals like Doc are *immoral* monsters. Whatever the Doc's formula for living forever is, if we follow his advice, we will have to kill or harm people to harvest enough organs. That's morally atrocious behavior. Worse, we could become mad like Doc Benton. We could end up rationalizing murder or removing someone's kidney or hand or pancreas against their will in the name of our own survival. We could even be convinced that our immoral acts are good, stealing organs being necessary for discovering what all of humanity wants to know, namely, how to thwart death.

On the other hand, Dean could be saying that medical immortals like Doc are *physical* monsters: he does not physically resemble a human being enough to make living forever desirable. Doc Benton is essentially Frankenstein's monster. He is a living entity made up of parts from other human bodies. Doc has the *form* of a human being: he has hair on his head and a face, he moves like and has the body shape of a human being. But really, Doc Benton is a composite creature. The "living matter" that constitutes Doc's body is not his original body. Doc has lost contact with his original physical matter, so much that we should hesitate to call him a human being. He is some other kind of entity that happens to contain human organs. And besides, Doc is hideous—he doesn't *look* like a normal human being. If living forever means performing multiple self-surgeries and effectively becoming a different species with heavily stitched faces, then it's just not worth it.

Dean seems not to be saying the first thing. There is no reason to think Dean is worried that he will turn evil if he learns Doc Benton's formula. Dean says nothing like that to Sam. Also, Dean has no reason to dwell on Doc Benton's character or psychology. Even if Dean cares to be a good person, he is going to Hell no matter what. That's the deal—it does not matter how many good deeds he does. Dean could behave like a moral saint for three weeks, or he could behave like Gary Ridgway. Either way, per the terms of the contact, the hellhounds are coming to kill Dean in three weeks.

Sam and Dean are interested in the formula only because of Dean's predicament. If Dean knows how to keep his body "forever young," he will be less susceptible to a mortal wound, and therefore better equipped to survive a hellhound or a demon attack.

Also, it wouldn't make much sense for Dean to assume that he would turn evil like Doc Benton. Someone does not become evil simply because they learn something from an evil person. True, evil teachers can be a bad influence, but how much influence they have depends somewhat on who's learning. Let's suppose Sam and Dean accept the Doc's bargain. They will spare his life in exchange for the formula. Let's also assume that Dean is committed to being good. Upon learning the formula, Dean could surely say, "Okay, I know what body parts I would need to replace and how often. I also understand how to do it. But I refuse to kill or harm anyone, and I won't steal from organ and blood banks either. I will acquire new body parts through moral and legal means only—like donations." In other words, someone could learn the formula from Doc Benton without becoming evil like Doc Benton. They could try to carry out the formula differently. Or, they could choose not to follow the formula at all: it could be an extremely valuable piece of knowledge they just don't act on for moral reasons.

Doc Benton's Physical Nature—No Thanks!

Dean seems to be saying that living forever is undesirable because, well, just *look* at Doc Benton's physical appearance and composition. Dean can't comprehend living for hundreds of years looking like that. (Which is certainly understandable when you have Jensen Ackles's good looks!) Indeed, Dean believes he would not be recognizably human if he modified his body and appearance to the point that he resembles Doc Benton. But Dean is not speaking only for himself—he is not saying that living forever is undesirable only for him. Dean is suggesting that living forever like Doc Benton would be undesirable for *any* person. How do we know? Sam and Dean bury Doc Benton alive *with* the lab book. As the dirt hits the fridge, Doc repeatedly screams that he can help Dean. Nevertheless, Sam and Dean keep shoveling.

It's as if Dean is saying, "Doc Benton, you wouldn't be helping anybody with this formula. That's why we're burying it along with you." Hence why Dean thinks that death and Hell are no worse than living forever Doc Benton's way. The

Hell of *Supernatural* is a place of endless torture. Except for a lucky few—like John Winchester and Bobby—there's no hope of getting into Heaven eventually ("All Hell Breaks Loose Part 2," "Taxi Driver"). If a condemned person heals having learned from their crimes, they will just be tortured again. This vicious cycle continues until the soul loses its humanity completely. From Dean's point of view, if Doc's formula has the same effects as Hell—it doesn't improve anyone's lot, and anyone who lives like Doc will just lose their humanity anyway—then there's no reason to prefer living forever to Hell. Doc Benton's plans are tantamount to creating Hell on Earth.

Dean's attitude toward immortality, then, seems to be this. In order for living forever to be desirable, a human being must not damage, maim, or replace too much of their original body. If they do, they will not be able to identify as human, which is a bad result. A good immortal life *at least* requires that a human being be physically continuous with their original body and appearance. Naturally there are questions of how much bodily alteration is "too much," and there may well be additional conditions that need to be satisfied for living forever to be truly desirable. Dean can be seen as articulating a bare minimum for living forever to be attractive to anybody.

Dean the Philosopher?

Dean's argument echoes a famous philosophical discussion of immortality. For a long time, philosophers have asked if we should want to live forever. Several of them have answered in the negative. One such thinker is Bernard Williams, a twentieth-century English philosopher. Williams famously argued that immortality—specifically, medical immortality—is undesirable because it would be boring. Suppose you could take an elixir that keeps your body young and healthy and adds three hundred years to your life. Williams thinks that with all that extra time, at some point you will run out of things to do. You will have exhausted all your interests and done everything that could make sense to you personally. Once that happens you will be stuck with hundreds of extra years. You will have nothing to do for the rest of time and you will be, pardon the pun, dying for a way out. (If you're familiar with the TV show *The Good Place*, this is precisely what happens to everyone in the afterlife in the final season.) And this wouldn't happen only to you. Williams thinks the terminal boredom is inevitable: it would happen to *anyone* who took the elixir. No one would sign up for that!

Williams is what John Fischer calls an "immortality curmudgeon," someone who believes that living too long *is* necessarily a bad thing. Fischer understands immortality curmudgeons like Williams to be concerned that an immortal life would not be recognizably human (*Death, Immortality, and Meaning in Life*, p. 104). An immortality curmudgeon will tell you that we need death in some sense. Death is not necessarily bad—because death gives our lives meaning and shape, or a definitive ending to our life stories. Without death our lives would be meaningless. Williams certainly believes that. Without a reasonable limit on how long we live, no rational person would take the elixir because no one would recognize a state of terminal boredom as a meaningful life for a human being.

Like Williams, Dean is an immortality curmudgeon. At least if we are talking about living too long the way Doc Benton does it. Dean's argument assumes that people have souls, but we don't have to believe in souls to take worries about medical immortality seriously. Although Dean doesn't mention boredom, Dean and Williams share the same fundamental worry—that a medically immortal life would not be recognizably human. Yet Dean and Williams clearly have different ideas about what it means to be "recognizably human." Dean is not worried about becoming bored while he lives longer. He seems only to be worried about what will happen to his body.

Thus, Dean was inadvertently challenging one of the great thinkers on immortality when hearing Doc Benton out. What does it mean for an immortal life to be "recognizably human" and worth living? Who has the right idea—Williams (we need to be interested in and actively engaged with the world around us) or Dean (our bodies need to function and look a certain way)? Might they both be partially correct?

Bernard Williams on the Makropulos Case

Williams's elixir example comes from an opera by Leoš Janáček titled "The Makropulos Affair." (Janáček's opera is based on a 1922 play with the same title by Karel Čapek, a Czech playwright. Williams loved opera; he even wrote a book on it toward the end of his life.) In Janáček's opera the main character, Elina Makropulos, or "EM" for short, becomes a medical immortal. At age forty-two she takes an "elixir of life." She stays aged forty-two for the next three hundred years. By the time EM is 342 she is miserable. As Williams describes it, "Her unending life has come to a state of boredom, indifference and coldness. Everything is joyless: "in the end it is the same," she says, "singing and silence." She refuses to take the elixir again; she dies; and the formula is deliberately destroyed . . ." ("The Makropulos Case," p. 82).

EM chooses to die because she has run out of what Williams calls *categorical desires*. A categorical desire is a desire that makes sense only if we assume that we want to keep on living. One day I hope to visit the annual Ice and Snow Festival in Harbin, China. This is a categorical desire for me. No matter how difficult or unsatisfying my life might be in other respects, I must want to continue living so I can eventually go to Harbin. The prospect of attending the festival gives me a reason to go on, as it were—as do other projects like writing books.

Not all our desires are categorical, however. With many of our desires we have them simply *because* we will continue to live. Our desires for food, shelter, and even medicine are like this: they do not give us reason to live, but so long as we are alive, we will desire these things. Else we will experience pain. Williams calls these *conditional desires*. A conditional desire makes no assumption about whether we *want* to continue living. A terminally ill cancer patient might prefer that their life ends soon—so no categorical desires—yet still want to eat when they are hungry. Even though the patient has lost interest in life, their desire for food makes sense *on the condition* they continue to live; that's the sense in which the desire is conditional.

For Williams, being recognizably human doesn't simply mean "not bored." There's more to it than that. For Williams, being recognizably human involves two things:

- **The person has a human body (numerically the same human body they have always had), and**

- **The person has categorical desires—"projects," things they care about doing that motivate them to want to keep living.**

Williams thinks the second point is more important when arguing against medical immortality. EM's body is fine, but for Williams, recognizing our humanity largely has to do with our nature as *valuers*. Human psychology is such that we need projects. Your projects and value commitments control your beliefs (including your moral beliefs) and your behaviors. Without projects we do not function like normal human beings.

This is precisely why we treat depression. A depressed person is unable to find enough satisfaction or enjoyment in any project to be actively engaged with the world around them; they are not functioning in the sense that they aren't valuing *some* aspect of the world that propels them into action. The problem with medical immortality, Williams thinks, is that we would all reach a point where nothing grabs us. We wouldn't be valuing correctly because we aren't moved to act.

Is Doc Benton Recognizably Human?

EM's life is not recognizably human according to Williams— but surprisingly, it would seem that Doc Benton's life is recognizably human by Williams's standards. Although Doc Benton has replaced many of his original body parts, he is still working with the one and only body he's had since birth. He hasn't switched bodies, like if he removed his brain and transplanted it into a fresh body. Doc Benton also has projects that are keeping him engaged. They are evil projects, but projects still. Doc values living forever, and he wants to continue living so he can keep killing and acquiring organs to perfect the formula for immortality.

If Doc Benton is recognizably human, would Williams then say that we should want to live forever Doc Benton's way? No! The killing aside, Williams could say that Doc Benton would end up like EM eventually. At some point the Doc will get bored—all his categorical desires will become exhausted—so even if his formula is working, medical immortality is ultimately undesirable.

We know that Dean thinks Doc Benton is "not human." But which of Williams's points would Dean disagree with? It probably isn't the second point about projects. Dean would likely agree that it's crucial for a human being to have projects (like killing zombies and Hunting down demons!). Dean might say that when contemplating medical immortality, Williams's first point about bodies matters more for wanting to live forever than Williams himself realizes.

But what did Williams overlook? Unfortunately, Dean doesn't explain why he's so disturbed by the idea of having an extremely altered physical nature. So, we have to do a little guessing. There are a few possibilities. One is Dean believes that Doc Benton is not recognizably human in the sense that he is not the *type* of thing we should call a "human being." Just as a bird with no wings, no beak, and no feathers would not be recognizably a bird, a human being who's had this replaced and that replaced would not be recognizably human. On this reading of "not human," Dean's worry is about the truth: he thinks he would be saying something generally false when describing Doc Benton as human. The idea is there are certain physical requirements a person must meet to be correctly described as human per the facts of science, and Doc doesn't meet them.

But that's just not convincing. The fact is, Doc Benton still meets a lot of the basic physical requirements for being human. He stands upright, walks and talks normally, has functioning organs, does not have misplaced parts (like a foot where a hand should be), and is quite strong. And as a trained doctor, Doc Benton's body is working as medical science dictates. Doc Benton physically resembles a human being in all the basic respects. He just *looks* scary. Maybe we should add that the replacement body parts must be in good condition for the description "human" to be true. But that's not very convincing either. Imagine a world where "Terminator transplants" are a real thing: I can buy bionic transplants so that my limbs look just like the robots from the *Terminator* movies. Let's say I have both my arms and legs replaced. Those replacement parts aren't just good, they are in mint condition. Yet no one would say I'm recognizably human post-transplant. Even if we stipulated that the replacement parts must be *human* parts in good condition, there are still problems. We would never say a double amputee with normal prosthetics is not recognizably human just because their replacements aren't human parts; and that's true whether their prosthetics are fashioned to look like human limbs or not.

Another possibility is that Dean believes that Doc Benton is not recognizably human in the sense that he's not the rightful owner of all his parts. If you own anything in this life, it's your own body. So whatever body we're born with, both it and all its parts belong to us—head, shoulders, knees, toes, organs, and so forth. No one can claim original ownership of those body parts except the individual who was born with them and to whom they rightfully belong, so that ownership is what makes us uniquely human. On this "ownership reading" of "not human," Dean's worry would be that Doc Benton's formula would cause us to turn into something that isn't *us*. The creature that we are calling "Doc Benton" is not really Doc Benton. This creature is just a collection of people parts that actually belong to other individuals. There isn't enough left of *him*, original Doc, to be the real human being who is Doc Benton.

The ownership idea also is not convincing. When exactly does an old person end and a new person begin? How much replacement is needed? It's impossible to say. (Although if full brain replacement were possible, that would probably make you a different person.) And besides, why think that being the original owner of my parts is what makes me human? If I need a kidney transplant and I rely on a donor, certainly I will be recognizably human after surgery. That's true whether the surgery is successful or not. If I have concerns before surgery, I don't think they'll have to do with me being "less human" on account of having someone else's kidney. Mainly I'll want to know if the new kidney will work, and what are the potential side effects and risk of my body rejecting the organ. Consider also the kidney donor. Are they less recognizably human just because the kidney they originally owned belongs to somebody else? Surely no! Very often, we describe organ donation as a great, "human" thing to do—especially when a living family member or close friend volunteers. That sort of praise suggests that my kidney donor is *more* human without the kidney they originally owned. (A defender of Williams might say that this case shows why categorical desires matter for being human. The donor is "more human" in the sense that they have a very praiseworthy project, one that shows the best side of humanity.)

Not "Recognizably Human," or Not Recognizably the Human I Am?

There is yet a third possibility. We have been trying to understand what Dean might have meant by "not human" in general. Maybe Dean didn't have anything general in mind. Maybe Dean was thinking mainly of himself and generalized about the choice he made.

Dean's choice to live forever is a personal choice. He isn't deciding for the rest of humanity whether to make Doc Benton's formula available. It's about whether *Dean* wants to live forever, whether *Dean* wants to go that direction with his life. After seeing Doc Benton's face maybe Dean thought, "I couldn't live like that. I wouldn't be able to recognize myself anymore. *I* would look like a freakin' monster."

This is a more personalized version of the ownership idea. How we understand ourselves involves many things, but a key one is the relationship we have with our own bodies—how we experience things "from the inside," our pains, our pleasures, and how we appear to ourselves. Knowing who I am isn't just a matter of waking up with numerically the same singular body every day. There's more going on. If I were to look in the bathroom mirror and see that I have a completely different face than the one I had yesterday, I would freak out. "WHAT HAPPENED TO *MY* FACE?!" I may have perfect kinesthetic awareness, and I may well feel like I'm in *my* body, but if my face is gone, I wouldn't be able to recognize the human I understand myself to be.

I emphasize faces because that's Doc Benton's scariest feature. But think about it. Let's say you want to live forever as badly as Doc Benton does and his method is the only known method. You need a new sinus cavity to continue living. The Doc says that replacing it will require facial entry which will leave a massive scar, one that looks like the Union Jack has been carved into your face. Imagine if you had such a scar, or if you had skin grafted. Do you think you would you be able to recognize the human you are? Sure, you could make your old self out, and you could explain what happened to your face, but would you still feel like you're *you* when you see your face?

The question is not limited to facial recognition and self-surgeries either. Consider a proud, accomplished pro football player who contracts cancer. The cancer takes him from 285 pounds down to 145 pounds. This player might still have strong categorical desires and an active life, but it's plausible to think they will not fully identify *as themselves*. They may feel only partly like themselves because of what's happened to their body—especially if football and physical prowess were the best parts of their life story.

The suggestion here is not that bodily alteration is bad *per se*. That's not true. Some people choose to radically alter their bodies for the better; we hear incredible stories about weight loss journeys all the time. The suggestion is that being recognizably human involves being able to fully *self-identify* in terms of one's own body. That's what Williams's EM argument misses. There are certain relations between our bodies and ourselves (other than numerical sameness) that need to exist in order to be who we are. Those relations are part of what makes us uniquely human. Being able to recognize this body as *mine*—or better, as *me*—is what I risk losing were we to live forever like Doc Benton. (Perhaps this is part of our concern about people who get *too much* cosmetic surgery: they are tampering with that ability to recognize!) Many of our waking moments would likely be spent just trying to get a foothold on who we are—comparing our past appearance to our present appearance, loving or hating our past selves compared to our present selves, remembering how things used to be and wondering if we are really the same person now. What a confused, awful existence!

If that's what Dean means by "not human," we can see why he and Sam bury Doc Benton's lab book. This isn't so much about the aesthetics of looking like Doc Benton. Living every day being unable to fully self-identify in terms of our own bodies would, for a lot of us, interfere with our ability to fulfill our categorical desires and have meaningful lives. The *experience* of living every day like that, *forever,* would be like Hell. For *any* human! That's why Hell wouldn't be worse than living forever Doc Benton's way (not to mention the constant pain from incisions and healing and regeneration).

Back to Williams's view of being "recognizably human." Dean would say that we should add a bullet point onto Williams's view. For Dean, being recognizably human involves three things:

- **The person has a human body (numerically the same human body they have always had),**

- **The person has categorical desires—"projects," things they care about doing that motivate them to want to keep living, and**

- **The person must be able to fully self-identify in terms of their own body.**

What Makes You "You"?

Would you choose to live forever? *Supernatural* helps us see that part of what goes into the choice is whether we would recognize ourselves in an immortal life. I might like the sound of living forever right now at thirty-eight, but will I still be *me* with hundreds or thousands of extra years?

While we're very grateful to Dean for making us aware that body recognition is important, there's no question that categorical desires are also important for the question about who we will be; Williams is right about that at least. I mention this because many people think that's part of Williams's main point about EM. Many have read Williams to be presenting a *dilemma* about medical immortality, a choice situation where all the available options aren't clearly acceptable. The dilemma is this:

- Either you could become permanently bored like EM,

- Or you could avoid boredom by forming new interests and projects over time, but this would require you to change your character and values constantly; if you do this enough times, the you that existed at the beginning (when you took the elixir) no longer exists; you are literally another person now.

Philosopher John K. Davis explains the second horn of the dilemma:

> You might find new interests and values to keep you engaged, but what you find interesting and engaging depends on your character and values . . . You can't take an interest in competitive sports unless you enjoy competition or an interest in meditation if you have no spiritual side. To acquire a new set of interests to replace the ones that bore you after a few centuries, you need to make some changes to your personality and values. Once you have changed your personality and values so that you can acquire entirely new desires and interests and passions, you avoid boredom—for a while. However, eventually you get tired of the interests that go with the altered version of your personality and values, and you need to alter your personality and values once again so you can acquire another new set of interests. (*New Methuselahs*, pp. 38–39)

The point is that your personality shapes your categorical desires and vice versa. Changing your categorical desires over and over would cause you to change your personality so many times that you would effectively extinguish yourself—however you understand yourself now. Even though you would be physically alive, you would be unable to recognize yourself. Future "you" has values that are so utterly different from the current you that you couldn't identify the future you as *you*.

Categorical desires are crucial to recognizing ourselves as individuals. If I were to ask you who you are, I suspect I would hear a lot about categorical desires. You would likely tell me about your history, which will contain some anecdotes about things you've accomplished—"chapters," so to speak, about values and activities and projects (maybe family, relationships, career, sports, hobbies, pets) that have kept you going for certain periods of time and how those things got you to where you are today. You would also tell me about what you're working on now, what's important to you and currently keeping you going.

If you had no categorical desires and only conditional desires, would you be able to say what's unique about *you*? Would you be able to comprehend your own humanity? EM does not exit the world because she no longer feels human; Williams doesn't say anything like that. Still, it's very hard to say what makes you a unique human if you don't have categorical desires. Your values wouldn't be very interesting. A person who has only conditional desires is reduced mostly to the animalistic part of their nature—surviving, satisfying basic needs, pursuing pleasure and avoiding pain. *Everyone* has these desires, so arguably, they can't be all that makes a human individual unique.

Is Dean's Argument Convincing?

Taken together, Williams's and Dean's arguments tell us that recognizing ourselves as human involves two things—recognizing our own values and recognizing our own bodies. But how important is body recognition, really?

Very important, if we take Liam Love's word for it. Liam Love was a truck driver from Grimsby, England. He suffered a horrendous injury in 2017. While drinking at a pub one night, Love had an argument with another man, Daniel Skinner. The argument got heated and a fight broke out. Skinner bit off the end of Love's nose. Skinner was sentenced to 20 months in jail for the attack, but Love's face was left mangled. He underwent three excruciating operations to reattach parts of his nose. Skin from Love's forehead was taken to repair the tissue damage, but unfortunately, Love's surgeons were unable to fix his nose completely. In addition to a large bulging tip on the end of his nose, Love has a huge, highly visible scar that runs from his hairline (near his left temple) to the bridge of his nose. Love struggled with life after the injury, quitting his job and not leaving home much. About his injury, Love said this:

> "*I don't feel human.* I feel horrible. I am in constant pain all day and every day. I feel depressed and anxious about the way I look."
> "*I feel monstrous.* I don't like people staring at me."

"What's a twenty-month sentence when I have to look like an idiot for the rest of my life? Really?"

"People will always be asking me questions—literally one bite across my nose changed my life. I don't want to go out anymore, I don't want to see anyone. I used to just cry all the time." (Naylor, "Nose Bite Victim," emphasis added)

Love's tragic words are striking—"monstrous," "don't feel human." These are almost exactly the same words Dean uses. The terrible incident altered Love's body to where he had difficulty recognizing his own humanity. Fortunately Love recovered somewhat, but his inner life as well as his social life was in a constant state of turmoil. Liam Love was not trying to live forever. Yet if a mortal life where we struggle to recognize our physical selves is as difficult as Love's sounded, who wants to live forever like that? Stories like Liam Love's make Dean's argument—that we should not want to live forever if we have to damage, maim, or replace much of our bodies—more convincing.

Medical Immortality in the Twenty-First Century

We may not be far away from actually achieving medical immortality. During the past two decades there have been major advancements in biogerontology, the scientific study of the biology of aging. Several mainstream scientists believe that we may soon be able to slow or halt aging, and perhaps reverse it altogether. Some even think that the first person to live to 150 or older is here among us.

One such scientist is Aubrey de Grey, a biologist and chief science officer of the SENS (Sensibly Engineered Negligible Senescence) Research Foundation. de Grey believes that we can prevent and perhaps eliminate many age-related diseases—Alzheimer's, cancer, diabetes, COVID-19—by targeting the biological mechanisms responsible for aging in the first place. The key, de Grey thinks, is to repair cell damage. We know that human aging is mostly caused by changes in our cellular processes. de Grey thinks that if you intervene in those processes—if you address yourself to the aging in your cells directly—you are maintaining your body such that you will slow the natural aging process, keep yourself healthy, and add several, perhaps hundreds, of years to your life. (de Grey has given numerous TED talks. They are all over YouTube.)

de Grey analogizes the human body to a car. Most cars are built to last for ten to fifteen years. But they can last much longer if you do the right *maintenance* on them. If you stay on top of things—exchanging fluids, swapping out old parts with new parts, dealing with wear and tear before it worsens—you can keep the car from aging. Indeed, with the right maintenance you can make a car last twice as long. de Grey thinks the same logic applies to the aging of the body (*Ending Aging*, p. 21). Thus, de Grey's research foundation is devoted to finding the right maintenance strategies for the body, particularly cell and gene "rejuvenation therapies."

Doc Benton would agree with de Grey's idea of maintenance. Doc even says to Sam, "This whole eternal life thing is very high maintenance" ("Time Is on My Side"). You may rest assured that Aubrey is not a "modern-day Doc Benton." (I met him once—nice guy!) But could we see a maintenance strategy like Doc Benton's? Could we grow new organs and make new body parts? According to John Davis, this is already being done, though the procedure is still in the very early stages of development (*New Methuselahs*, p. 9). Davis is skeptical that replacement body parts will be a big part of life extension, but they could have a role in it.

Recently the Biostasis Research Institute, a private organization based out of Berkeley, California, launched two new research centers to study cryopreservation (storage at extremely cold temperatures) of human organs and tissues donated for transplantation (Burgess 2021). The centers will be located at the University of Minnesota and Massachusetts General Hospital. The stated aim of the research is to create "human organ banks," warehouses for donated organs including brains. The hope is that, with better organ storage technology, we will have more organs readily available and ultimately save more lives.

The goal of the Biostasis project is not yet to live forever, and it doesn't even address aging, but it does show there's some optimism about the role of organ replacement in human maintenance—recognizably human maintenance.

6
How the Hell Are We Supposed to Kill an Idea?

Nur Banu Simsek

"Hell House," Episode 17 of the first season of Supernatural, aired on March 30th, 2006.

Still in the early days of the show, when neither the showrunners nor the actors knew that their project would span fifteen years, "Hell House" doesn't stray too far from any other monster-of-the-week episode and is only notable for marking the start of the prank wars between Sam and Dean and the introduction of characters who affectionately parody *Ghostbusters*.

However, beneath the surface of this seemingly filler episode is one of the most powerful supernatural beings that ever appears on the show. The brothers come face-to-face with a tulpa, a monster that becomes real when enough people believe in it. Tulpas change as people's beliefs about them change, and over time they take on a life of their own and are incredibly hard to kill. Battling with a physical manifestation of a constantly changing idea which exists not on paper but in the minds of devoted fans is risky for the showrunners. Not only do tulpas represent the project of artistic creation itself, but they also pose a philosophical challenge about the power of ideas.

That's What You Think!

"Hell House" opens up with a group of teenagers on their way to a supposedly haunted house in Richardson, Texas. Craig

Thurston leads the group, telling a story about how something sinister lives in the root cellar, chasing after girls and stringing them up. The group is a little uneasy but ultimately doubtful about the whole story. Even though they badger Craig to learn where he found out about the house and the homicidal creature that dwells in the basement, they quickly overcome their initial disbelief when they find the body of a girl hanging in the cellar. By the time the police arrive, however, the body is missing, and news of the haunted house is spreading among local thrill-seekers.

Sam and Dean arrive in Richardson a couple of months after the incident to check out whether anything supernatural is worthy of their attention while they wait on news from their father. As Sam tells Dean about the legend of this misogynistic spirit who exclusively targets women, he highlights that the cops think the incident was simply a prank as they were unable to recover a body from the house. Dean shares the cops' intuitions but Sam says he read what he believes to be sincere first-hand accounts from the teens on a paranormal website called HellHoundsLair.

Throughout the episode, Dean exhibits more skepticism than usual for his character. He isn't exactly keen on visiting a haunted house and he remains unconvinced that there is any real danger because Sam's research on an online forum frequented and managed by teenagers does not seem exactly credible to him. Dean's skepticism is crucial because it sets us up to later analyze how belief can be extremely powerful, and in fact, deadly, when coupled with the right tools.

The brothers find the kids and question them but their answers don't reveal much and the details of what they saw in the house are full of contradictions. Despite their obviously comedic and unreliable retelling of the events, the teenagers do succeed in directing Sam and Dean to their friend, Craig Thurston. Craig tells the brothers that the Hell House used to belong to a farmer named Mordechai Murdoch who lived in the 1930s with his six daughters. At the height of the Great Depression, as his crops failed and he neared bankruptcy, Murdoch started becoming desperate. He couldn't bear the thought of his children starving to death so he decided instead to give them quick and minimally painful deaths. As they begged and pleaded with their father,

Murdoch strung up his daughters one by one and then killed himself in the end. The spirit of Murdoch is now trapped in the house forever, attacking and killing any girl who goes inside.

After listening to Craig's story, the brothers decide to go and investigate the farmhouse. Inside the house, they see inverted crosses on the walls, which have been used by Satanists for centuries, Sam tells Dean, but the sigil of sulfur didn't show up in San Francisco until the 1960s — decades after Murdoch killed his daughters. While investigating the house, the brothers run into Ed Zeddmore and Harry Spengler, self-identified paranormal investigators who go by the name of *Ghostfacers* and run the HellHoundsLair website. Neither the kids' stories nor the symbols in the house add up to a coherent story, and Ed and Harry exhibit no real experience when it comes to dealing with supernatural beings and phenomena. Before fully giving up on what seems to be a harmless local legend, the brothers check town records and the police station for some final clues. Dean confirms that there are no active missing persons cases while Sam finds out about a Martin Murdock from the town archives who was in fact a farmer in the 1930s but had two sons and did not kill anyone.

At this point in the episode, the brothers feel that they have hit a dead-end, so they chalk up the whole thing to Ed and Harry making up material for their website and they are ready to leave town and go elsewhere where their services might be more urgently needed. The very same day, two girls and a guy find themselves outside of the Hell House. One of the girls goes into the basement on a dare and meets her fate as Mordechai, wearing farmer overalls and a black hat, throws a rope around her neck and hoists her into the air. The girl kicks and screams but unfortunately, she doesn't survive.

Seeing as the girl's death is consistent with Mordechai's legend, Sam and Dean decide to stay in Rochester. The next day, they manage to sneak past the cops and into the house where they finally run into Mordechai in the root cellar. The farmer swings his axe at the brothers and is impervious to their rock salt bullets—which are usually successful at dissipating traditional ghosts. As Sam and Dean escape the house, they realize that the Mordechai from the legend and the Mordechai who tried to kill them are different. The legend said Mordechai strung up girls, and had hung himself, but the Mordechai in the house appeared with an axe, went after the brothers, and had slits on his wrists.

Typically, ghosts in *Supernatural* follow a set pattern. In any other episode with a ghost, Sam and Dean can rely on salting and burning the ghost's remains ("After School Special"), destroying haunted objects ("Hook Man"), or even resolving the ghost's issues ("Roadkill"). As Sam and Dean puzzle over the inconsistencies in Mordechai's legend, Sam sees a new post on the HellHoundsLair website. The post claims that Mordechai was actually a Satanist who chopped up his victims with an axe before slitting his own wrists. Now he's imprisoned in the house forever.

Dean suddenly realizes that one of the signs painted on the walls of the house is a Blue Öyster Cult band logo. The brothers go back to the music store where they first met Craig Thurston, who finally confesses that he and his cousin Dana orchestrated the original prank and started the legend of Mordechai. The police never found a body because the girl Craig's friends saw was Dana. They painted random symbols from albums and theology textbooks on the walls of the abandoned farmhouse, and then made up a story inspired by one of its previous owners. The story spread by word of mouth until Ed and Harry picked it up and put it on their website. After that point, "everything just took on a life of its own."

Seeing as Mordechai's weapon of choice and victims change typology, and that the real Martin Murdock was not guilty of filicide, Sam finally realizes that they are dealing with a tulpa, a Tibetan thought form. He tells Dean that in 1915, a group of twenty monks visualized a golem in their heads and meditated intensely enough that they brought the golem into life out of thin air. As Craig and Dana's story found its way to the HellHoundsLair website, the number of people who believed it exponentially increased. With a Tibetan spirit sigil on the farmhouse wall and on the website concentrating thousands of people's belief in Mordechai, the legend transformed from being a mere story to being an actual monster. The connection between Mordechai and the forum members remained dynamic and he continued to change as the legend changed and people came up with different stories about who he was and what he did.

One Case Where Destruction Is Harder than Creation

Thousands of people theorizing and strengthening the tulpa through their convictions poses a tough challenge to the brothers. Simply deleting the sigil off the wall or off the website wouldn't destroy Mordechai because once he came to exist, he was no longer dependent on the sigil. This is when Dean delivers the million-dollar line for the episode: "How the hell are we supposed to kill an idea?"

Their plan is to take advantage of Ed and Harry and manipulate them into posting a piece of information about Mordechai that will supplant a way of killing him in the fans' minds. They give Ed and Harry a death certificate from the 1930s saying that Murdock died of a self-inflicted gunshot wound and thus has a deadly fear of pistols. If enough people on the website are exposed to the idea, the brothers think they might get to kill Mordechai.

That night, Dean and Sam sneak into the Hell House again, thinking the new intel has stewed online long enough. Their pistols drawn, they search for Mordechai in the house and find him with his axe, screaming as he lunges for them. Both brothers empty their guns into Mordechai, but he turns to mist as he did with the rock salt, reappearing moments later. Dean and Sam learn that even though the information was on the site, it wasn't there for long because the HelloundsLair servers crashed. Once they realize that the pistols won't work, they decide to escape the house. After an intense fight where Mordechai almost kills Sam, while Dean splashes kerosene everywhere, the brothers manage to leave and Dean sets the house on fire.

Dean reasons that since Mordechai cannot leave the house, and the brothers don't know how to kill him, it was better to improvise. By burning the house down, he ensures that nobody else will go in and Mordechai won't have a house to haunt. Sam asks "what if the legend changes again and Mordechai is allowed to leave the house?" and Dean simply retorts, "Then we'll just have to come back."

It's a weak ending for "Hell House." Over the show's 327 episodes, only about sixty creatures make a one-time appearance—leprechauns, elves, and unicorns being some of the other one-timers. The brothers mention the tulpas a few times in the later seasons but they never encounter a tulpa again. Of course, as the show's fate changed and they stepped away from doing monster-of-the-week episodes and moved into pre-apocalyptic storytelling, it made sense to drop some of the more comical monsters. However, I suspect the reason they haven't brought back tulpas has nothing to do with humor and everything to do with how powerful tulpas can be.

People who are thinking about tulpas essentially create something out of nothing, and they can do this completely unwittingly. In "Hell House," we see how Craig and Dana's story, accompanied by band logos and random sigils lifted off of a theology textbook, still played a crucial part in Mordechai's conception. As tulpas aren't universally affected by silver bullets, salt circles, or angel blades, they also have the advantage of being incredibly hard to kill. Biblical evil like demons or Cain or even Lucifer have been much easier to deal with because they obey certain rules within their universe. There are ways to kill and defeat them, written in ancient scrolls or Men of Letters research and Sam and Dean have succeeded at every turn, even when it has required great sacrifice. In fact, even in the series finale of the show, which fans felt conflicted about for many reasons, the brothers were able to defeat a character like the God of Abraham.

In contrast to ritual and physical means of killing banshees, archangels, or wendigos, to kill Mordechai, Sam and Dean have to uproot an idea or drastically change it as it exists in other people's minds. They have to introduce a radical notion and have the means to distribute it. With the HellHoundsLaid forum goers, a simple comment or post could not make a difference. They needed Ed and Harry's help as website owners to garner attention for the death certificate and superficially create a weakness for the tulpa among the fans' collective imagination. Without such a weakness, there's no way to kill a tulpa. Another reason the episode can feel unsatisfactory and hastily wrapped up is probably because killing an idea is hardly that easy. In fact, Dean and Sam's plan does not work, Dean ultimately resorts to brute force, and the uncertainty of whether Mordechai is dead or whether he'll come back remains looming over them.

Part of the incredibility and weakness of the episode stems also from how cleanly the chain of events that lead to Mordechai's inception is explained. Sam and Dean's first tulpa is one whose story is promulgated via a single news source: the HellHoundsLair website. This is both a curse and a blessing for the brothers. On the one hand, they can conveniently make a plan (albeit an unsuccessful one) to reach all the believers of Mordechai through Ed and Harry's website, and on the other hand, because the website's servers crash, there is no other way for the fans to access the new information and change Mordechai's legend. Because of these unreliable developments in the story, the real force and potential of the tulpa doesn't fully shine through to the viewer. In fact, the last scene where Dean sets the house on fire deliberately underplays the tulpa species.

IoT as the Internet of Tulpas

Especially in a modern setting, the tulpa presents an interesting case study as it sheds light on what the advent of the Internet has made possible for us. In the real world, ideas spread far more rapidly and ambiguously than we can keep track of and the issue of censorship is not a new one. In most cases, ideas aren't confined to a single source, but spread out over many sources with many branches.

Socrates famously argues in the *Republic* for a kind of refinement and censorship of the arts such that children are not told stories and myths that depict the gods as treacherous and vicious beings. He goes further to say that mothers and nurses should also be careful what sorts of stories they tell children in case those stories instill fear and cowardice in them instead of piety and courage.

Now of course we don't live in Plato's *Republic*. Where we live, censorship mostly serves as further publicity and bolsters public interest in whatever is being censored or hidden, so much so that the phenomenon itself has a name: the Streisand Effect. Whether it is an offshoot conspiracy theory or a social manifesto, modern technology has immortalized even our most inane thoughts and ideas. Contrast this for example, with medieval and pre-modern manuscript replication, before the conveniences of the printing press. It used to be that only the thoughts, theories, and knowledge deemed worthy by a church, monarch or wealthy patron, would be reproduced by hand and collected. The dissemination of ideas was a mightier effort than today's heavily circulated social media or blog posts, which suffer no real restrictions. However, what saves a lone tweet or a blogpost from losing itself to the internet black hole is an audience. Just as Craig and Dana's made-up story became a sensation enough to conjure up a physical being, we witness similar trends with memes, cryptocurrencies, and even broader and structural realities like gender norms and racial biases.

There's also a tension in what the creators of an idea or character intend versus what comes to be. Craig and Dana fashioned a story around Mordechai just for fun, which is understandable for a couple of teenagers from a small town in Texas. However, once the story garnered enough believers through the HellHoundsLair website and manifested Mordechai into physical reality, it no longer mattered what thrill-seeking teenagers on an online forum intended. Mordechai himself never knew that he was the result of a superficial legend created solely for entertainment purposes; he only knows he's supposed to kill any girls who wander into the basement, or chop up any person that faces him. Mordechai's disconnect from the forum-goers' intentions is reminiscent of all characters in the public sphere (including Sam and Dean Winchester).

Even though the showrunners are the primary creators of Sam and Dean's story, what they create takes on a life of its own once a fandom forms and claims audience ownership of those characters. The fans then can overlay their own collective imagination onto the show's storyline. They can make up parallel universes with altered canons, and they can even have enough sway to change the outcome of the show, to demand new storylines, and even petition specific roles for their favorite actors. It's exactly this force of compulsion that could have scared the showrunners away from making tulpas a recurring monster on *Supernatural*.

"Hell House" aired exactly nine days after Twitter was created. What would the brothers have done if there were a network of sites and forums that spanned across the US and the world, all engaged in tulpa creation and manifestation, with hundreds of thousands of members and contributors? Even though the brothers have been to Hell and back (quite literally) multiple times, a problem of that scale would still be well above Dean and Sam's pay grade unless they tried to invoke divine intervention where a God or multiple gods fought and banished the tulpas along with the thoughts in people's minds. To battle with a tulpa in today's world where viral tweets or instagram photos can get hundreds of thousands of likes would have been akin to the brothers trying to topple the patriarchy or end racism by themselves.

When Socrates criticizes the poets and the playwrights in the *Republic*, he does so to point out that fiction, poetry, and even nursery rhymes can affect people's moral development. Yes, reading Homer's epics or Aeschylus's plays aren't perfectly analogous to tulpa creation, but it's true that the ideas we create and consume tend to impact our reality one way or another. Medical racism and sexism among healthcare providers cost black and brown women their lives, while incel manifestos circulating in anonymous corners of the web encourage mass shooters.

What our society thinks about human dignity and environmental justice can either cultivate flourishing communities that live in harmony with the Earth or launder colonialism and imperialism motivated by fear and scarcity. "Hell House" asks us the question: what do we do when it's better for us to kill an idea? When that idea has come to life and is killing people? The episode can't give us an answer, but it does start the conversation.

7
More Mothers, Lovers, and Other Monsters

PATRICIA L. BRACE

In a November 2014 interview with *Variety*, the film and television industry magazine, on the occasion of the show's two hundredth episode, *Supernatural* creator Eric Kripke recalled the notes he got from the network after the first season of the show:

> We always had to fight to stay on and in Season Two, that was very true. We moved over, it was the new CW, and we were a bubble show. A big note that the network had at the time was "We should really give the boys a home and some recurring characters and bringing in some women would be good." ("Supernatural at 200")

Kripke's response to that criticism was to add Ellen, Jo, and Harvelle's Roadhouse, but he did it under protest. He felt it took the show away from its core, which was two brothers, alone on the road, with no ties, especially not to anyone who could be a potential permanent love interest or even a mother figure. If the boys were truly happy and settled, they could not be true Hunters. Their life was one of rootless road trips, sacrifice, and honor. Their reward was knowing that they saved lives, sometimes even the whole world.

In the early seasons of *Supernatural*, to be a female recurring character or guest star on *Supernatural* was usually the equivalent of wearing a red shirt on *Star Trek*. The same usually held true for their bases of operations. By the end of

Season Two for example, Harvelle's was burnt to the ground ("All Hell Breaks Loose") and both Ellen and Jo are killed in "Abandon All Hope . . ." (Season Five), sacrificing themselves to save Sam and Dean so they can try to kill Lucifer.

As the show continued through a record-breaking fifteen seasons, the audience learned that dead did not always mean dead and characters often returned as the time honored sci-fi-fantasy tropes of parallel universe twin, or ghost, or secretly protected by a powerful witch's spell so cannot be killed, or even resurrected by a god or God-like being. Both Ellen and Jo returned, briefly, made use of for poignancy in their respective episodes, "My Heart will Go On" (Season Six) an alternate reality where Ellen is married to Bobby Singer and "Defending Your Life," (Season Seven) with Jo appearing as a ghost, to be a witness in Dean's trial before the god Osiris.

The female characters in the later seasons of the show, Nine to Fifteen, fit within the same rubric as used in my first essay on the subject, "Mothers, Lovers and Other Monsters," back in 2013. Here I'll look more closely at mother figures in Sam and Dean's lives, and several characters overlap categories as their relationships with the boys evolve to become both monster/antagonists and mother figures.

Warrior Mothers

Probably the most important mother figure in Sam and Dean's life, Mary Winchester dies in flashback in the Pilot episode of the show. As part of a deal she made to save her future husband John, Mary gave the yellow-eyed demon, Azazel the right to come into her home in ten years' time, starting the chain reaction of events that led to John and his sons becoming Hunters. When she interrupts his visit to Sam's crib, the demon kills her. Avenging her death is what motivates the Winchesters in the first two season of the show, culminating in the deaths of both John and Azazel.

Mary appears several more times in later seasons, in ghostly form, as a hallucination or in flashback, as her younger self, Mary Campbell. As a ghost, she's protective and self-sacrificing, defending her sons from a poltergeist in their old home ("Home," Season One). She embodies everything that Dean wants home to be in his djinn-induced hallucination in "What Is and What Never Should Be" (Season Two) with hugs of welcome and making him Dagwood sandwiches. Sam hallucinates her approval of his drinking demon blood to kill Lilith, in "When the Levee Breaks" (Season Four). She's also used by the manipulative angel Zachariah to torture them in "Dark Side of the Moon" (Season Five) as he flips the script from her first appearance in the episode, in PB&J crust-cutting mode, and has her tell Dean he was nothing but a burden to her.

When first Dean and Cass and later he, Sam, and Cass time-travel back to the Seventies to meet up with young Mary, they learn that the Campbell clan, including their mom, were Hunters and that Mary was hoping John would take her away from that life ("In the Beginning," Season Five) and "The Song Remains the Same" (Season Five). Her deal with Azazel is shown in the former and their inability to alter Mary's fated death is seen in the latter.

Kantian Objectification and Free Will

In each case, Mary's appearances are used to evoke a strong emotional response from her sons. They love her and are extremely protective of her and her memory. If an antagonist wants to get a rise out of the boys, bringing up their mom is often the best way to do it. This objectification of her and her use as tool is what the philosopher Immanuel Kant (1724–1804) warned against. As a memory, a ghost, or a time-travel younger version whose memory gets wiped so the angels can have their Apocalypse, she has little agency or choice in her fate.

These glimpses into the character of Mary Winchester made her a popular and beloved mother figure for the boys. When God's sister Amara brings her back to life, in the finale of Season Eleven, it changes the dynamic of the show. Mary's appearance to Dean in a graveyard is underlined by the fact that earlier in the episode he visited her gravesite in preparation for what he thought would be his own death, going off as a bomb to slay Amara. Now here she is, still dressed in the angelic white nightgown she died in during the first scene in the Pilot. It's a reboot, a second chance to get to know the mother they have mourned, avenged, and missed for most of their lives. Dean was four when Mary died, and Sam was six months old. Can the real woman, making her own choices, live up to the memory? Amara believes she can.

At this point, Season Twelve, Sam and Dean have had a permanent base of operations in Lebanon, Kansas, in the Men of Letters secret Bunker since Season Eight, and now they have their mom back. Except for the time they spent in Sioux Falls, South Dakota, at Bobby Singer's scrap yard, before it was destroyed and he was killed by Leviathans in Season Seven,[1] this is the only fixed home and parental figure they have had.[1] However, how much "mothering" do they now need?

Other Mothers for the Brothers

By this time, Dean is thirty-seven and Sam thirty-three. They are self-sufficient adults, raised by an absentee vengeful father who trained them since they were children as Hunters. In their travels they encountered a variety of women who have mothering aspects to their characters and served as positive examples to the Winchester boys. Ellen Harvelle is one from the early seasons of the show. Her love for her daughter has her sacrifice her life so that Jo does not die alone. In her episodes with Sam and Dean, she holds them to a high standard and refers to them as "her boys." Likewise, Mrs. Linda Tran, mother of the holy prophet Kevin Tran, is willing to sell her soul to save her son ("What's Up, Tiger Mommy?" Season Eight). She shows courage and resourcefulness in her later appearance in Season Nine ("Captives"), defeating the demon who was holding her hostage and then welcoming Kevin's ghost to live with her, despite knowing he could turn vengeful.

One of the longest running recurring female characters in the show is Sheriff Jody Mills, of Sioux Falls, South Dakota. From her first appearance, she sets the standard for the many female sheriffs, deputies, and police who appear on the show, such as Stillwater, Minnesota's Donna Hanscum

---

[1] In the finale of Season Five, Chuck argues in his description of the final showdown between Lucifer and Michael that Baby, the Impala, was the Winchester brothers' home, the only constant in their wandering lives.

(Briana Buckmaster). Tough and fair-minded, Jody has great agency and control. She is skeptical of the Winchesters because of their association with local "town drunk" Bobby Singer until she is witness to a supernatural happening in her own home: the return of her dead little boy, Owen ("Dead Men Don't Wear Plaid," Season Five). Unwilling at first to stop whatever brought him back, she impedes the Winchester's investigation into the resurrections around town, but when her son's zombie nature is revealed by him killing her husband, she becomes their ally. She appears in all the remaining seasons of the show, eventually "adopting" three teenage girls who have had encounters with monsters and crossed paths with Sam and Dean: Claire Novak, Alex (Annie Jones), and Patience Turner. These "Wayward Sisters," along with Jody and Donna were supposed to star in a spin-off, but it was not picked up by the network.

Since her family's horrific deaths, other than a brief flirtation with Bobby right before his death and an almost fatal dinner date with the demon Crowley, Jody's focus has been on her career in law enforcement and her sideline as a Hunter. The entry of the girls into her life pushes her towards the mothering part of her nature that she gave up when her son died. Her experiences working with Bobby, Sam and Dean give her the skills necessary to understand the horrors that each of the girls go through that lead them to her: Claire with angels and demons, Alex with vampires and Patience's psychic gifts that make her the target of a serial killer wraith. Patience's grandmother, psychic Missouri Moseley, was also a caring mother figure for Sam and Dean in the Season One episode, "Home."

Sam and Dean get drawn into the family they create, acting as mentors and taking a brotherly (or perhaps avuncular) role with the girls, in "Don't You Forget about Me" (Season Eleven). An awkward dinner discussion at Jody's table about birth control may be played for humor, but the familial bond expressed in the episode is also in counterpoint to a dark mirror image represented by Alex's time with her vampire family. It literally comes back to bite her with a vengeance when one of their victims returns ready to kill everyone she cares about now. After defeating them, Alex's guilt overwhelms her, and she is crushed under the weight of her guilt for the part she played in killing so many people in her past life. Jody mothers her, telling her, "Alex, you were ready to give up your life for us; that's goodness . . . and that's what's scary about family. It gives you so much to lose." Her compassion and understanding creates a strong foundation for the ties that bind her new family together.

Who's Your Mommy?

When Mary and Jody meet in "Celebrating the Life of Asa Fox" (Season Twelve) it's under difficult circumstances. At this point Jody is more of a mother to Sam and Dean than Mary, gently chiding Dean for not telling her that their mom had returned from the dead and then telling him she is there for him any time if he needs to talk. In contrast, Mary's demeanor to her sons is cold and distant. Her transition to the twenty-first century is rough. As she tells the reaper Billie, it was not her choice to come back.

Learning that John raised the boys as Hunters, (something she never wanted) and that he died avenging her, she blames herself for making the demon deal with Azazael. This guilt compels her to leave the Bunker and go out Hunting on her own, and eventually hooking up with the British Men of Letters, one of the Big Bads of Season Twelve, headed by the evil Dr. Hess, former headmistress of the Men of Letters version of Hogwarts. As the head of an organization that requires children to kill their best friend to be admitted, she is a human monster. Her assistant, Lady Bevell is a close second, following orders and leaving her young son in England to come to America and sadistically torture Sam.

Wanting to contribute, Mary embraces the more sophisticated Hunting techniques of the British Men of Letters (as does Sam initially) and even has a sexual relationship with one of their more vicious members, Mr. Ketch, though when she becomes suspicious of him, he captures her, and she is subjected to conditioning by Lady Bevell to remove her free will and sense of morality. The loss of agency makes her into an object to be used by the British Men of Letters. As Lady Bevell tells Sam and Dean: "You see her as Mummy. We see her as one of our best killers." We see Mary brutally murdering an American Hunter in flashback in "There's Something

About Mary" (Season Twelve) and after that she unsuccessfully tries to commit suicide to keep from endangering her sons. At the completion of her "realignment," just as she feared, she has no loyalty to her sons and tacitly condones their deaths, watching emotionlessly as Ketch locks them inside the Bunker and cuts off their air supply.

In "Who We Are," (Season Twelve) brainwashed Mary shows up in Sioux Falls with orders to kill Jody and any other Hunters she encounters. The initial confrontation between the women is not shown on screen, but Jody is able to capture Mary with Alex's help and hold her until Sam and Dean arrive. The women play a little "good mom" vs. "bad mom" when Jody comforts a wounded Dean and Mary snarks, "Aw, you want to play mother to my son? He's all yours." Jody replies, "Dean, that's not your mom," reassuring him and supporting him. We also see her tender farewell to foster daughter Alex when she heads off with Sam to attack the British Men of Letters headquarters while sending the girl to a safehouse.

To break her conditioning Dean dream-walks into Mary's mind and he finds her "hiding out" in a vision of their house in Lawrence, checking on fat baby Sam in his crib and making little boy Dean lunch. Here we see the resentment that he felt at her for making the deal with Azazel finally come out: *"I hate you . . . I had to be more than just a brother. I had to be a father and I had to be a mother to keep him safe. And that wasn't fair, and I couldn't do it."* He blames every bad thing that happened to Sam on her, from Jessica's death to losing his soul and then tells her he hates her, *and* he loves her, a feeling most people with fraught family relationships can easily understand. Then he does what he needs to do and tells her he forgives her and wants to start over, so she needs to fight, to see him as he really is. Just as she does, Ketch shows up, ripping apart the dream and gleefully beating Dean down. Just as he is about to shoot Dean, Mary takes him out, agreeing that both she and her son are killers. In a parallel, it is Jody who kills Dr. Hess, in the exact same way, with a head shot. Good warrior mothers again, both protect their children.

At the end of the episode, with her free will restored, Mary explains to Dean that the way she's been acting—cold and distant—since she's been back, is because she was trying to make things right. Her guilt over what her actions caused to happen to her sons makes her fear that they can't forgive her. In response, the Winchester boys hug it out with their mom, ready to renew their family bond.

Lucifer's Baby Momma

In Season Twelve Mary is shown as a sexual being, a powerful and smart Hunter and a mother who is trying to do better. This is reinforced in the show's emotional Season Fourteen two hundredth episode, "Lebanon," in which Dean's wish on a magic pearl grabs John Winchester out of 2003 and brings him to the Bunker in 2019. Their brief time together is cut short because of the temporal paradox. If John does not return to the proper time, Mary, and all the people they have saved over the last fifteen years, will cease to exist.

John says he chooses to be grateful for the time they have, and gives some closure to his sons, telling them he is proud of them and loves them. When Mary and John reunite, they share a passionate kiss, and soon thereafter the boys head out to get the ingredients for Winchester surprise, the only thing Mary knows how to cook. Although this is not stated explicitly, it has been thirty-six years since husband and wife had some alone time. We can only hope that their private reunion was as fulfilling as the joyous meal they share with their sons before John is sent back in time.

Other mother figures on the show are allowed to have a sex life, but it almost always becomes problematic. In Season Twelve, Kelly Kline was the widowed American President's mistress. As his aide, Kelly travels with her boss and is always on hand as a sex partner. It is a dangerous game she plays, sleeping with the most powerful man in the world. Seeking that power, Lucifer possesses the Commander in Chief and in that guise conceives a child with Kelly.

The arrival of Kelly and Lucifer's son, teen Jack Kline, also brings out the motherly instinct in Mary. She welcomes him to the family and is protective of him as if he is her own. When she comforts Kelly at Jack's birth, we get a foreshadowing of both women's sad futures ("All Along the Watchtower," Season Twelve):

KELLY: I'm dying.

MARY: I know.

KELLY: But that's okay . . . 'cause wouldn't you die for your sons?

MARY: Yeah.

Kelly will not survive the birth, but because of her son's powers she bonds with him in utero and later is able to meet him in her Heaven. It is her belief in his potential for goodness that gave her the strength to follow through with the pregnancy. She chooses to be grateful rather than resentful.

If Cass, Sam, and Dean are Jack's fathers, then Mary becomes his other mother. While trapped in the Apocalypse world, Mary and Jack bond by working together as part of the Resistance against the evil archangel Michael. She is proud of his ability to help in their fight, but also worries about him and his problems with controlling his powers. Mary makes the unfortunate decision to use "tough love" on him when she is horrified by his cruel killing of Nick, Lucifer's one-time vessel. She keeps at him, pushing him to say he understands that what he did to Nick was wrong and that causes the Nephilim to lash out, wiping her from existence. In effect Jack commits matricide twice—his birth causes Kelly's death and his careless wrath, Mary's.

The Queen of Hell and Mrs. Butters

A list of "Mother Monsters" in *Supernatural* could include The Mother of All, Eve who created the Alpha monsters; The Darkness, Amara, twin to God and imprisoned by him at the dawn of Creation; and Alex's vampire "mother" of the Nest, Celia. Each of them creates or births evil into the world and guards it jealously, making them antagonists to the Hunters. All are defeated by the Winchesters and their allies. Amara may be the exception after her reconciliation with her brother, but in the end, she is subsumed by him and then absorbed into Jack when he takes Chuck's grace in the penultimate episode of the show.

Crowley's mother, Uber-witch Rowena MacLeod and Wood Nymph Bunker House-Mother Mrs. Butters are examples of supernatural women trying to hold their own in a man's world while also mothering their respective "sons." Each has an important role to play in the series and act as both ally and antagonist to the Winchesters.

The three-hundred-or-so-year-old witch Rowena is brought into the series as an antagonist in Season Ten and shows herself to be a selfish, highly sexual, manipulative yet powerful wielder of the dark arts. At various times she aligns herself with dark forces including Lucifer and Amara. At others she's a reluctant ally of the Winchesters, using her magicks to help them battle Lucifer, Amara, and Chuck, God himself. She is an admittedly terrible mother. She abandoned her son, Fergus, (the name Crowley had as a human) as a young child and though she says she's proud of his rise to power, she actively works against him in secret, plotting with Lucifer to overthrow him. For his part Crowley loathes her but buys in to her flattery and sets her up in Hell as is befitting his mother until she shows her true colors, and then he kicks her out.

Rowena is the bad mother personified and betrays Crowley and the Winchesters several times. She also kills many innocents in her selfish quests for power and advantage. However, there are cracks in her bad persona. She had a favored foster son, a peasant boy, Oskar, to whom she granted immortality in return for his parent's kindness to her ("Brother's Keeper," Season Ten). When a spell to remove the Mark of Cain from Dean needs her to "sacrifice what the spellcaster loves" we see that she is capable of motherly feeling, but willing to override it for her own needs. She also murders her own grandchild, Gavin, to show Crowley what it is like to lose a child in revenge for him bringing Oskar to the Winchesters' notice.

It's only after Crowley's death that we see her show the same kind of motherly wrath in service of her son when she starts killing Reapers to attract the attention of Death to return him to life ("Funeralia," Season Thirteen). Though her plan doesn't work, it does show that she cared for her son perhaps even more than she knew. When questioned about her motives by Sam she admits she would rather have him alive and hating her than dead and a hero. By the final two seasons, Rowena has become an ally to "Team Free Will" and works with them during the Apocalypse World arc, even saving them all by holding open the rift at the risk of her own life so that they can return before Chuck destroys the alternate universe.

Rowena's death at Sam's hand in the final season is a true self-sacrifice ("The Rupture," Season Fifteen). Chuck opened Hell and the dead souls are streaming out in a "Ghostpocalypse." The temporary barrier around the town is collapsing. Like her earlier spell, the one to close the Hell fissure requires a death, that of the spell caster, (which is exactly how Cowley died to seal the first dimensional tear to Apocalypse World). She tells Sam she cannot do it herself, but she knows they are fond of each other so she can count on him to do the right thing.

This is a very different woman than the one we first met. She no longer views others as objects to be used and manipulated for her own selfish needs. She has learned and grown and treats Sam as a foster son/apprentice. After her death we learn that she left all her magical implements and journals to Sam, which gives him a boon. He finds a spell in the journals to resurrect his love interest, the dead Hunter, Eileen Leahy. Dragged to Hell by a Hellhound, she was released by the fissure, and Rowena's spell reincorporates her. Though this is later revealed to be another manipulation by Chuck, allowing him to use Eileen as an unwitting undercover operative against the Winchesters ("Our Father, Who Aren't in Heaven," Season Fifteen).

Our last glimpse of Rowena is in her capacity as Queen of Hell ("Our Father, Who Aren't in Heaven," Season Fifteen). She finally seems to have found the place where she belongs. When Sam, Dean, and Castiel visit her there, hoping to talk to Michael in the cage, she takes it upon herself to counsel Dean and Cass, sensing tension between them. Whatever it is, she tells them, they need to work it out before something like death comes between them, just as it did for her and Fergus. This kind, motherly, commanding woman is the final evolution of the character.

In "Last Holiday," the boys' attempt to reboot the problematic Bunker systems causes the Wood Nymph known as "Mrs. Butters" to appear. Sidelined after Knight of Hell Abaddon's murder spree in 1958, this magical being has been held in stasis ever since. After she was captured by the Thule

Society and killed over two hundred Nazis, she was offered a job protecting the Men of Letters Bunker. This she takes very seriously, acting as both Housemother and guard dog for "her boys." For the first time in their lives, the Winchesters have a 1950s style stay-at-home mom catering to their every need. The montage sequence showing her magical decorations and feasts for every holiday and the lunch sacks she presents them with every day as they head off to Hunt highlights the boys' ecstatic and grateful expressions at her care.

Of course, there must be a catch, and in this case, it is in her overdeveloped protection skills. She was programmed by the World War II–era Men of Letters to destroy anything that threatened the organization. Their method of achieving this was coercive, physically torturing her and convincing her that her home in the forests of Europe had been destroyed so she would not try to escape. Her considerable power also augments the Bunker's systems, so she became a sort of perpetual battery booster for the Men of Letters. They took away her free will and graft any sense of agency she has to her new mission. Jack discovers all of this is an old film which shows Butters literally ripping the head off a Thule officer and then offering everyone tea and cookies. She is their Golem; her life is dedicated to them.

When Butters feels threatened by Jack's presence as the son of Lucifer, she plots to take him out, weakening him with a Trojan Horse set of Smoothies that dull his powers and make him vulnerable. The Winchesters refuse to go along with the scheme. Even though Jack accidentally killed their mother, they still take a parental protective responsibility for him and so she imprisons Dean and tortures Sam. This is the same way she was treated by the Men of Letters.

In the end the Winchesters convince Mrs. Butters that the OG Men of Letters had deceived her. They free her and she returns to the forests from whence she came. Sadly, for the legacies, she takes her extra power boost and her packed lunches with her.

She's my Mother, No My Sister

One final character that fits this discussion of motherly relationships with the Winchesters is Celeste Middleton, the computer hacker known as Charlie Bradbury. When we first meet her, she is a computer tech at Richard Roman Enterprises, the front that the Leviathans use in Season Seven to prepare humans to become their cattle. Young, quirky, extremely pop-culture literate, feminist, proud, and out, she is not presented as a potential love interest for either Winchester, so we are free to enjoy seeing the friendship and familial love grow between her and her "boys."

Charlie uses her mad skills and free will to help the Winchesters take down numerous supernatural threats including a power hungry LARPer who covets her Crown as Queen of Moondoor and later a djinn keeping her and Dean in a loop only solved when she faces her own mother's death. She is taken to Oz with Dorothy for a time in Season Nine, battles with her own evil twin after being split by the Wizard and finally, works with the Mark of Cain removal team to help find a way to save Dean from the curse in Season Ten. Charlie is actually killed by the Wicked Witch, but is brought back to life by the angel Gadreel, who is inhabiting Sam's body at the time. It is her decryption of the Nadia Codex text that allows them to find the spell in the *Book of the Damned* to remove the Mark. As Dean tells Ketch in "Bring 'Em Back Alive" (Season Thirteen), "Charlie was like family. She was a sister to me. She did more for me and Sam than I can say."

Like Ellen, Mary, Rowena, Kelly, Jody and Mrs. Butters, Charlie is dedicated to helping and protecting the ones she loves, even at the cost of her own life. She literally travels the world searching for knowledge and learns Hunter skills to help the Winchesters. Doing this, however, earns her the Frankenstein family as enemies and she works up to the last second to get the Codex decryption to Sam before they find her and brutally kill her. Dean and Sam are devastated, knowing that they failed to protect her. There is some consolation in the fact that they meet her "alternative" double in Apocalypse World in Season Thirteen and they are able to bring her to Earth Prime before the other one collapses.

Part III

"Dude, you were hallucinating sheep on the road."

8
Which Brother Is the Good One?

GERALD BROWNING

Throughout their journeys on the road and all the adventures they have had, Sam and Dean Winchester have made many decisions—some brash and some calculated—that have decided the fate of humanity many times over. These decisions have often revealed important personality traits that set them apart from one another. However, the question remains: which brother is the "good" brother?

The "family business" that the Winchester boys have inherited from their parents has forged them into the ethical warriors that they are. Both brothers have made decisions that have put their lives in peril. These decisions have shown us who they are. It is obvious to see that their views of "right" and "wrong" are different. And it appears that Dean Winchester's moral compass, as dark as it may be, is more suited to their ongoing war than is Sam's.

Deontological Ethics, Consequentialist Ethics, and Idjits

One of the major debates that seems to be recurring throughout the series is the notion of what, exactly, is the right thing to do. Sam and Dean both see their actions as being morally correct, even though they often strongly disagree. Even though they are making a lot of the same life or death decisions with each Hunt, their attitudes towards the ethics in their decisions are addressed in different ways.

Dean's moral compass is consequentialist: he judges whether an action is right or wrong by all the consequences, good and bad, that follow from it. If there is a great good to be gained, then the action is right. Sam is more in line with what philosophers call "deontology," which is the view that some things are right and wrong on their face, no matter what the outcome. A deontologist would say, for instance, that it's just wrong to torture an innocent person to death, even if, due to specific circumstances, the net results would be better than the results of failing to commit that horrible act.

As Dean re-introduces Sam into the world of the Hunters, Sam brings up moral problems of his new life. In the first episode, "Pilot," we see that even the lifestyle of the Winchesters was rampant with moral dilemma. Dean steps into an investigation conducted by the local sheriffs. Sam flinches when Dean pulls out fake federal credentials—lying and deceiving are near the top of the list of things deontologists don't approve of. Also, as the boys check into a motel (the same motel once used by their father), Dean rifles through a box full of phony credit cards. Sam makes a snide comment, which Dean brushes off.

Again, Sam Winchester's ethical concerns stem from a deontological attitude. Sam judges stealing and lying to be morally wrong. This seems to be his moral compass throughout much of the series. As he grows into the Hunter that he will become by the end of the series, we see that Sam has changed (sometimes not for the better). Later in the series, we see Sam dabbling with the dark arts, and finding himself addicted to dark magic. However, looking at the Sam Winchester in the initial few seasons of the show, even though he has been jaded by his childhood experiences hunting, he is much more subject to moral doubts than his brother, Dean.

A consequentialist like Dean Winchester believes that the ends—meaning the predictable results—may justify the means. In "Bugs" (Season One) Dean exits a bar with cash won from hustling pool. Sam suggests that they get "honest" day jobs. Dean replies that Hunting is their day job. Dean is aware of the ethical problems that hustling pool, credit card scams, and the like entail, but the "day job" of fighting evil is the moral focus, and it takes moral priority.

Even though he commits petty crimes, Dean sees these as means to an end. They allow him to continue his fight against the forces of evil.

Many of the moral actions that Sam and Dean do are matters of life and death. It is these harsh situations that really highlight the differences in their characters. In "Heart" (Season Two), the Winchesters are hunting a were-wolf in San Francisco. They meet a young woman named Madison. Madison, once an innocent victim who needs to be protected, gets bitten and becomes the target of Dean Win-chester. Sam, who has fallen in love with Madison, doesn't want to kill her. When they find out that Madison is infected and has become a shapeshifting werewolf, they tie her up. Dean knows that this is a temporary solution and that the only way to stop Madison from eventually harming a lot of people by infecting them is to kill her. The consequentialist in Dean is taking charge.

Knowing that Sam has strong feelings for Madison, Dean wanted to spare him the pain of killing her. Throughout the series, Sam and Dean constantly struggle with the notion of killing human beings and killing monsters. While that line was very easy for Dean to draw, Sam struggled with the dis-tinction many times. To Dean, Madison the Human Being was very different from Madison the Werewolf. To Sam, the difference was more blurred. Madison, who loved Sam, as well, wanted him to end her life so she could not hurt anyone. Sam, reluctantly, killed her. Sam had resigned himself to killing beings that were visibly monsters, but Madison was a shapeshifter, a werewolf. Therefore, she was visibly a human being. This made the line *very* blurry for him. How-ever, Dean, whose ethics focuses on the consequences of their actions hated the idea of killing Madison, but had no prob-lem doing so because he knew that her werewolf urges would get the best of her at some point and she would seriously harm people in the future.

Ethics through Sam's Eyes

The show, *Supernatural,* allows the viewer to be introduced to the world of the Hunters through Sam Winchester's eyes. Dean has been acclimated from years of hunting monsters.

However, Sam, living a mundane lifestyle, seems to need to be re-introduced into the life. Sam has an ethical viewpoint that is much like that of most people who are watching the show. He "knows" the concept of right and wrong. He "knows" that killing is wrong (in any circumstances). So, the moral question of what makes someone, or something, a "monster," is seemingly very straightforward. However, the further along in the show we watch, the less "black and white" the issues become.

The phenomenon of the gray line between what makes someone a monster and what doesn't is seen throughout Season Four when Sam becomes addicted to demon blood. Way back in Season One, we see that Sam has psychic abilities. In "Home," Sam has a dream that a demon stalks a family in their old home. What seems at first like a wild goose chase turns into the boys saving a young family from a poltergeist and seeing the ghost of their deceased mother (who was trying to protect the family from the malevolent spirit). This plot point turns into a major storyline throughout Season Four when Sam finds out he was fed demon blood as a baby, giving him preternatural powers, which he uses to combat evil, in partnership with a "rogue" demon named Ruby. In Season Four, Ruby hooks Sam on demon blood as a way to gain more power to exorcise demons with his mind.

In "Faith" (Season One), Sam and Dean have another conversation about what makes someone a "monster." In this episode, Sam and Dean uncover a Reaper who is letting a faith healer decide who lives and who dies. A blind faith healer named Roy heals Dean's weak heart of an affliction that occurred during a Hunt. Dean is suddenly filled with remorse when he finds out that a Reaper rescued him from death, but in order to do that, an innocent person had to die.

In the middle of their investigation, Dean coldly decides that Roy (who is actually an innocent, since he genuinely believes that he is a faith healer) is a monster. Dean says, "Sam, the guy's playing God. He is deciding who lives and who dies. That is a monster in my book." Sam quickly reminds his brother that Roy is a human being. Dean realizes that the decision to stop the killings (the "long game" if you will) is ultimately the right choice, even though killing a human being is part of the plan. Sam quickly dismisses any idea of killing an innocent human being, though this would stop the Reaper's killings, showing us that Sam is judging the action itself, as opposed to the consequences.

A major dilemma that arises for Dean is that slowly Sam is turning into a monster and Dean feels that he must try to save (or kill) Sam in order to save his soul. The same dilemma that Sam had with Madison becomes a major storyline again when Dean has to decide whether or not to kill Sam. Both brothers ultimately make different decisions. Ironically, Sam who sees the act of killing as an ethical problem, ends up killing his target. Dean, however, does not kill Sam, even though he was constantly looking at the action as a consequentially "good" thing.

Another storyline that illustrates Sam's and Dean's differing views of good and evil can be found in "Bloodlust" (Season Three). Gordon Walker is a vampire hunter who doesn't see humans and vampires as "shades of gray." Walker's sister was turned into a vampire, which led to Walker killing her. From this he concluded that every creature who was "supernatural" was inherently evil and deserved to be destroyed.

The Winchesters came across Walker while investigating cattle mutilations. They encounter Walker in the middle of a Hunt and save his life. Still mourning the death of his father, Dean embraces Walker's attitude and hunts the nest of vampires with Walker. However, they fail to notice that Sam gets abducted by vampires. In order to prove to the Hunters that the vampires are not a threat, they let Sam go. He tries to convince the other Hunters that these vampires are no threat, but they don't listen.

In this episode, we see the argument over what is good and what is evil. Sam believes that since the vampires tried to live a life without killing humans, they weren't evil and should be allowed to "live." Walker and Dean believe that every supernatural creature should be eliminated. Sam sees killing of anything as a "bad" action. Walker and Dean believe that "the ends justify the means," the "ends" being that humanity would be safer without the vampire predators around. This would "justify" their methods of killing the monsters. However, as the story progresses, Dean sees that the vampires that Walker is hunting are actually innocent of killing people. Dean sees the light. He faces off with Walker in a showdown, which culminates in Walker's capture.

Dean the Consequentialist

Dean Winchester was born and raised as a Hunter. Unlike Sam, he has little interest in finding a life outside of Hunting. He lives for the next hunt and is eager to terminate as many demons and monsters as he can. He rationalizes his kills as "for the greater good." His "good" comes from the consequences of his actions. The fewer the monsters on the planet, the better off humankind will be.

Early in the show, we see that Sam is struggling with the idea of killing. In "Simon Said" (Season Two) the Winchesters are hunting a man with the ability to make people do whatever he says. They know that the target was born on the same day Sam was, has psychic abilities like Sam, and was chosen by the same Yellow-Eyed Demon that killed their mother. As such, Dean is more than willing to kill those who are using their powers to hurt others, whereas Sam is hesitant. A running theme throughout the season is Sam wondering whether he is evil and will do evil because of the powers. He sees a vague line between himself and those he hunts.

Dean mentions that Sam "doesn't have it in" him to kill people. However, Sam replies with "You've seen the things I've Hunted." Dean's consequentialist beliefs allow him to draw a line between those they kill and the killings that they (the Winchesters) commit. Sam, on the other hand, is not as certain as his older brother.

To Murder or To Kill

A recurring theme throughout the series that further serves to highlight the moral differences between Sam and Dean is the "I am a Monster" theme. Each brother encounters his own moral and ethical threshold in different ways. Both come very close to becoming the very monsters that they instinctively Hunt.

A major question that comes up in *Supernatural* is "What makes someone or something a monster"? A related and very important theme is the distinction between a "kill" and a "murder." On many occasions (one being the episode "Simon Said"), Dean tells Sam that he is "no murderer." However, on many occasions, they refer to each other's "kills." So, what's the distinction between a "murder" and a "kill"?

Dean refers to stalking and killing monsters as a "hunt" or a "kill." However, when someone is killed in cold blood (especially a human), he refers to them as "murdered." While this may be mere semantics to some, the implications may allow Hunters such as Sam and Dean to be able to sleep at night. Dean has executed many monsters, but in Season Three, he dies and is sent to Hell. When he is brought back, we learn that he was given the opportunity to torture, and did torture, damned souls. Once he returns to Earth and he reflects on what he has done, he feels guilt and remorse. He even goes so far as to contemplate the possibility that he himself is a monster. Even though they were mere souls who were corrupted, Dean tortured helpless beings. The line between humanity and monstrosity grows very thin for the Winchesters throughout the series.

In "Croatoan," Sam argues with Dean about the cavalier attitude that he seems to have towards killing. A demonic virus has spread through a town, infecting many of the citizenry. The people become controlled by demons. Neither Sam nor Dean can be absolutely sure which person is infected. However, Dean seems to kill indiscriminately. "We are supposed to struggle with this. That's the whole point." Sam impresses upon Dean the "struggle" with keeping one's humanity by not killing innocent people. He seems to want Dean to focus on the moral implications of killing innocents rather than just focusing on the end result (the extermination of the demons). To Sam, the struggle is necessary for keeping one's humanity. Sam even goes so far as to tell Dean that he is acting like one of the monsters who are holding everyone in the room hostage. The episode culminates with Dean nearly shooting an innocent person. Right as he is on the brink of shooting, he pulls himself from the edge. Both Sam and Dean see the importance of the distinction between humanity and monstrosity. Again, as we see throughout the series, both Winchesters struggle with their humanity by constantly coming to the brink of it, and both have been very close to their monstrous sides, from which they must time and time again fight their way back.

A glowing example of this is when Ruby gets Sam hooked on demon blood and he develops the ability to exorcize demons with his mind. Dean tells Sam that he is scared that Sam has actually become a monster and that Dean might have to Hunt and kill his own brother. Just like the demons, the cravings that Sam feels actually begin to cause him to physically look similar to the very monsters that they Hunt.

Dueling Thoughts

In Season Three we actually see Sam beginning to think in similar ways to Dean. In "Fresh Blood," the boys are being stalked by their old foe Gordon Walker. The Winchesters go after a vampire who's turning women so that he can have a "family." Echoing fears that we've seen with Dean, this vampire is afraid of being alone and tries to do whatever he can to keep a family. Gordon Walker mercilessly attacks and kills members of the vampire's family. As an act of brutal revenge, the vampire captures Gordon and turns him into the very creature that he hates the most.

When Sam and Dean find out that Gordon is involved, Sam tells Dean that they need to kill Gordon. Dean is shocked by Sam's argument and wonders what is wrong with him. When Sam tells Dean that they have no other option because Gordon will always go after him, Dean agrees. It initially appears that Sam is becoming a consequentialist, but self-defense is one of the rare instances in which deontologists justify killing.

Later in the season ("Malleus Maleficarum"), Sam and Dean learn of a coven of witches operating out of a suburban neighborhood, we see Sam actually moving toward consequentialism. Sam tells Dean that even though the women are human, they are still acting out of evil and must be stopped. "Burn, witch, burn" is Dean's reply. In that same episode, Dean voices his concerns about Sam's change of heart. "You seem less and less worried about offing people." Sam asks where has caring about life gotten him. "It's just what you're *supposed* to do," Dean replies.

Typically, at times like this, they find themselves arguing about "the sanctity of human life." Sam, it seems, is coming to realize that the most practical way of "fighting the war" against evil is to change his viewpoint about morality. He needs to be more like Dean. He seems to realize that the hesitation that he shows by distinguishing between murder and Hunting is not very conducive to fighting the war against evil—especially if Sam has to fight the war on his own.

Doing Good by Killing Things

Dean and Sam Winchester are warriors whose philosophical outlooks on what they do differ almost as much as their personalities (at least most of the time). They work well together focusing on their strengths and doing whatever they can to protect the other partner. Both men understand that as they face the dangers that they face in each episode, they may change, becoming darker characters who teeter closer to that abyss that can turn them into the very things that they hunt.

The very fact that they feel as if they are making a difference in the lives of innocent civilians and that they are on the side of "good" or "righteousness," is what inevitably makes them good Hunters. As a deontologist, Sam Winchester looks at each of the actions that he takes and decides whether it's good. He constantly questions the motives and actions of himself, as well as those of others. The consequentialist Dean, on the other hand, looks at the end result of an action. He does believe that even though he has killed many beings, since he did it for the greater good, that's what matters the most. On several occasions, he has mentioned that Sam, questioning every little movement he takes, can create hesitation and even doubt, which can prove to be fatal, when your life is on the line. Both seem to be driven by the goal of doing good.

One of the main differences between Sam and Dean is that Sam dwells on a lot of the moral dilemmas more than does Dean. Sam seems to analyze each kill that they commit. He wonders about the difference between murder and killing. There are many references to this distinction—an important distinction to the Winchesters because it marks the difference between being a Hunter and being a monster.

The term "monster" doesn't only apply to the supernatural. In "The Benders" (Season One), Sam gets abducted in Minnesota by a sadistic family of Hunters who have decided to hunt humans for sport. The brothers think that it could be a supernatural phenomenon, but when Dean and Sam find out that the Benders are merely sadistic backwoodsmen, they attack in much the same way as they would any creature. So, even though they weren't "monsters" in the literal sense of the word, the Benders were "monsters" in their own right.

One of the most important parts of *Supernatural* is the internal fight that the brothers have. The line between humanity and monstrosity isn't as bright as we thought. Each episode we see some sort of struggle where this line gets grayer. It appears that with each episode, the Winchester boys get closer and closer to leaving their humanity behind. This fight seems to begin and end with the parallels between the demons that indiscriminately hunt humans, and the Hunters who indiscriminately kill monsters.

Both Winchesters see the need for hunting monsters and killing them. The Winchesters have killed humans who kill other people, and have let monsters live who try to live "good" lives. So, it turns the life of a Hunter into shades of gray. The consequentialist's point of view would be very conducive to the lifestyle of a Hunter, but the deontologist's point of view towards morality would allow the Hunter to think through the decisions and to be able to live with the life-or-death decisions that they have to make.

Both Sam and Dean deal with the same dilemmas of their lifestyle: death, morality, fear, and anger. Ultimately, both have to struggle with the same problems even though they rationalize their dark decisions. Both realize that their causes are ultimately just and these wayward sons still have a long road to drive.

9
God the Programmer Is Dead

Michelle DeVries

Good and evil, right and wrong, moral and immoral, ethical and unethical, repetitive and superfluous, righteous and wicked, *Supernatural* writes each foe that the Brothers Winchester face as another page in the story of a constant battle between forces of light and darkness. But who determines what fits into each category, and how?

Monster Ethics

If *Supernatural* has shown us anything over its fifteen seasons, it is that monsters come in all shapes, sizes, and moral dispositions. During the early seasons, many of the enemies that Sam and Dean faced took the forms of mythical monsters from a myriad of cultures, murdering and torturing for fun or for selfishness or for no real reason at all. Much like the first levels of a video game, these monsters were the show's way of teaching us that evil is in the world and how we can spot it.

For *Supernatural*, the concept of a "monster" is an ethical concept, defined as a creature whose actions and values disregard the basic ethical standards accepted by the wider society. In short, they break the social contract time and time again for their own personal gain.

From werewolves to wendigos, from vampires to djinns, many of these monsters are dispatched, but some are left to coexist with humanity, provided they kept their monstrous ways to a minimum. The brothers spare those who have the capability as well as the willingness to uphold the social contract. This opens the door for monsters to arrive in a more familiar form: humanity. If monsters can have human traits, such as the capacity to live in peace with human society, then it stands to reason that humans can also have monstrous traits, such as greed, selfishness, brutality, and a torturous or murderous intent. This is true in our universe, and it is true in the universe of the Winchesters.

As the show and its story evolve, we see these layers being added to deepen the definition of "monster." The brothers spare, help, or even work with creatures that may be physically monstrous but morally humane; selfish and cruel tendencies become exposed in the brothers and in other human characters that on the surface seem unflinchingly "good"; and obviously evil forces became allies for the Winchesters at different times. Throughout the series, the writers have continued to make a grand commentary on the concepts of good and evil, showing that they aren't simple or even perfectly binary. With God becoming the ultimate villain in the final season, the ideas of good and evil, of moral and immoral, are ideas in a near-constant state of flux.

The Winchester Contract

Sam and Dean live as true deontologists, putting duty as the highest moral obligation on their scale of action. Fierce loyalty, getting the job done, and doing what they see as the right thing above all else form the rigid backbone of their deontological ways. We know that they do not always follow the law, as they regularly steal and lie in order to do the job of Hunters—as it turns out, the pay is less than a livable wage—but their moral standards allow them to ignore these small infractions, writing them off in the name of a greater good.

It seems logical to let these small-time crimes slide when Hunting is an all but thankless enterprise. It gets hairy when the boys start killing things. There have been times, such as with a werewolf co-ed, where the Winchesters have chosen to let a monster or beast go on the promise that it will not wreak havoc on the nearby population. Yet, there are plenty of times where we hear them talk of killing all non-human beings as a very black and white concept, such as when Dean deems the Phoenix as evil simply because of his species, despite the fact that the Phoenix was trying to live a quiet and peaceful life.

To complicate things even further, Sam and Dean regularly kill human hosts possessed by angels or demons even when the human host could potentially be saved. Perhaps one could argue that not killing the demon, even at the cost of the host, means that the demon could go on to possess others and inflict more pain and suffering on the world. That is a fair point, but one that does not apply when the possessed person is a loved-one of Sam and Dean. Then, the brothers go to great lengths to save the host at all costs. Consider the fact that Sam convinces Dean to avoid being banished to another realm, resulting in Dean killing Death and releasing Darkness upon the world.

The brothers are human, humans are imperfect creatures, and imperfect creatures make mistakes, hopefully learning something in the process. This is the redeeming theme that allows the *Supernatural* audience to return to the Winchesters' defense time and time again. This theme of making mistakes, learning a lesson, and doing better next time is a hopeful one, and would be enough to excuse their actions, except for the fact that they do not view others in this way. Even those close to them, such as Castiel and Jack, are not immune to the wrath of a wronged Winchester.

The series sees many heroes made into villains, and the angel Castiel is no exception. Yet, even when he was in a position to end the Winchesters, he spared them. Sam and Dean did not extend to him the same courtesy, binding Death himself to kill Castiel without even trying to save their corrupted friend. Jack made his fair share of mistakes as well, but tried to make amends by bringing Mary back to life. Rather than recognizing his remorse, instead of attempting to understand, the brothers tried to lock Jack away forever and then tried to kill him.

These examples of conflicting ethics and double standards could go on and on. The brothers jump to conclusions because they've been betrayed so many times. What about when Sam betrays Crowley after Crowley admits that he has been trying to tone down his evil ways? The brothers fight against manipulation and control at all costs. What about when they manipulate Amara into thinking they want to trap Chuck, and then plot to kill both Chuck and Amara even though she is not a villain at that point? I think you're picking up what I'm putting down.

So how can we call Sam and Dean Winchester deontologists? Because they adhere to a rigid system of duty as moral obligation without wavering and without fail. The variable is not the duty, but rather to whom the duty is done. Because their first and only lasting loyalty is to family, to each other, all of their actions are born from that bond. It is easy, then, to change the lenses of reality to fit morals to this philosophy. Does this make them bad men? No. It makes them relentless followers of a moral code that supersedes all others. It makes them fiercely rigid to a social contract of two. In the end, this social contract proves to be beneficial to the rest of humanity—and maybe even some monsters too—but that is just a fringe benefit to the brothers. One could argue that, if they were not good men, things would not have ended up so neatly packaged for the world.

Authoritarian Utilitarian or Capitalist Democrat?

Sam and Dean aren't the only duty-driven troublemakers in the series. Angels and demons also have their own moral codes that govern their actions, and it is worth taking a quick look at how the writers depict these sublime and super-natural creatures and how they interact with mundane humanity.

If ever there was a perfect image of bureaucracy at its best—or, arguably, its worst—the angels in *Supernatural* fit the bill. Switching from act utilitarianism to rule utilitarianism when the situation suits them, the angels are willing and eager to sweep aside individualism in order to assure the greatest good and happiness for the greatest number. Never mind that they have very little understanding of humanity and life on Earth. There's no bending of the utilitarianism morals for angels, and Castiel is no exception.

There are many times throughout the series where he and the other angels use and abuse humans for their own ends, or a perceived end goal. As often as not, this puts them squarely in the Winchesters' sites as obstacles to be overcome and enemies to be defeated. It's also worth mentioning that the angels' utilitarianism lends itself well to a bureaucratic state of checking boxes and following orders, provided the orders come from one professing absolute knowledge and perfect understanding of what will result in the most good for the greatest number. This is evidenced in the fact that Heaven falls into chaos during God's absence. They cannot seem to live in harmony without a central and absolute authority to act as the keystone of their social contract, falling into a Hobbesian state of nature.

Hell, on the other hand, gets its moral direction from democratic leadership mixed with a capitalist economy. When Lucifer is in the cage, demons build a society through contracts and civility, though to each other rather than to all creatures including humanity. Each demon willingly agrees to enter into the civil society of Hell, creating a contract similar to that of the Winchesters—one that does not seek to include, nor provide terms for inclusion of anyone outside of themselves.

It Ain't Easy to Be a Saint in Heaven

It would be nearly impossible to talk about the ethics of *Supernatural* without discussing the ethics and actions of gods, plural because in the end, the main God of the series is replaced by another, very different one. These two gods take strikingly opposite approaches to the rule and watch of humanity.

Chuck, who represented a traditional Christian god for most of the series, is an author writing the fates and fortunes of all living things, intervening and interfering where and when he sees fit or disappearing to watch the world fall subject to his whims and machinations when he feels like it. This does not make Chuck a clockmaker god who sits back to watch what he has built as it works indpendently of him without need or want of interference. It makes him a programmer god: one who writes a code and then watches the machine try to keep up its computer power as he makes tweaks and inserts puzzles, enemies, and games for entertainment.

He's similar to a child playing with action figures, and his child-like petulance definitely shows. Is he all-knowing? Sure, he knows all the code and all of his tweaks. Is he all powerful? Yes, within the system he has created he has total control. Is he all good? Let me refer you to the problem with the angels' ethics as described above. Chuck's absolute knowledge does not equate to absolute understanding of humankind. Chuck is all good as Chuck understands goodness, but his understanding is imperfect in that it is perfect. Humans are imperfect creatures, as proven by the Winchesters and their actions and inconsistencies and failings. Perfection can neither understand nor tolerate imperfection. That's why, from an ethical standpoint in *Supernatural*, this human life on Earth is the best possible life for humans. Obviously, Hell and Purgatory are undesirable places, but so is Heaven. When Dean finds himself in Paradise, he likens it to *The Matrix*, being unerringly and unbendingly perfect, and therefore far from nirvana. Because there cannot be understanding between perfect and imperfect, Chuck cannot create a perfect place for imperfect creatures. How much good could a good Chuck chuck if a good Chuck could chuck good?

When Jack becomes the new God, he absorbs Darkness. He explains that he will be in every drop of rain and speck of dust, that people don't need to pray to him and should instead trust that he is already part of them. Yet, at the same time, he makes a point of saying that he will not be "hands on," having already learned that when people have to be their best, they can be. The center of his theology is humanity because humanity understands itself better than any personification of a deity. Jack's paradise is the continuation of the best possible life for humanity: this life, but without the meddling of a programmer. Instead, the deity has made the clock and sits back to admire his ticking work.

God Is Dead—Here Comes Nietzsche

All the supernatural *Supernatural* creatures, except those that fell under particularly strong human influence, showed, and often acted on, an immense potential for evil. Even God Chuck himself, as an ultimate supernatural being, finds himself in violation of a moral code toward his creations, and in the end, he is destroyed by the unflinching duty of the Winchester brothers.

According to Nietzsche, in the absence of divine expectations, people can pursue life as they desire, free from restrictions that might prevent them from becoming the person that they would otherwise be. To experience true freedom is to not be ashamed of who you are and to accept your circumstances without obligation, dread, or fear, no matter what. This is its own system of ethics, and here is what Nietzsche had to say about it:

> I want to learn more and more how to see what is necessary in things as what is beautiful in them—thus I will be one of those who make things beautiful. Amor fati: let that be my love from now on! I do not want to wage war against ugliness. I do not want to accuse; I do not even want to accuse the accusers. Let looking away be my only negation! And, all in all and on the whole: some day I want only to be a Yes-sayer!

Nietzsche also has much to say about the role of willpower in *shaping* those circumstances or the lack of strength that prevents people from being able to shape their circumstances, but that is another story for another day.

While it's unlikely that Nietzsche had seen into the future and picked out the exact plot point that the writers of *Supernatural* employed in their final episodes and while it's unlikely that the literal death of a fictional God was what he was referring to, we can still draw the conclusions from Nietzsche that the writers most certainly did about freedom, individualism, morality, and the power of humankind. The Winchesters' fight is a fight for freedom of expression, regardless of who is standing next to them while they engage in the battle. Angels, demons, Death, werewolves, and tricksters are just the flavor. *Supernatural* reminds us that loving fate doesn't mean that bad things won't ever happen, or that humanity and the natural world will always be weak and at the mercy of the supernatural one. It means that we must find our code, our morality, our social contract in order to do the right thing in the face of the bad, and that code is what allows our story to also end in a profoundly human place.

10
Cas Is Family

DARCI DOLL

From the earliest seasons of *Supernatural,* Sam and Dean Winchester demonstrate both their aptitude as Hunters and the strength of their familial bond.

In Season One, the brothers are on a mission to find and rescue their father, John Winchester, and to aid him in avenging the death of their mother, Mary Winchester. Though John is noticeably absent through most of Season One, he shows his dedication to his family when in Season Two, episode 1, he offers the demon Azazel his life in exchange for Dean's survival after a car accident.

We learn in Season One that Azazel is the demon who killed Mary; the demon that the Winchesters have been Hunting for all of Season One. We later learn that in order to give Sam psychic abilities, Azazel had given Sam demon blood when he was a six-month-old. It is when Mary walks in on this act that Azazel kills Mary. Even further on, we learn that Mary had entered a deal with Azazel to save John's life when they were first dating; this deal is ultimately what opened the door for Azazel to give Sam the demon blood and to kill Mary.

John's love for his boys and his desire to protect them is so strong that he is willing to make a deal with the very demon he had been Hunting, foregoing the opportunity to avenge Mary's death. This is the depth of the Winchesters' love. As a family they fight for what's right, use their strength to defend those in need, and when someone they love's life is on the line, they will give everything they have, even their own souls and lives, to save them. Moreover, this dedication to the ones they love extends beyond blood relatives.

We ought not to ignore the problematic relationship that John had with Sam and Dean. In many ways he was neglectful, bordering on abusive. His ultimate sacrifice showed the love that he had for them; however, one could fairly question whether such a gesture would be necessary had he acted more lovingly throughout the boys' lives. Later in the series, there are instances that show that Bobby Singer was more of a father to the boys than John was. With pride, Bobby says, of Sam and Dean, that he raised two boys and they were heroes. As Bobby poignantly said, "Family don't end with blood, boy" (Season Three, Episode 16).

The Winchester brothers form strong bonds with their Hunter family and in doing so, put their lives on the line for those they love. While the Winchester brothers may put their lives on the line for their non-blood chosen family, they do not go to the extreme lengths of offering their souls or lives for these "family" members as frequently as they do for Winchesters.

In Season Twelve. Episode 6, "Celebrating the Life of Asa Fox," Sam and Dean have the opportunity to meet a network of Hunters gathering to celebrate the life, and mourn the loss of, fellow Hunter Asa Fox. At this event, Sam and Dean discover that in the hunter world, they are legendary. The brothers have inspired others to the point that they have nearly become an urban legend. More than just their Hunting abilities give the brothers this fame. The returns from death, the self-sacrifice, the ending of the apocalypses are all part of what the Winchesters stand for with faith and family and it is what makes them legends. This is not to say that the sacrifice comes easy. In "Prophet and Loss," Season Fourteen, Episode 12, Sam argues and physically fights with Dean over Dean's decision to lock himself and Michael in the Ma'lak box. Sam tells dean that they need to believe in themselves and keep playing their cards. Sam followed Dean to Hell and back and not to give up now. Dean is ready to make this sacrifice, but Sam cannot let him go. Dean promises to try to find an alternative, but makes Same and Castiel promise that once they are officially out of options, they have to "put him in the box." This is an extension of the brothers' love. As much as they are willing to sacrifice for one another, they are equally reluctant to let each other go.

Once someone is accepted as a "Winchester," the brothers extend this two-sided coin of self-sacrifice and protection to the newly inducted members. While the Winchesters *do* see their fellow Hunters as family, the actual "Winchester" moniker only extends to a few, mainly: Bobby Singer, Castiel, and Jack. The journey of Castiel becoming a Winchester was not an easily fought one. It was an arduous journey, fraught with mistakes and missteps (mostly on Cas's end). These missteps, though, were eventually atoned for and replaced by a Castiel worthy of being a Winchester.

Born Under a Bad Sign

At the end of "All Hell Breaks Loose—Part 1," Sam dies at the hands of another child under Azazel's blood influence (Season Three,, Episode 21). In a typically Winchester move, Dean summons a crossroads demon and makes an agreement to exchange his soul for Sam's resurrections. While Sam and Dean attempt to break the contract with the demon, they are unsuccessful and at the end of Season Three, we see Dean in Hell. In "Lazarus Rising," Dean is resurrected without an immediate explanation. While Sam and Bobby are unaware of Dean's resurrection, they continue Hunting and trying to learn what they can about Dean's state in the afterlife. Dean works his way back home where the next goal is to try to determine *how* it is that Dean was able to resurrect from Hell, with a physical body intact, albeit with a new scar of a handprint on his upper arm. After an incident that left psychic Pamela blind, the boys eventually learn the source of Dean's resurrection. They encounter a man with dark hair, garbed in a trench coat and tie who reveals the presence of wings. When asked who he is he says, "I am the one who gripped you tight and raised you from Perdition" ("Lazarus Rising").

We learn that this is Castiel, an angel of the Lord who has brought Dean back from Hell because God commanded it. Skeptical, Dean denies the existence of angels and God at first, but he reluctantly accepts Castiel's account. In Season Four, Episode 2, Castiel states that Dean is part of a larger picture and that he had pulled him from Hell and can send him back again. In these first meetings, Castiel challenges the common perception of angelic grace. Castiel is cold, logical, mission-driven. He bears no affection for Dean (or anyone for that matter) and is solely content with using Dean as a pawn for a greater good, as dictated by God. Purpose-driven, Castiel does not get bogged down with sentiment, emotions, or worldly attachments. So devout is his faith in the "bigger picture" that he is apparently willing to destroy a town for purely utilitarian reasons (Season Four, Episode 7).

Utilitarianism is the ethical theory that morality is determined by producing the best consequences for the most people. Under this approach, we ought to maximize the greatest good for the greatest number of people. In this view, there are no actions that are inherently good or bad; all that matters is the consequences generated. In this case, Castiel would be justified in destroying a town of innocent civilians to stop the summoning of Sam Haine. That being said, Castiel later reveals that his ultimate orders are to follow Dean's commands, so his instinct to destroy a town are vetoed by Dean's willingness to save a town of innocent people.

This cold, calculating way of assessing moral requirements is one that does not sit well with the Winchesters, Dean in particular. It is through Dean's insistence that the town is spared from Castiel's wrath. In this episode we start to see the doubts below Castiel's calculating veneer. He confesses to Dean that he's merely a tool, a hammer, of the Lord and his job is to follow orders unquestioningly. He does, however, still have doubts on occasion. Yet, his faith gives him the strength to do what is willed of him. He tells Dean that he doesn't know what right or wrong is and he does not envy the weight on Dean's shoulders when it comes to making the "right" decision. I believe that Dean saw this as room for potential and that is why he continued to not only work with Castiel, but began to rely on and trust him over the course of the series.

The Angel's Alright

Working with the Winchesters continued to chip away at Castiel's armor. By Season Four, Episode 16, the angels were commenting that Castiel seemed too close to the humans. To the angels this affection, or attachment, towards humans was impairing Castiel's judgment and was seeding doubt. At the end of this episode, Castiel tells Anna that he is considering disobedience; Anna tells him, "It's time to think for yourself." The conflict is not so easily resolved with Castiel. In "The Rapture" Castiel returns to Heaven, but is called down by Sam and Dean when Castiel's host, Jimmy Novak, and his family are threatened by demons.

Jimmy is shot and begs Castiel to use him, and not his daughter Claire, as a vessel. Castiel explains that this will be painful and permanent, but Jimmy agrees. As Castiel leaves, Dean asks what message he was trying to share. Castiel merely responds that he has returned above and serves Heaven, not man, and certainly not Dean. It appears that the doubts previously plaguing Castiel have subsided and been replaced by his original focus on angelic purpose. Despite this, and his insistence that the strained relationship with Dean is destiny, that everyone will be at peace in paradise and therefore do not need saving, Castiel acquiesces and helps Dean once more (Season Four, Episode 22).

It seems that despite his best protests, Castiel has not abandoned doubts or rebellion. In fact, the next time we see Castiel, Lucifer tells him that Castiel should support him; after all, they both rebelled. Lucifer was cast out, Castiel was cast out. If Lucifer is beaten, Castiel becomes the new evil. Castiel, not renouncing his rebellion, merely says he will die before he lets that happen. The development of Castiel's "conscience" seems to be progressing which is confirmed when Anna tries to compel him to kill Sam. By Anna's reasoning, Sam is Lucifer's vessel—no vessel, no Lucifer, no apocalypse. In a change from the Castiel we first met, he declines. He is no longer a cold, calculating, utilitarian follower of Divine Command, despite his earlier objection that he is a servant of Heaven. Anna takes note of this and remarks how he's changed. He agrees, "perhaps too late," that he has (Season Five, Episode 13).

In Season Five, Episode 18, with Dean considering giving everything up to surrender to the angels, Castiel confronts Dean. He tells Dean he rebelled, he gave everything for Dean and Dean did not hold up his end. In just under two complete seasons, we have seen Castiel metamorphize from a rule-following angel of faith, to a doubting rebel acting on behalf of the later named "Team Free Will." He has transformed so much that he no longer is an angel of the Lord, *per se*; rather, he is a devotee to Team Free Will, willingly investing in Dean. Like Lucifer, Castiel has embraced rebellion in the name of doing what's right. He is learning to think for himself, albeit with the guidance of the Winchester brothers—primarily Dean.

Castiel previously mentioned that his relationship with Dean was destiny. As the relationship develops, the destiny seems less about Castiel using Dean as a fellow tool to prevent the apocalypse. Rather, they collaborate together to identify what is right and then proceed to take actions that correspond with that assessment. No longer is Dean following John, no longer is Castiel following heavenly orders. Both are dedicated to identifying, pursuing, and protecting the good.

This process of assessing what is good and then acting on behalf of it echoes Aristotle's *Nicomachean Ethics*, where Aristotle states that there is a chief good that all humans strive for. (I.1, 1094a) It is in pursuit of this good that all people are motivated; it guides thoughts and action. For Aristotle, it is important to understand the chief good because unless you do, you cannot act in a way that is in accordance with the chief, or ultimate, good. As all humans crave this good, not living in accordance with it will be harmful and painful. (Aristotle is talking about the chief good for "humans." He doesn't talk about a chief good for angels, so I am assuming that Castiel, in using the Winchesters as moral guides, is seeking the chief good for humans as well.)

If you can identify the chief good, you can act in ways consistent with it, thereby increasing your odds of attaining it. It's through this process that humans can attain *eudaimonia,* or flourishing. It is this *eudaimonia* that people truly crave; for Aristotle, it is the chief good. As such, a *eudaimon* life is not possible without knowing the chief good. Castiel as we first saw him was one who had no concern of a chief good. To him, the only good was unquestioningly following the word of the Lord.

As he spends more time with Dean, Castiel begins to give more attention to his doubts. He learns to think for himself and begins to act in ways that he, after some consideration, believes is good. In this Castiel is working in accordance with Aristotle's moral prescription that we ought to contemplate the good, identify the good, and then act in accordance with it in order to *become* good, or *eudaemon* (II.2 1103b).

The angels were correct in their suspicion that Castiel had been impacted in a way that alters his way of thinking and behaving. The question, however, is whether such a change is wrong. From the side of the angels, this was a fall from grace in the same family as Lucifer's fall. Such a fall is a disgrace and goes against Castiel's angelic nature. For the Winchester's and the Hunters, though, this is a sign of improvement. It is this willingness to examine what is good and to act in ways in accordance with it that encourage them to trust, and work with, Castiel. And for an Aristotelian, Castiel is on the right track.

The desire to seek out the good and act in ways you *believe* are good is not the end of Aristotle's theory. You cannot merely act in ways you *believe* are good (as the Castiel we first met did); you have to have confirmation of which thoughts, actions, and activities are *actually*, and not just apparently, good. This requires moral and intellectual education as well as a community and environment that is on the right track and can guide the individual on the right path to *eudaimonia*. For Castiel, Dean is the primary source of this exposure and "education." While both Winchesters are dear to Castiel, he says "Dean and I do share a profound bond" (Season Six, Episode 3). For that reason, my emphasis is on Dean's influence more than Sam's. Whether Dean is the *ideal* moral compass is up for debate.

After choosing to re-sink the *Titanic* to save Dean and Sam specifically, Castiel says "You're the ones who taught me that you can make your own destiny. You don't have to be ruled by fate. You can choose freedom. I still believe that's something worth fighting for" (Season Six, Episode 17). The Winchesters have directly helped Castiel evolve into an agent of free will who focuses on doing what is right instead of what is commanded.

To say that Cas is getting better about trying to identify and pursue the good is not the same as saying he's perfected the act. Throughout his development, he struggles with understanding what the right thing to do is. He fluctuates, struggles and agonizes in his decisions. In Season Six, when he rescues Sam, he has to plead with the Winchesters that he did what he believed was the right thing. Additionally, in Season Six, Castiel works alongside Crowley, but when confronted by the Winchesters and Bobby, he denies the collaboration. They respond that he did a poor job of saving Sam. Castiel, while improving, still has a ways to go to achieve the true good and *eudaimon* life.

Free to Be You and Me

In Castiel's development the Winchesters recognize that he's developing into something more than just a tool promoting an angelic sense of Heavenly fate. As Cas gets closer to the Winchesters, he goes beyond being a fellow Hunter or collaborator. By Season Six, the Winchesters see him as family, though with some complications. Despite lying about working with Crowley, Castiel still observes the Winchesters from a distance and works behind the scenes to help them. When Dean questions his loyalty to the Hunters, Cas says, "Dean, I do everything that you ask. I always come when you call, and I am your friend. Still despite your lack in faith in me, and now your threats, I just saved you, yet again. Has anyone but your closest kin ever done more for you?"

Although Castiel has been ignoring the prayers of the Winchesters throughout Season Six, Castiel still feels dedicated to the Winchesters and still uses them as a guide for what to do. Sometimes, however, he misses the mark. This is a mark of someone who is on the path to goodness, but has yet to attain it. Because Castiel is still in pursuit, he will make mistakes and rely on the Winchesters to help guide him back to goodness and right action. More than just being moral guides, Cas has started to see the Winchesters as friends and even as family. He mentions he's done for Dean what only the closest kin would do. He is seeing himself as being part of the Winchester family, though it may take time for that to be fully developed. In Castiel's mercurial ways, he struggles with these connections to the Winchesters.

In Season Six, Episode 22, Dean pleads with Cas, asking him to get rid of the "juice" before he kills everyone. Dean tells Cas that he's family and Dean would die for him. After all Dean has lost, he doesn't want to lose Cas too. Dean's pleas do not convince Cas and he replies, "You're not my family, Dean, I have no family." Castiel, empowered with the souls from purgatory has had his judgment clouded. While still on the quest for the good, he has strayed from the Winchester's way of life and has instead molded himself into a new god. A "better" god. And those who do not bow to him will be destroyed.

This transformation continues on to Season Seven, Episode 1. Here, Cas says that the Castiel they knew is gone. Having once been convinced that free will was the answer, Castiel now realizes that the subjects need a firm hand, a father. He is the new father and tells the subjects to be obedient or die. In trying to be good, Castiel again has sided with obedience to authority. The difference is that this time *he* is the godly authority. As with many of Castiel's attempts to improve the world, his attempts to be a god fail and the Winchesters again bring him back to the right path. Cas's blessing and his curse is having too much heart; Samandriel (Alfie) says that this is Cas's main problem. This big heart is what encourages Castiel to care for the Winchesters, to listen to their guidance, to try to save the world in any way he can. It's also why he goes astray from the Winchesters' guidance. He believes his heart and good intentions will be sufficient; however, he needs the Winchesters to help him see that doing the right thing is more than just good intentions. Despite Castiel's failings, the Winchesters still maintain their bond and faith in Castiel. They believe in his good intentions, they believe in Castiel. They are likely aware that Cas doesn't have the critical thinking skills to evaluate what's actually good from what's just apparently good. While his skills get better under the tutelage of the Winchesters, he remains a work in progress. By Season Eight, Dean unquestioningly sees Castiel as family. Pleading with Cas about the tablet, Dean tells Cas that he is family, that Dean needs him. Cas drops his angel blade and takes the tablet to Dean. The appeal to family has reached him and has brought him back to Team Free Will.

As Castiel develops, he becomes more reflective, which is useful to his understanding of what is actually good. When extracting Gadreel's remaining grace from Sam, Castiel realizes the procedure poses a threat to Sam. He says that the old him would have jammed the needle in Sam's neck, even if he died, because the end justifies the means. But what he went through—being human and appreciating a PB&J—taught him that angels can change and "Who knows. Maybe Winchesters can too" (Season Nine, Episode 11).

Castiel is getting closer to understanding how to be good and is acknowledging that the Winchesters have room for growth too. His fellow angels recognize this growth and separation from being a tool of the Lord. Bartholomew calls Cas the ultimate rebel (Season Nine, Episode14). Gabriel says, "most angels aren't like us, Castiel, they can't handle the whole 'free will' thing" (Season Nine, Episode 18). Gadreel says that having seen Cas through Sam's eyes, he knows that Cas has a reputation of honor (Episode 21). Josiah says when he looks into Cas's eyes, he doesn't see an angel looking back at him (Episode 22). Metatron, trying to recruit Cas's followers says that Cas cares about no one but himself and the "Hardy boys" (Sam and Dean) (Episode 22).

In questioning whether Castiel's loyalty lies with the angels or the Winchesters, Hannah demands that Cas punish Dean. At the risk of losing his flock, Castiel refuses to harm Dean. From our perspective, this shows the love and bond that Cas has with Dean. Metatron, however, says that this is evidence of Cas's true weakness: he's in love with humanity. Castiel's desire to do the right thing, the love of his human family (the Winchesters) has overridden his attachment to his angelic family. The influence of the Winchesters on Castiel has continued to help bring him closer to loving the good because it's good and not because it's been ordered. While Castiel uses the Winchesters as models and guides, he resists following him blindly as he did while an acting angel of the Lord. The hierarchy of ruler and subject is being chipped away at by his relationship with the Winchesters.

When told by Hannah that the Winchesters are a bad influence, he defends them. The Winchesters may be rough around the edges, but they're the best men he's ever known "and they're my family" (Season Ten, Episode 2). In these later seasons, Cas is being more open and reflective about the influence that the Winchesters have on him. He's acknowledging that, while imperfect, they are amongst the best of men. These are men that he is proud to serve with, proud to learn from. Claire notes his development and changes for the better. Cas, according to her, "was super stuck up—and a dick. And you just wanted to punch him in the face." But now, he's just "I don't know, nicer. And kind of a fool, no offense" (Season Ten, Episode 9).

Through his time with the Winchesters, with his big human loving heart, Castiel has transformed from the man who killed Claire's father, to someone she can sort-of like. Furthermore, in this episode, Dean has a crisis of identity and tells Cas that he's the furthest thing from a role model. Cas disagrees, as do I. Under the guidance of the Winchesters, Castiel has evolved from a mindless fool to a thoughtful caring person.

I Believe the Winchesters Are Our Future

When Castiel lets Lucifer use his vessel to join with Chuck to stop the Darkness, he says it's torture but worth it to save the world. Dean agrees with Cas that it was right to let Lucifer ride "shotgun" because it gave everyone the best chance of beating the Darkness (Season Eleven, Episode 23). In this move of Castiel gaining power, he is not wanting to use the power to rule or carry out a mission as he had previously. He has grown to the point where his main emphasis is doing what will help. Dean assures him that Castiel helps and says, "you're the best friend we've ever had. You're our brother Cas, and I want you to know that" (Season Eleven, Episode 23). The Winchesters have started to articulate to Cas that over the past six seasons, he has become a best friend and brother. They rely on him, they trust him, they look out for and would die for him.

Yet, when Mary asks Cas when he started to feel like he fit in, like he belongs, he replies he's "still not sure I do" (Season Twelve, Episode 3). While he feels an affection and loyalty to the Winchesters, his past mistakes are still causing him to be hesitant about his role in the Winchesters' world. This hesitancy diminishes soon. When Billie (the reaper) demands the death of a Winchester to seal a deal, Castiel kills her. He says, "You know this world, this sad doomed little world, it needs you. It needs every last Winchester it can get. And I will not let you die. I won't let any of you die. And I won't let you sacrifice yourselves! You mean too much to me, too everything" (Season Twelve, Episode 9). His friendship, or familial bond, with the Winchesters has made him stronger, he tells an angel who says humans are dangerous (Episode 10). It is the strength of this bond to two good men that gives Castiel the opportunity to grow stronger and into a better person.

As Castiel lay dying from being stabbed with a silver-tipped spear (the Lance of Michael) by a Demon, he uses his remaining strength to express his gratitude to the Winchesters:

> Look, thank you. Thank you. Knowing you, it . . . it's been the best part of my life. And the things that . . . the things we've shared together, they have changed me. You're my family. I love you. I love all of you. Just please . . . please, don't make my last moments be spent waching you die. Just run. Save yourselves. And I will hold Ramiel off as long as I can. (Season Twelve, Episode 12)

Fortunately, the Winchesters' influence over others was not limited to Castiel. Crowley, the King of Hell, realizes that he can save Castiel by destroying the Lance and does so. Like Castiel, Crowley grows into a better person through his time with the Winchesters.

The love of the Winchesters also extends to Jack. When Jack is born, Castiel becomes a father to him. The father that Jack says will help him find peace on earth (Season Thirteen, Episode 1). When Lucifer comes to find Jack, Rowena tells him that his real fathers are Sam, Dean, and Castiel (Season Thirteen, Episode 21). The Winchesters have welcomed Jack into the family and take care of him like they would any other loved one. When Jack is still learning, Dean tells him, "even when we're strong, man, things are going to happen. We're gonna make mistakes. Nobody's perfect, right? But we can get better. Every day we can get better. So whatever your dealing with, you know whatever. . . . Whatever comes at us, we'll figure out a way to deal with it, together. You're family, kid, and we look after our own" (Season Thirteen, Episode

21). This is the love and guidance of the Winchesters. They don't expect perfection, they just expect an attempt to be the best version possible.

His time with the Winchesters has taught Castiel the power of love, of goodness, and of sacrifice. When the Empty comes for Jack, Castiel offers to take his son's place. The Empty agrees, but conditionally. Castiel is not to go now, but only when he can suffer. The Empty wants Castiel to forget about this deal. When he gives himself permission to be happy, that's when the Empty will drag him to nothing. While believing that Sam and Dean need not worry about this deal, he is at peace with his decision. He has learned to sacrifice for family for the good, not just for following rules. While the Winchesters' trust in Jack wanes over time due to some bad choices and accidents, Castiel's never fades. Even when he believes that Jack has lost his soul, Castiel regards him as family and protects him the way a Winchester would.

After Jack accidentally kills Mary, Castiel feels that Dean no longer trusts him, that Dean blames him for Mary. When Dean asks Castiel where he's going, Cas replies "Jack's dead. Chuck's gone. You and Sam have each other. I think it's time for me to move on" (Season Fifteen, Episode 3). While Castiel still loves the Winchesters and regards them as family, Castiel feels too much like a burden to stay with them at the moment. Slowly, he returns to Hunting and back on the mission to fight Chuck. While he needed a break, he cannot totally break off from the type of man the Winchesters have helped him become.

Blood Brothers

While I have stated that the Winchesters have helped Castiel become a better person, it may still be unclear how their relationship enabled this to happen. In Book 8 of the *Nicomachean Ethics,* Aristotle discusses his theory of friendship. For Aristotle, friendship, or *philia,* is a type of love. It differs from erotic love, but is still a powerful motivating force.

According to Aristotle, there are three types of friendship: friendship of utility, friendship of pleasure, and true friendship. For Aristotle, all three forms of friendship require some degree of mutual well-wishing. That is, the friends should want goodness for each other in some capacity. The friendships based on utility are relationships formed based on a mutual benefit or usefulness. Likewise, the friendships based on pleasure result from mutually advantageous pleasure. Both of these friendships can be formed quickly and will dissolve when the utility or pleasure ceases to exist.

The true friendship, the primary one that Aristotle is concerned with, is between people of virtuous character. These friendships are formed out of a recognition of good moral and intellectual character. Because it is so difficult to attain goodness of this sort, the friendships will be rare and will be difficult to attain. However, once they are formed, they will be just as difficult to dissolve.

In *Supernatural*, the relationship between Castiel and the Winchesters starts out as a relationship of utility. The three work together to attain a goal and only interact insofar, or so long as, they are useful to one another. When the usefulness ceases, they tend to limit interaction. At some point, the friendship becomes pleasurable and the three seem to enjoy each other's company. Yet, over the seasons, the friendship develops even further into a true friendship.

Castiel starts out flawed, with angelic utilitarian intentions. But as he recognizes the good character of the Winchesters, he becomes closer to them and his bond becomes stronger. The more time he spends with the Winchesters, the better his own character becomes. Recognizing this, the Winchesters see more goodness in Cas and become closer to him. Throughout the series the three of them make mistakes, but ultimately, they strive for the actual good which makes them of admirable character. This mutual recognition of admirable character serves as a benefit to Sam, Dean, and Cas in a variety of ways. First, the goodness in the three and their resulting friendship will help each of them identify and reflect upon their own goodness. This will help them confirm which of the things they do are good and which are not. This outside reflection provides the three with a tool that aids in moral and intellectual development. Second, the friends can help guide each other through the different levels of good character. By engaging with people of good character, the friends can supplement each other in areas of weakness. For example, if Dean has sufficient courage and Castiel doesn't, Dean can help provide a model of courage for Castiel to follow. Cas can then mimic Dean's courage until he develops the character trait himself. This type of interaction, reflection, and action are pivotal in what helped the Winchesters have an influence on Cas. Castiel recognized in them good moral character. He learned from and emulated this (and made some mistakes that he also learned from) and in the process became a better person himself.

In the end, it is this friendship, this bond, that allows Cas to become the best version of himself. Trapped by Billie, Dean doubts himself and his value. He blames himself for getting Castiel and himself cornered and unable to escape. He blames himself for not being able to defeat Chuck. Dean worries that everyone will die and he can't stop it. This man of good character is in a position where he has the weight of the world on his shoulders and feels that he is lacking. Yet, Cas's love and respect for Dean gives him the means to beat Billie. He tells Dean:

> When Jack was dying, I . . . I made a deal to save him. The . . . the price was my life. When I experienced a moment of true happiness, the Empty would be summoned and it would take me forever. I always wondered, ever since I took that burden, that curse, I wondered what it could be, what—what my true happiness could even look like. I never found an answer. Because the one thing I want . . . it's something I know I can't have. But I think I know—I think I know now. Happiness isn't in the having. It's in just being. It's in just saying it. I know. I know how you see yourself, Dean. You see yourself the same way our enemies see you. You're destructive and you're angry and you're broken. You're— "Daddy's Blunt Instrument." And you think that hate and anger that's—what drives you. That's who you are. It's not. And everyone who knows you sees it. Everything you have ever done, the good and the bad you have done for love. You raised your little brother for love. You fought for this whole world for love. That is who you are. You are the most caring man on Earth. You are the most selfless, loving human being I will ever know. You know, ever since we met, ever since I pulled you out of Hell, knowing you has changed me. Because you cared, I cared. I cared about you. I cared about same. I cared about Jack. I cared about the whole world because of you. You changed me, Dean. (Season Fifteen, Episode 18)

Dean asks, "Why does this sound like a goodbye?" "Because it is. I love you." With those final words, Castiel is able to sacrifice himself in the one way that can protect Dean from Billie; being so happy that the Empty is summoned to claim him. As he is taken, Castiel smiles with tears in his eyes, happy for the life he's lived, the sacrifice he's made, and for the mark he's left on the world. In Season Nine, Episode 22, Castiel in a moment of doubt asks Dean if "we three" will be enough. Dean replies "Always has been." These three, with the aid of Jack, ultimately are enough to save the world. Always has been.

11
Why Sacrifice Yourself?

GERALD BROWNING

Throughout the series, *Supernatural* has constantly upped the stakes of its storylines. Each season, the Winchesters have escaped the jaws of death. However, there were times when they did not escape, and Sam and Dean have sacrificed their lives for one another (or even for the fate of the world).

In many cultures, the notion of self-sacrifice is looked at in a noble light. Yet *Supernatural* repeatedly raises the question, "Just how noble an action is this?" How selfless is this self-sacrifice? Is it sel*fless* or sel*fish*? Is there any ego or logic behind the motivations of risking their lives for the "greater good"? Are their actions really . . . just (or morally right)?

Even though self-sacrifice and suicidal intentions are perpetuated throughout the series, there are ethical problems that arise because of self-sacrifice. On several occasions (and for several reasons), the rationale behind the Winchesters' decisions on ending their lives may not be the most noble reasons. This can be connected to the egos of the brothers. When thinking of the notion of self-sacrifice, we may see it as being the ultimate sense of selflessness. But if our identity, and the identity of family, connects to the idea of putting the family above our own self, then is it a sense of selflessness and humility, or is it a type of dysfunction? Sam and Dean Winchester have committed several acts of self-sacrifice in the name of love and family. These may seem like selfless gestures of love and devotion, but some of their reasons may be less than noble.

Many fans of the show believe that Sam and Dean have a dysfunctional, co-dependent relationship. The boys were raised by a single, absentee parent. From the very beginning there was a strong relationship between the two. Sam relied on Dean to take care of him. Dean needed someone to take care of. So, when their father John Winchester went missing, it made sense that Dean (who has been used to Hunting on his own) would drag his younger brother back into the world of the Hunters.

Was Dean's bringing Sam back into his world done out of selfishness? In "Skin" (Season One), while Hunting a shape-shifter, Dean admits to Sam that he hopes that after they find their father that they would "be a family again." This acts as an admission of his motives. Dean seems to be trying to bring Sam into a world that might get him killed in order to keep their family together.

Soon after his confession, Sam informs Dean that he had no intentions of staying in the "family business." This echoes the very first episode, when Sam periodically reminds Dean to bring him back to Stanford so he could take a medical exam. As such, we see a bit of selfishness in Dean's actions. Dean has committed heinous actions in the name of being a family and "taking care of family." This seems to create an unhealthy relationship within the family dynamic. This "codependency" between the brothers also creates a trend that will be repeated on many major plot points throughout the series. However, there are other potential reasons for the Winchesters to sacrifice their own well-being for the sake of one another.

Another potential motivator for the actions that we see the brothers perform is a simple fear of being alone. In "Croatoan" (Season Two), Dean Winchester is willing to sacrifice his own existence so that Sam won't be alone when he becomes infected with a demonic virus that forces the infectee to come under the influence of demonic possession. Even though Dean sees himself as a "lone wolf" type of character, one of his greatest fears (which he mentions several times throughout the series), is Hunting alone.

An infected Sam tells Dean to leave him so that he can commit suicide without hurting his brother, or anyone else. Dean tells Sam that he is "tired" of the Hunting. This shows that he is all too willing to lay down his life to help his brother. Not only do we see this in "Croatoan," but we also see it near the end of Season One in "Devil's Trap," where Dean decides to use one of the powerful Colt bullets to save Sam. This bullet can save the world from a demon and Dean Winchester uses it to protect his younger brother.

In a twist of irony, in "Crossroad Blues" (Season Two), Sam and Dean hunt for a crossroads demon—an entity who makes bargains with humans for their souls. In one scene, the brothers encounter a man running from the demon to save the soul of his wife. The man's wife was dying. He bargained for his soul to save the woman he loved. "I would die for her on the spot," he says to the Winchesters. In response, Dean says, "I think you did it"—sold his soul—"for yourself. So you wouldn't have to live without her." He adds, "Guess what, she's going to have to live without you, now." This serves as a foreshadowing of decisions that the Winchesters make. More than once, they have made this very decision to save the life or soul of the other. It's easy to see that Dean's anger at the man comes from the anger he feels for his father making a deal with a crossroads demon to save his life. Now, Dean's feelings come from a self-loathing due to the pact his father made for him. And later in the season, we will see Dean make the same decision to save his brother, Sam, from death and Hell, only to see Sam fall into that same path of self-loathing.

That scene in "Crossroad Blues" occurs after the boys lose their father because of a bargain. At the beginning of Season Two ("In My Time of Dying"), John makes a deal with the Yellow-Eyed Demon, who happens to be the same demon that killed his wife. He bargains Dean's life for his own, and the mysterious Colt that can kill anything. This seems to set the theme for many large story arcs which culminate in a season finale where one brother attempts to bail the other brother out of a particular life-or-death situation by placing themselves in harm's way. And when we connect this notion with the idea that one of Dean's fears is being alone (and Hunting alone), we may come to the conclusion that Dean's motives for self-sacrifice may not be for the right or noble reasons.

In "Home," the Winchester siblings investigate their childhood home when a demon terrorizes the family that currently lives there. Mary Winchester, Sam and Dean's mother, sacrifices her spirit to save the family and her sons from a poltergeist that has attacked them. We understand that Mary Winchester's motives for sacrificing her spirit may have come out of her love for her boys and protecting the family. However, we've seen that there are characters within the series who may have less than honorable reasons.

The Season Two finale sees Sam locked into a showdown with other children like himself. These children have gifts due to drinking the blood of the Yellow-Eyed Demon when they were infants, and whose mothers were killed in the same gruesome way that Mary Winchester died. One of these children were prophesied to lead Lucifer's army in a war against God. The Yellow-Eyed Demon knew that child was Sam Winchester. In the showdown at the end of Season Two, Sam gets killed by another child with super powers, Jake Talley (played by Aldis Hodge). Without a second thought, Dean makes a deal with a crossroads demon to exchange his life for Sam's.

In Season Three, we see that Sam learns of the pact Dean makes with a crossroads demon. In this season, we see the guilt eat away at Sam. Worst of all, we see this guilt feed into a sense of duty that Dean has (not to mention the fear that overwhelms him) throughout the show. We see the desperation that has to find something to stop Dean from leaving. In Season Four, when Dean returns from the dead (when Castiel rescues him from "the pit"), Sam confesses to Dean that he contacted a crossroads demon but no one would accept his deal. So we see that Sam was willing to sacrifice himself to bring his brother back from Hell. It would seem that the cycle never stops.

Utilitarianism is a type of ethics that is directly connected to consequences—as opposed to deontology, which says to follow rules regardless of consequences. Utilitarianism sees the right action as the one that creates the greatest amount of "good" for the most amount of people. In many seasons of *Supernatural*, the boys seem to do what's "good" (even if it means committing heinous actions). These horrible actions are considered to be justified because they ultimately benefit the greatest number of people. However, there are those who argue against utilitarianism because some would say that utilitarian morality might ultimately require a great amount of "self-sacrifice."

Is it moral to sacrifice my life to save my brother's, when my brother has been involved with saving the world? According to the utilitarian thinker, the answer would be "yes" if and only if saving the brother would create a "greater good" than the alternative. One may ponder the rightness of deciding such an action from a utilitarian perspective. Is saving one brother ethically appropriate? Does that mean that Dean believes that Sam is a better person than he is?

I think that Dean actually *does* believe that. One example of this is in Season Three, when Sam is preparing himself to fight a war alone since Dean sold his soul to save his brother's life. Sam starts making decisions that Dean would make. He decides to kill Gordon Walker in "Fresh Blood." Then, in "Malleus Maleficarum," Sam makes the same decision to kill witches, and Dean becomes concerned. "You're supposed to go on about the sanctity of human life . . . !"

The expectation of Sam making the "good" decisions and being the moral compass of the duo is there. This may have been a contributing factor to Dean Winchester's decision to trade his life for his brother's. However, the question still remains: what good comes from self-sacrifice?

Nothing Good Comes Out of It

In "Mystery Spot" (Season Three), Sam and Dean cross paths with a trickster demigod. This demigod, whom the Winchesters have dealt with before (so he has a grudge) places the Hunters in a time loop, where Sam has to constantly watch Dean get killed. This triggers the day to start over again. With so many *Back to the Future* and *Groundhog Day* references, the episode is a deceptively light and comedic one. This is one of my favorite episodes of the first three seasons of the show. The writing is spot on for the characters, but it also allows the trickster to not only be the antagonist of the episode, but also to be a teacher for the characters. He seems to want to teach Sam that he cannot save his brother and that Dean himself is Sam's greatest weakness. The fact that the Winchesters constantly place themselves in harm's way and rescue each other seems very self-defeating and, in a way, selfish.

Later in the episode, the trickster deceives Sam by letting him believe that he is out of the time loop and then has Dean killed in a botched, random robbery. Sam spends six months Hunting down the trickster with a myopic focus. Bobby Singer, another Hunter who helps Sam and Dean (and becomes a surrogate father figure to the Winchesters), warns Sam not to go after the trickster alone. Bobby even mentions that Sam scares him at times.

The Sam Winchester who survives his brother's deaths becomes an obsessive Hunter who focuses all of his energy on finding the trickster. When he does find him, Sam begs the demigod to bring Dean back. The trickster tells Sam that he was trying to teach him a lesson. The lesson was that nothing positive comes from the self-sacrificing attitude. "Nothing good comes from it." The pattern of a Winchester throwing his life away for the other Winchester is nothing more than a path to self-destruction. And throughout the series, we see this exact thing happen again, and again. Dean had sold his soul to save Sam and Sam was willing to do the same to save his brother. As we saw, this pattern seems to stem from John Winchester selling his soul to a crossroads demon to save Dean (that demon being the Yellow-Eyed Demon who killed Mary).

The Ego

Whether it be love of family or fear of being alone, the motive behind a Winchester's compulsion to sacrifice his life and safety for the sake of someone that they care about is not always a positive thing. Is it noble? It sure looks that way. However, the motive seems to be something borne out of an emotion a bit darker and deeper than loyalty, love, or humility. One emotion could be a sense of ego.

Dean's emotions were very influential in his willingness to sell his soul. One of the often-used statements that Dean makes in Season Two is how tired he is. Dean was tired of being a "good little solider" of John Winchester's. As the episodes progress, we start to see the anger and resentment that Dean has for his father. It would appear that Dean's potential to have a "normal life" was gone the moment his mother was killed by a crossroads demon. The resentment in Dean Winchester grows to the point where he confesses to Sam, "I'm tired, Sammy." Moving from job to job, kill to kill, has exhausted Dean. He's tired of fighting a fight that he's likely not to win. The blood, secrets, lies, and magic have all gotten to Dean Winchester's psyche and he seems to want out. So, whether you call it "self-sacrifice" or "suicide," Dean's emotions, and pessimistic outlook on life has had a major influence on his life and belief system.

How immortal are the Winchesters? Sometimes I wonder whether they take their lives for granted. One of the key points to mention here is the fact that the demons know the brothers by reputation. If they haven't gotten into an entanglement with the demon before, it's a safe bet that the demon will have heard a story or two about the legendary Winchesters. Once a being (human or otherwise) meets the Winchesters, there's usually some talk about the exploits of Sam and Dean. At times, we have to wonder whether they're even afraid of dying at all. The Winchesters have seen a lot of killers in their path. This would show that there is a certain amount of ego involved in the notion of self-sacrifice. The irony is that the Winchesters seem to be so willing to throw their lives away, and this could be out of some sense of ego.

The egos of the Winchesters are certainly fed in Season Four when we see the introduction of the archangel Castiel. Nothing would prove that your fight is for the right reasons than partnering up with an actual, honest to goodness angel. "Maybe you've been saved by one of the good guys," Sam tells a skeptical Dean when Sam learns that Dean "is important to the man upstairs." Whether the Winchesters were thinking like Consequentialists or Deontological thinkers, having an angel on your side is a great indicator that you are indeed on the side of the righteous. If there are actual demons straight from Hell and Dean happened to find himself in it, then there has to be a Heaven with angels. However, the ethics gets more complicated as we start to see that many of the angels in Heaven have an actual disdain for humanity and some of them have no problem killing people for the "common good."

The introduction of Castiel, the angels, and God puts a seemingly more definite spin on the notion of good and evil in *Supernatural*. However, once we start to realize that even the "good" and "heavenly" characters on the show are not infallible, this spin seems a bit less concrete. The people who are good on the show may not *really* be good, and the people who are evil may not *really* be evil. From a psychoanalytical perspective, ego is about testing one's reality and the concept of personal responsibility.

Intentions

The road to Hell is paved with good intentions, and we see a lot of this coming to fruition in *Supernatural*. However, we can see that the reasons for self-sacrifice (or suicide) are many. With all of the darkness in the series, the storylines that involve self-sacrifice are the darkest, and they seem to take up a large part of the overarching storyline.

We have seen many characters make demonic pacts that cost the use of their soul. In "Playthings" (Season Two) Sam and Dean investigate a rash of deaths at a gothic-styled Connecticut inn. It turns out that the ghost of the owner's deceased aunt was haunting her daughter. The aunt (who died when she was roughly seven or eight), tried to kill her grand-niece to ensure that she was not alone (sound familiar?). However, the grandmother of the child in danger (who was virtually catatonic), sacrificed her life to save her family. The grandmother put on hoodoo protection spells to save her family from her sister and when that didn't work, she promised her sister that they would be together forever. At the end of the episode, we see the two little girls playing in the inn which has been closed down and vacated.

In "Wishful Thinking" (Season Four) Sam and Dean investigate strange occurrences in a small town only to discover a wishing well that actually grants wishes. In this episode, a little girl wishes for her teddy bear to come to life, and it does. However, the bear is going through an existential crisis due to the fact that his total existence seems to be revolving around having tea parties with a little girl? "Is that all there is?" the depressed bear screams in response to the girl telling him that all he will do is have tea parties with her. In a fit of despair, Teddy, the Suicidal Teddy Bear (thank you, Internet Movie Database) puts a shotgun into his mouth and shoots himself in the head. Unfortunately, for Teddy, the shotgun blast does not kill him. To which he wails "Why?"

In most of the desperate actions of suicide and self-sacrifice in this show, many resort to this as a "way out." However, the irony is that there doesn't seem to be an end after the act. Either before or after John and Dean made their pacts, they confessed to being "tired." Recall that one of the victims of the hellhounds in "Crossroads Blues" wanted his wife to be cured of her cancer, to which Dean accused him of being selfish. In this section we see two other characters who commit self-sacrifice or suicide. Interestingly enough, the one that is the closest to reality was committed by a teddy bear. And even more fascinating, that teddy bear asks the best question of all: why?

Self-sacrifice or suicide? Which would you choose to identify the actions that these desperate people took? Did John and Dean (and later Sam) commit suicide by choosing to walk into "the pit"? Or was it self-sacrifice because they did it on behalf of another person? Did the teddy bear commit suicide (he is even credited with being "suicidal" in his very name)? If the difference between self-sacrifice and suicide is the fact that there is a "self-less" reason for self-sacrifice, then can we say any of them committed self-sacrifice? Are they selfish or selfless?

If we look at life as a "gift" as the theologian John Milbank suggests, self-less or self-ish is an important distinction. On the surface Dean gives his life as a gift for Sam. According to Immanuel Kant, a real "gift" is one where there is no expectation of something in return. So the deals that Dean and John make are for the other person with no expectation of getting anything in return. Also, anyone is vulnerable to death and to exchange one's vulnerability for another's is the "ultimate ethical agent." One interesting query is that when we factor in the possibility that death isn't the "ultimate" end (as in *Supernatural*) then does this really mean that self-sacrifice is no longer the "ultimate ethical agent"?

There are other characters who have sacrificed their own lives for self*less* reasons (which are *not* questioned). In "Abandon All Hope" (Season Five), Ellen sacrifices her life to save the Winchesters and stay with her daughter, Jo, who

143

was attacked by a hellhound. We see in this action that the fear of being alone is an integral part of this storyline. In "What's Up Tiger Mommy?" (Season Eight) Linda Tran sells her soul to buy her son Kevin in a "supernatural auction." These supporting characters both made decisions that created an "end" for them, and both decisions were for family.

Spot the Motive

Through fifteen seasons, Sam and Dean have been to Hell and back . . . literally. And through these years, they have had each other's backs time and again. At times that means sacrificing one's life and safety for the other. With them being family, this is something that they are more than willing (and almost eager) to do. What's the motive behind doing this?

What appears to be done out of love, family loyalty, and the noble action of saving the world, may turn out to have been done out of fear of being alone, family guilt, or even ego. As such, the nobility that we may think we see in the action of self-sacrifice isn't so noble. If that's the case, then what's the point? Is it to show that there's nothing wrong with saving yourself? Is it the fact that family, while important, should not be more important than self-awareness? Is the overall point that at heart we are all motivated by selfishness? It wasn't accidental that when he found out Sam was dead and he would be alone, Dean made a deal to sell his soul and was given one final year to spend with Sam. And soon after, being left alone was an important theme throughout the following season.

"The end" isn't always *the* end. Even though desperate characters may choose to end their journey, or use their lives to allow someone else to continue theirs, the action of self-sacrifice (no matter the motive) does not guarantee that their end is *the* end. There's no denying that self-sacrifice (as opposed to suicide), is a noble action. The fact that one Winchester (as well as other characters in the story) makes a conscious decision to place himself in the path of danger and be more than willing to pay the ultimate price for his loved ones, is a noble and very righteous action.

So, if we decide to pick apart the motives and reasoning behind the actions of desperate characters such as Dean

Winchester or John Winchester, including minor figures such as Linda Tran, there can be noble actions in even the most flawed of characters. Whether performed for self*less* reasons or self*ish* reasons, these actions can further the plot and tap into the depths of our emotions.

Part IV

"There's no higher power; there's no God. There's just chaos and violence and random, unpredictable evil that comes out of nowhere."

12
Finally Free

Trip McCrossin

"I ain't touching this one with a ten-foot pole," Bobby begs off, responding to an unexpected bit of theological ranting that Dean's directed at Sam, in "Are You There, God? It's Me, Dean Winchester," the second episode of *Supernatural*'s fourth season. Unexpected, but also unsurprising eventually.

Supernatural lures us in initially with an entertaining story of two brothers, Sam and Dean Winchester, in "the family business," monster Hunting. A little past midway through Season Two, however, in "Houses of the Holy," we begin to have an inkling that something broader's afoot. They're Hunting an unusual monster, the vengeful spirit of the late Father Gregory, who believes himself to be an angel, righteously orchestrating the deaths of local sinners, which puts them at odds: Sam's nonchalant profession of faith, that is, and Dean's ardent defense of atheism in response. The inkling becomes more forceful early in Season Three, in "Sin City," as Dean's atheism begins to give way, initially to a more theism-curious agnosticism, in his exchange with demon Casey, in which he confesses that he'd "like to believe." Finally, by the beginning of Season Four, the first episode to carry an overtly scriptural title, "Lazarus Rising," the monster-of-the-week storyline is clearly being subsumed by what one might call, in the spirit of a similar two-track structure that *The X-Files* popularized, a "mythology" story-line, but involving extra-terrestrials of a decidedly more theological sort.

149

The mythology storyline begins by taking one kind of monster in particular, demons, and putting them in conflict with angels, who Castiel, the first to arrive on the scene, describes as "warriors of God" (4:2). Cas, as we come to know him, has just, on God's orders, resurrected Dean from Hell, where he'd been dragged, by Hell Hounds no less, in Season Three's finale. This, following a deal with a cross-roads demon to bring Sam back, who'd recently been killed in a more standard bit of monster Hunting, in Season Two's finale. What ensues over the following dozen seasons is an ever more, at times bewilderingly complex rumination on all manner of things biblical. The most persistently vexing question at issue, however, is God's nature and role in humanity's flourishing, or, as the case may be, foundering.

Unsurprising indeed, then, that an old problem would arise anew here and persist, which is the problem of evil— the perniciously difficult to satisfy "need to find order within those appearances so unbearable that they threaten reason's ability to go on," as Susan Neiman described it a few years before the pilot aired ("What Is the Problem of Evil?"). How in the world can we "get behind God," Dean rants, given the abject misery that routine plagues humanity? "Bad crap happens to good people," that is, on the one hand, and in God's absence, we reasonably assume that "that's how it is, there's no rhyme or reason, just random horrible evil, I get it, I can roll with that." If God is "out there," however, on the other hand, "what's wrong with Him? Where the Hell is He while all these decent people are getting torn to shreds? How does He live with Himself? You know, why doesn't He help?"

Can we blame Bobby for wanting to pass? After all, ever well-read, he surely knows that the problem's as old as the Old Testament's Book of Job. Worse, it seems to have grown no less intractable with age. Immanuel Kant, for example, not typically thought to be an "idjit," went so far as to write of the "failure of all possible attempts at theodicy," 'theodicy' being Gottfried Leibniz's word for the business of reconciling God's ways with "bad crap." As angel Joshua bemoans in "Dark Side of the Moon," "you could drive yourself nuts asking such questions."

Still, while Bobby may well be forgiven for wanting to pass, through Sam and Dean's long and arduous struggle, *Supernatural* itself becomes *our* ten-foot pole.

Long, Arduous, and Unusual

Dean's version of the problem of evil's not, it turns out, the only one. Midway through the Enlightenment, Neiman contends, as Bobby just as likely knows, the problem evolved to include, in addition to Dean's *theological* version—in which, as Dean testifies above, human reason strains, in the above "find order" spirit, to reconcile human suffering with faith in divine wisdom, power, and benevolence, which either makes or allows it to happen—a more *secular* version as well (*Evil in Modern Thought*, pp. 7–8 and *passim*). Here, while it's no longer in response to suffering's ostensibly divine pedigree, reason strains similarly nonetheless. In both versions, we worry that the strain may be sufficient to call into question reason's *ability* to make the order it so fervently desires.

Supernatural's not alone in addressing the problem within popular culture, but in light of the problem's two versions, it occupies a provocative place nonetheless. There's no shortage of storylines that, while alluding occasionally to the theological version, address the secular version primarily— Mary Shelley's *Frankenstein*, for example, Thomas Harris's Hannibal Lecter quartet, and David Goyer, Chris Terrio, and Zack Snyder's *Batman v Superman*. A smaller number address both a bit more even-handedly—Margaret Atwood's *The Handmaid's Tale*, for example, especially George Miller's television adaption, and Stephen King's *The Stand*, especially in the finale of Josh Boone and Benjamin Cavell's own adaptation, penned by King himself. *Supernatural* is the rare storyline that addresses, by contrast, primarily the *theological* version. In at least three related ways, this is more provocative still.

On the one hand, the series ran for an impressive fifteen seasons, airing from early fall of 2005 through late fall of 2020, racking up, equally impressively, three-hundred-plus episodes. (Were it your job to watch *Supernatural*—and how *excellent* would *that* be?—working a standard forty-hour week, it would take over five weeks to complete the task!) All the more impressively, its average viewership throughout was two million plus per episode. This has to go at least some way, in other words, toward settling the question of whether the theological version of the problem continues to be of interest even in light of the secular version's development.

On the other hand, over the course of its run, *Supernatural*'s overall storyline developed in an ostensibly provocative way. Serial television's overlapping storylines develop more or less organically, season by season, as a series is renewed some way into each, by a staff of writers, under a showrunner's direction. This much is familiar. What's less so, however, is online fandom's recognition of four distinct "eras" within the storyline, defined by a succession of showrunners or teams of showrunners and their respective visions (see, for example, under "Seasons," http://supernatural.fandom.com). This, and the attention it draws to an overarching distinction between what develops in the first of them and what develops in its aftermath, makes the series into a theology incubator of sorts.

Finally, while some of the perspectives hatched are relatively familiar, the cumulative effect is ostensibly novel—an ostensibly novel *theodicy*, that is. No small potatoes this.

Gone Missing

Before we get on to the size of the potatoes, and in the service of this, a broader exploration of *Supernatural*'s incubating eras, we can't help but pause a moment to reflect on Bobby thinking back to Job, as we've imagined he does in response to Dean's rant, and a certain tension in the storyline that results.

As the parable of Job begins, God wagers the Avenging Angel—Lucifer, by the more familiar name at hand—that Job, as the most righteous of subjects, can withstand whatever torment may come. Unaware of the rivalry, while he has no desire to "curse God," he nonetheless wants, and insists he deserves, a story as to why, given his righteousness, he is being let to suffer so remorselessly. "What have I done to you, Watcher of Men," he pleads, "Why have you made me your target and burdened me with myself?" (Stephen Mitchell, *The Book of Job*). And to his "comforters" then, who've come from afar to console, but also, as it turns out, to chastise, he insists similarly. However pitiful, his I-want-my-day-in-court grievance is clearly impious, as God clearly can't be held to account. Rather, Job must accept blame for his own suffering, however unimaginable the inducing transgression. "Can an innocent man be punished?," Eliphaz insists, for example, "Can a good man die in distress?," he and Bildad and Zophar becoming ever more strident in this as the exchange continues.

"I will never let you convict me," he says to Bildad ultimately, "will hold tight to my innocence; my mind will never submit," because "if only God would hear me," in the summation to the three, "I would justify the least of my actions." When God turns up finally, however, as the famous Voice from the Whirlwind, Job capitulates. "Where were you when I planned the Earth?," God asks, poignantly, but also rhetorically, needless to say, and a divine onslaught ensues. "I will be quiet," Job concludes by the end of it, suitably awed, "comforted that I am dust." Job's capitulation, relatively contrite either way, is nonetheless interestingly ambiguous.

He *was* saying that he's owed an explanation, but what's he saying *now*? The more conventional take is that he's *rejecting* what he said earlier, believing now that God, majestic and inscrutable and all, doesn't, indeed can't owe him an explanation beyond his comprehension in the first place. The less conventional take is that he's more modestly *refraining* from saying so, believing that while he may not be *owed* an explanation, still he *cannot help but want, indeed need one*.

Dean's heartfelt, sometimes vehement grievances in the wake of giving up not only his atheism, but his agnosticism, are in the spirit of Job's own, generally speaking. "So, He's just going to sit back and watch the world burn," he rails at Joshua, for example, in "Dark Side of the Moon," "just another dead-beat dad with a bunch of excuses." And while there's no one in the storyline corresponding in any obvious way to Job's comforters, Dean himself takes on this role to an extent. "But why do *I* deserve to get saved," he says to Cas, "I'm just a regular guy?" Finally, we're not without God doing at least a bit of the where-were-you-at-the-beginning chastising. "You and your brother, always breaking the rules," He says to Sam, "but there's still so much about the fabric of the universe that you don't know, that you can't know, 'cause you're only humans. But I'm God" (15:09). What's harder to find is the *overall* structure of the Book of Job—either the more or the less conventional interpretation of Job's response to the Voice from the Whirlwind, that is.

Then again, maybe we're just looking at the wrong parable?

What's in a Title?

Not for nothing, "Raising Lazarus" is titled "Raising *Lazarus*." We're reminded of *his* parable, that is, parables actually—of Lazarus of Bethany, most notably, raised from the dead in the New Testament's Gospel of John, but also of Lazarus and the rich man, in Luke's, relating to one another postmortem from Heaven and Hell respectively. As it turns out, the two parables share a helpful moral thread.

Lazarus of Bethany, the more famous of the two, Saint John tells us is dying. His sisters, Martha and Mary, send word to Jesus, but instead of setting out straightaway, as they likely expect, and as we likely would as well, Jesus puts the trip off for a few days, knowing that—indeed with the intention that—Lazarus will be several days dead and buried by the time he arrives. Why the delay?, the disciples ask, as again we likely would as well, to which he offers simply that Lazarus's suffering and death is justified by God's glory. Later is better than sooner, that is, as it will allow Jesus to bring him back to life more revealingly than merely back to health.

Before he does, Martha comes along to confront Jesus similarly, that if only he'd arrived sooner, Lazarus would still be alive. To this he famously answers, "I am the resurrection and the life. He who believes in me will live, even though he dies; and whoever lives and believes in me will never die. Do you believe this?" She does, of course, as she confirms, and that's the point, but perhaps, while we may applaud her faith, we may also imagine that if we were her, we might find it no less *reasonable* to wonder, "but I *already* believed, and so wasn't my brother's suffering and death a bit of, well, *overkill*, as it were?" If virtue's what we're after, then even if suffering's somehow helpful, shouldn't we balk nonetheless at a world in which it's otherwise meaningless?

Saint Luke's parable tells us, on the other hand, about the rich man who lives a life of luxury, presumably in ignorance of the likes of Lazarus, a beggar at his gate, content with the meager scraps falling from his table, and of the plights that await them as a result. Eventually they die, of course, and take up residence in Hell and Heaven respectively, as we're told, and it seems their new accommodations are more or less as expected. Except that the rich man, able to see Lazarus in Heaven, sitting blissfully alongside Abraham, is moved.

May Lazarus, he asks, please "dip the tip of his finger in water and cool my tongue, because I am in agony in this fire?" He may not, Abraham answers, as "in your lifetime you received your good things, while Lazarus received bad things, but now he is comforted here and you are in agony." Good things happen to good people, that is, and bad things to bad, *eventually* at least, and also permanently, as a "great chasm has been set in place, so that those who want to go from here to you cannot, nor can anyone cross over from there to us." But it seems the real problem is that Lazarus wants Abraham to take pity not only on him, but also on his five brothers, still living, in ignorance of what's befallen him, and so at risk of the same. Who better to set them on the straight and narrow, the rich man figures, than someone who visits from the dead with first-hand knowledge of the importance of this?

Again no, Abraham insists. He'll just have to settle for Moses and the prophets, and besides, it's six of one, half dozen of the other. "If they do not listen to Moses and the Prophets," Abraham insists, "they will not be convinced even if someone rises from the dead." If he agrees, we may applaud his faith, but again we may imagine that if we were him, we might find it *reasonable* to wonder, "but I *know* they need the better example, because after all, they're *my* brothers." Again, if virtue's what we're after, and it's illusive for the rich man, his brothers, and for the rest of us, then shouldn't we balk at a world in which we're routinely deprived of the exemplary help we need?

This now seems closer to the mark. Dean wants what Job wants, a story that makes his and Sam's suffering intelligible, but doesn't act as Job does, as he does curse God, often. "You tell [God] I'm coming for him next," he says to Cas as the first of our four eras concludes. Still, as cursing God doesn't make suffering any more intelligible, or at least much more, and doesn't help us much, if at all in responding to it, Dean wants what Lazarus wants, for the world itself to include better guidance. The question is, if not from God, whence such guidance?

The Ends of Eras

For decades, fans of *Blade Runner* (1982) wondered about the fate of its central protagonists, Rachael and Deckard, until finally, its writers were tasked with developing what they thought would be the most plausible, compelling, and provocative version of their story thirty years hence, as reflected in *Blade Runner 2049* (2017). Similarly, *The Handmaid's Tale* (1985) and *The Handmaid's Tale* (2018ff) and *The Testaments* (2019), *Twin Peaks* (1990–91) and *The Return* (2017), *Star Wars'* original trilogy (1977–83) and sequel trilogy (2015–19), *Dexter* (2006–2013) and *New Blood* (2020), and on and on. Out of the ends a storyline achieves, that is, flourish an array of possible ends to which to dedicate its successor.

As noted above, a similar phenomenon occurs in serial television, subject as it is to season-by-season renewal, *Supernatural* being no exception. In its case, however, it occurs not only season by season, but era by era. Hence the whither-does-where-we've-been-point-us-now incubator business. Out of the ends that the first, second, and third eras achieved, flourished an array of ends from which the writers chose those they dedicated the second, third, and fourth to respectively.

The first of the four eras, the "Kripke Era," led by series creator Eric Kripke, with the assistance of co-showrunner Robert Singer, consists of the initial five seasons, driven by the "five-year plan" he originally envisioned the overall storyline to reflect. Its overall storyline revolves around Dean's eventual question to Cas, as to why he's been resurrected, and Cas's answer, "because God commanded it, because we have work for you" (4:1).

The work, we learn in the course of the following episode, not for Dean alone, but for Sam and Dean together, is to prevent demon Lilith from breaking the remaining unbroken seals of the sixty-six that lock Hell away from humankind. By the end of Season Four, having failed to co-operate as they should have, the effort has failed, and Lucifer and his demons walk the Earth, Season Five being Sam, Dean, and Cas's struggle to return Lucifer to "the cage," and by doing so stave off the ensuing Apocalypse. By the end of Season Five, and so the end of the era, they've ultimately succeeded.

It's at the expense of Sam's life, however, who, as Lucifer's "vessel," along with Archangel Michael, possessing the body of Sam and Dean's younger half-brother Adam, is condemned to the cage. Dean's abandoned by Cas as well, who returns to Heaven, to address the anarchy he anticipates resulting from Michael absence, exacerbating God's own.

What's the era's overarching theme? It's this. Even as the world's increasingly Hell on Earth—and not just figuratively, because there're monsters about, but literally, because, well, the Apocalypse—still God's at best occasionally involved, at worst not at all.

Who's the Boss?

The middle two eras—the "Gamble Era," consisting of Seasons Six and Seven, led by Sera Gamble, with Singer continuing as co-showrunner, and the "Singer-Carver Era," consisting of Seasons Eight through Eleven, led by Singer and Jeremy Carver for the first three, Singer alone for the fourth—while increasingly complex, have nonetheless a common reactive thread. Heaven, it turns out, this version at least, abhors a vacuum as much as nature does.

We begin a year after the events that conclude the previous era, during which time Dean has been living the "normal, apple-pie life" with Lisa and her son that he promised Sam he would, free of monster-Hunting. Sam, by contrast, who we learn in the closing moments of the previous era was mysteriously resurrected shortly after his apparent demise, has returned to it. As always, they are soon enough reunited, and the ensuing storyline, through roughly the first quarter of the era (6:5–11), is, in part, a fascinating rumination on what it would mean to be soulless, Cas having unintentionally resurrected Sam as such, and what it would mean to be made whole, which Sam eventually is.

Our attention turns for a stretch then (6:12–22) to what's developed since Cas returned to Heaven. The anarchy he anticipated has turned to civil war, between his vision and Archangel Raphael's, who wants to free Michael and Lucifer from the cage and reboot the Apocalypse. With a comparable conflict raging in Hell, between Crowley, the King of Hell, and demon Meg, who's looking to depose him,

Cas and Crowley strike a deal to discover the location of Purgatory, empty it of the souls of the demons consigned there, each of them immensely powerful, divide the spoils, and use them to prevail in their respective struggles. Cas ultimately outsmarts Crowley, gobbles up not just his half of Purgatory's souls, but all of them, and with the resulting power, appoints himself Heaven's "new sheriff," as Dean had earlier chided the aspiration (5:22). Turns out, it's worse than he feared.

"I'm not an angel anymore," Cas warns, in a tone reminiscent of when we first hear him engage with Dean (4:1–2). "I'm your new God, a better one, so you will bow down, and profess your love unto me, your Lord, or I shall destroy you." As Lord Acton famously warned, long ago, "Power tends to corrupt; absolute power corrupts absolutely." Except that Cas comes to realize that he's at risk of such corruption, when he finds himself having slaughtered innocents in exercising his new powers, as a result of one of the denizens of Purgatory he has internalized overpowering him (7:1). These would be the "Old Ones," or, in more biblical fashion, the Leviathans, God's earliest creations, banished for fear that they would consume the remainder of Creation. Cas decides to return the gobbled souls to Purgatory, but the Leviathans remain, later released into the world, wreaking havoc on humanity, his part of the storyline another fascinating, though more allegorical rumination, on the consequences of anthropomorphic conceptions of non-human animals, the environment generally (7:9–23).

For our purposes, however, the principal lesson is the wages of hubris. Cas wanted to make peace in Heaven, a laudable goal, and to this end internalized Purgatory's souls, though by dishonorable means, leading him to imagine himself God, only "better." The state was unsustainable, putting humanity in peril, even once he'd overcome his hubris. The era ends with the boys overcoming the peril, with the defeat of the Leviathan, but at a price—Dean and Cas being expelled to Purgatory, to spend eternity fending off demons trying to kill them, and each other.

Now Who's in Charge Here?!

The overarching theme of angels aspiring to rule Heaven, to questionable effect, is a continuing theme in the subsequent era, the third, "Singer-Carver." Again, we begin a year after the culmination of the previous era, Dean escaping from Purgatory, though without Cas, who escapes only later, and Heaven and Hell continuing to be embroiled in conflict. Against this background, we turn our attention to "The Word of God," which we know from the conclusion of the previous era (7:21) consists of tablets recorded by God's scribe, the Angel Metatron.

Sam and Dean use the "Demon Tablet," on the one hand, in an effort to close Hell, and so prevent the emergence of additional demons (8:14ff). Cas, on the other hand, having finally emerged from Purgatory himself, is enticed by Metatron to use the "Angel Tablet" in an effort to close Heaven, in order to prevent its conflict from spilling out to humanity's detriment (8:22ff). Both efforts ultimately fail (8:23). In the former, in the midst of completing the third of three "trials," Angel Naomi reveals that doing so will kill Sam, and Dean convinces him that no matter what the stakes, it's too high a price. In the latter, Metatron deceives Cas into closing Heaven in an unanticipated way, by expelling all angels but himself, in retaliation for their behavior forcing him from Heaven, eons ago, in the wake of God's departure. Both failures have longstanding consequences.

Chaos reigns in Hell, that is, and Heaven's not doing so well either. Crowley has been absent, as a result of being part of Sam and Dean's trials, and in his absence Abadeen, not just any demon, but one of the original Knights of Hell, is vying to replace him. In Heaven, the hostile take-over's already happened, Metatron having cast out Heaven's angels, their fall to Earth the series's most sublimely tragic image. As a result, Heaven's a de facto autocracy, Metatron now alone in Heaven, which he soon tires of, making a play to let back in a select few, appropriately fawning angels, while he also returns to Earth to perform miracles in order to get humanity on board with new management. Abadeen and Metatron being both immune to more routine angel-blade smiting, a more powerful weapon is needed, which turns out to be the so-called First Blade, which can be wielded only by one who bears the Mark of Cain, as in Cain and Abel.

A long search for Cain ensues, resulting in the Mark and the Blade passing to Dean, who uses it to kill Abadeen, Cas having succeeded in deposing Metatron on his own. What becomes apparent in the aftermath, however, is the corrupting influence of the Mark on Dean, much of the remainder of the era given over to various machinations to rid Dean of the Mark. Ultimately successful, what's freed in the process is what was destined to be if Dean rids himself of the Mark without passing it on to another, which is The Darkness. "The truth," Metatron offers Cas, in explanation of this novel bit of cosmology, with no small admiration, "it'd make the Bible thumpers' heads explode. I mean, they want their God to be a finger-snapping, all-powerful Creator, you know. And they want magic . . . Mary Poppins. But what He did, Creation, that took *work*, took *sacrifice*. In order to create the world, God had to give up the only thing He'd ever known. He had to betray and sacrifice His only kin: The Darkness, His sister," Amara by name. Bad news is, yet another vying to fill the void, this time in a way that will not only alter Heaven, but the whole kit and caboodle, and seriously not for the better.

A long search for, and eventually struggle against Amara ensues, this time with a divine weapon called the "Hand of God." Unlike the struggle with Cain, however, Amara is not defeated. The new struggle's not without consequences, however, which will help to define to the next and final era. On the one hand, Lucifer's rereleased from the cage (11:10), adding himself eventually to the list of those attempting, and ultimately failing to rule Heaven. On the other hand, Chuck Shurley, the erstwhile prophet, able to channel Sam and Dean's goings-on, recording them as pulpy *Supernatural* novels under the pseudonym Carver Edlund, reveals himself to have been God all along, first to Metatron, and later to Sam and Dean. While they're predictably shocked, we can't help but be less so, remembering Chuck's then mysterious vanishing in the conclusion to the Kripke Era.

Undercover Boss (and the Unexpected Grandson)

The final era, "Singer-Dabb," consists of the final four seasons, Twelve through Fifteen, led by co-showrunners Singer and Andrew Dabb. Here again, there's *so* much going on in the storyline, much of it new—the reincarnation of Mary Winchester, the British Men of Letters, the Thule Society, and Apocalypse World, to name only the most conspicuous complexities. What becomes clear eventually, however, is that at times frantic momentum is building toward an eventual convergence of the two storylines above, and what that convergence ultimately yields.

On the one hand, Lucifer's most recent escape from the cage leads eventually to the emergence of the Nephilim, whom we know as Jack, the offspring of Lucifer, possessing US President Jefferson Rooney, and Rooney's aide, Kelly Kline (12:8ff). More powerful than the Archangels, themselves more powerful than regular Angels, the latter want Jack captured and killed, assuming that, as Lucifer's offspring, he can't help but be evil. Demons want rather to capture and raise him up, on precisely the same assumption. In the middle are Sam, Dean, and Castiel—mostly Sam at first, but Dean comes around, Castiel a bit more slowly still—who assume precisely the opposite, which is that Jack's partially human origin leaves him susceptible to corruption, but fundamentally good nonetheless.

On the other hand, God's re-emergence, as in Chuck outing himself, leads eventually to a telling confrontation with Dean, whom He has incited to kill Jack (14:20). "I'm hands-off," He offers by way of ostensibly well-meaning reassurance, "I built the sandbox, you play in it." Except "when things get really bad," he adds, which is "when I have to step in." Jack as we currently find him, having lost his soul, behaving erratically as a result—which, given his powers, is "a problem," and "dangerous"—is surely a case in point. Dean's initially convinced, but in the end balks, tossing aside the gun Chuck fashioned especially for the occasion. While he doesn't say so, we're left to imagine that he's reconnected with the above assumption, regarding Jack's fundamental goodness, presumably in light of his remorseful resignation in the face of his own execution. "I know what I've done," he admits, "and you were right all along, I *am* a monster." What Chuck reveals in response is TMI at a cosmic level.

"This isn't how the story is supposed to end," Chuck bellows, "the gathering storm, the gun, the father killing his own son, this is *Abraham and Isaac*, this is *epic!*" Sam left incredulous, Dean fills in the blanks for him. Chuck's "been playing us this whole time, our whole lives," he says, with withering contempt, "Mom, Dad, *everything*." "This is all you," turning to Chuck, "because You wrote it all, right? Because what? Because we're Your favorite show? Because we're part of Your story?" Chuck's re-emergence, in other words, isn't exactly that. However absent He may have been for some undisclosed period of time after Creation, as we learned already from Metatron (8:21), Chuck's been present more recently, over the course of Sam and Dean's lives in particular. More importantly, from Dean's perspective more worryingly, Chuck's been making happen not all, but much, if not most of what has happened to them, and in general. Chuck's not so much the celestial "dead-beat dad" Dean had accused Him of being (5:16), but rather the "helicopter parent" He'd told Metatron "no one likes" (11:20), intimating that He wasn't one, at least not when He "left" originally.

In rapid succession now, Chuck takes it upon Himself to smite Jack—unclear whether this is because of the supposed danger he poses, or out of spite in response to Dean's intransigence—Sam shoots Chuck, with the gun Dean was meant to kill Jack with, but not fatally, as expected, and finally, Chuck responds, disdainfully. "Fine!," He chides, "that's the way you want it? Story's over. Welcome to the end." At this point, Chuck opens up Hell, issuing forth what Dean will later call the Ghostpocalypse. The boys are nothing if not about silver linings, however, and so begins the final season, the beginning of the end of the final era.

In the End Is the Beginning

By the end of its premiere episode, the boys have managed to escape the most immediate manifestation of the Ghostpocalypse, in the cemetery where Chuck's shot and decides to end it all. Sam now busies himself consoling Dean, who's back on a "been playing us this whole time" tear. Their exchange foreshadows a later, and arguably more substantive bit of consolation, midway through the subsequent episode, Cas now the consoler. This later exchange recalls in turn their more confrontational one during the Kripke Era's conclusion, and the body of the conclusion more generally.

If "whenever we thought we had free will, we were just rats in a maze," Dean asks in the first instance, because "sure, we could go left, sure, we could go right, but we were still in [Chuck's] damn maze," then "everything that we've done, what did it even mean?" Not only did it "mean a lot," Sam insists, for the sake of those they've saved, but "when we win this," as in beat back the Ghostpocalypse, "God's gone. There's no one to screw with us. There's no more maze. It's just us. And we're free." Dean certainly appears to share Sam's confidence, as we enjoy that most emblematic of *Supernatural* moments, Dean asking "You know what that means?," Sam answering, "We've got work to do," as they close the Impala's trunk and the scene and episode fade to black. Dean's "playing us" doubt reappears not long after, however, in the very next episode, in response to Cas's apology for keeping from Dean certain troubling facts about Jack.

In the second instance, the metaphor's changed, to "we're just hamsters running in a wheel our whole lives" now, but the sentiment's the same: "everything that we've done is for what? Nothing." Cas's eloquent response, in the spirit of Sam's, is interestingly different nonetheless. "Chuck is all-knowing," he begins, "He knew the truth, He just kept it to Himself." And okay, now that "His cover's blown," how to avoid "everything we've done" despair? "Even if we didn't know that all of the challenges that we face were born of Chuck's machinations," however, he asks, "how would we describe it all? We'd call it 'life'. Because that's precisely what life is. It's an obstacle course, and maybe Chuck designed the obstacles, but we ran our own race. We made our own moves, and mostly, we did well with that. . . . You asked, 'What about all of this is real?' *We* are."

Cas's perspective, meant to console Dean emotionally, is also *philosophical* consoling. Kant—still not an idjit—proposed a similar one, not so much in a theological setting, but the regular old one in which we wonder how free we can be really if we're material creatures embedded in a material world. How can we reasonably choose, that is, given our natural limitations, between a description of the world, including human behavior, as thoroughly deterministic, on the one hand, and, on the other, one that includes human freedom? Then again, even if we can't as a result *know* that we're free, how can we reasonably *not* choose, *in spite of* such limitations, to *believe* in the latter?

Whether we're folks of faith wondering how we can freely choose to do this as oppose to that if God knows always already in advance which one of them we're going to do, or folks not of faith wondering how we can so choose if prior circumstances have already made one of them the more natural consequence, in the moment we still have to do the work of deciding—can't avoid it even if we wanted to, no matter how empirically compelled we are. But who decides, as we go along, whether "we did well" in the process? *We* do.

The language here—"doing well," in "life as an obstacle course," defined at least in part by our struggle with what it can mean in the first place to "make our own moves"—is interestingly reminiscent, in the third instance, of the language animating the five-minute conclusion to the Kripke Era. Narrated by Chuck, before his "cover's blown," he begins by bemoaning the fact that "endings are hard," in large part because "it's all supposed to add up to something" finally. It does, in a sense, He'll want to say, but as backdrop He offers a glimpse inside the Impala, Dean at the wheel, Cas riding shotgun, in the wake of the Lucifer-Michael struggle that's claimed Sam, or so they believe.

"I don't know what God wants," Cas admits, "if He'll even return. It just seems like the right thing to do" to return to Heaven. In God's absence, however, and more specifically some mitigating story from Him, Dean's suffering remains maddeningly unintelligible: "What about Sam? What about me, huh? Where's my grand prize? All I got is my brother in a hole!" But "you got what you asked for," Cas responds, referring it seems to the rant we began with, "no paradise, no Hell, just more of the same," asking then in conclusion, clearly rhetorically, "What would you rather have: peace or freedom?" Cas vanishes before Dean can respond, leaving him to complain memorably, "You really suck at goodbyes, you know that," and us to wonder what his response would have been. We don't really wonder, though, do we? Not really.

To be animated by the problem of evil, after all, is to reject the mere assertion of such a choice, without further reason why we should accept it. In this spirit, peace apparently out of our control, however much we may hope for it, we opt for what isn't—the exercise of our freedom more as opposed to less virtuously. "Every part of him," Chuck recounts, "wants to die, or find a way to bring Sam back, but he isn't gonna do either, because he made a promise," to leave monster hunting behind and lead a "normal apple-pie life" with Lisa and Ben. Dean and Lisa embrace, and we hear her quietly consoling him, "It's okay, it's gonna be okay," and are ourselves consoled. And it's at *this* moment that Chuck asks the "What's it all add up to?" question, which endings are supposed, annoyingly, to answer, foreshadowing Cas's later "doing well" in "life as an obstacle course" motif.

"I'd say this was a test," he confides, "and I think they did alright. Up against good and evil, angels and devils, destiny and God Himself, they made their own choice." He goes on to name it, "They chose family," following with, "Isn't that kind of the whole point?," seeming to suggest that that specific choice was the whole point. The use of "that" as opposed to "this," however, suggests that the "whole point" is rather choice in principle, regardless of what individual instances we may or may not enjoy in practice.

Homo Fabulans

Cas was wiser in his consolation than he may have realized, though he didn't live long enough to learn of this, sadly, assuming news doesn't travel to The Empty.

As it turns out, that is, "Chuck was all-knowing," in particular about Sam and Dean's lives as they transpired over the course of three hundred and twenty-five episodes and roughly twenty-eight minutes into the three hundred and twenty-sixth, and in this sense, yes, "He knew the truth, He just kept it to Himself," the immediate cause of Dean's despair. But then there's Chuck's fatefully malfunctioning finger-snapping, which is meant to eliminate Jack, but fails, revealing instead that He's, rather *he's* lost his powers, which Jack has subsumed, assuming as a result, as we're about to learn, the mantle.

Cas's question, then, again suitably amended in retrospect, is all the more telling. "Even given that we do know that all of the challenges that we face were born of Chuck's machinations, how would we describe it all? We'd call it 'life'. Because that's precisely what life is. It's an obstacle course, and maybe Chuck designed the obstacles, but we ran our own race. We made our own moves, and mostly, we did well with that" [especially as even if Chuck's machinations were our challenge's origins, it's turned out that they weren't also their *ends*]. . . . "We'd *call it* 'life'," emphasis added, in the following sense.

Metatron was also more right than he knew, that is, though he too lived not long enough to find out. And not just in challenging Chuck to see that He's "wrong about humanity," wrong to find us so "disappointing." "They are Your greatest creation," he insists, as "sure, they're weak, and they cheat, and steal, and destroy, and disappoint, but they also give, and create, and they sing and dance and love. And above all, they never give up" (11:20). More to the present point, he was also more right than he knew in an earlier bit of admiration, of a particular sort of thing we "create." Humanity sure was

> something to watch. What you brought to His Earth. All the may-hem, the murder, just the raw, wild invention of God's naked apes. It was mind-blowing. But really, really it was your storytelling. That is the true flower of free will. At least, as you've mastered it so far. When you create stories, you become gods, of tiny, intricate dimensions unto yourselves—so many worlds. (8:14)

Putting Metatron's admiration together with Cas's later consolation, storytelling is the "true flower of free will" in the sense that the latter's the ground in which it flourishes, but really, in another sense, how can we tell ultimately which is the flower and which is the ground? And if we can't in fact tell, as it seems, as long as we can smell the flowers, as it were, what does it matter?

But aren't we moved differently by Jack's closing soliloquy? Don't we hear something different there about storytelling, in his resistance to being "hands-on," which Chuck had similarly assured he was? In answer to Sam's question, "So, you're *Him*?," and Dean's insistence, in response to Jack's confirmation that He's indeed now God, "You got a lot of people counting on You, people with questions who're gonna need answers," Jack describes, eloquently, the new order of things.

I'm . . . everywhere. I'm around. I'll be in every drop of falling rain, every speck of dust that the wind blows, and in the sand, in the rocks, and the sea. . . . And those answers will be in each of them, maybe not today, but someday. People don't need to pray to Me, or to sacrifice to Me. They just need to know that I'm already a part of them, and to trust in that. I won't be hands-on. Chuck put himself in the story. That was his mistake. But, I learned from you, and my mother, and Castiel that when people have to be their best they *can* be. And that's what to believe in.

Jack insists that he won't be "hands-on," yes, distinguishing Himself from Chuck, who insisted similarly, but disingenuously. And He further distinguishes Himself by swearing off "Chuck's mistake," and so won't "put Himself in the story." But there *will be* a story, and while He won't "put Himself" in it, He's also "everywhere and around" in the most comprehensive sense conceivable, and so really, given recent experience, if they'd wanted to be sticklers, they might've wanted to be reassured, "okay, so you're not going to put Yourself in the story, but You're also not going to *write* the damn thing, are You?" But they didn't, perhaps because the rest of what Jack said left them sufficiently reassured that history wasn't about to repeat itself, or maybe Jack just bugged out too quickly. And perhaps He would've answered anyway, if at all, in the spirit of the Voice from the Whirlwind, "It's above your damn paygrade." Just as likely, it doesn't matter.

What matters is that Chuck, being Chuck, isn't any longer, leaving them, without evidence to the contrary, to *trust* that *they* are, regardless of whatever else may be happening. Hence the first of *Supernatural*'s conclusions, to the penultimate episode, in which Sam and Dean toast those they've lost, and the future. "You know," Sam begins, "with Chuck not writing our story anymore, we get to write our own, just you and me going wherever the story takes us— just us," Dean completing the thought, "finally free."

"'What about all of this is real?'," Cas asks. "*We* are," he answers. And who are *we*? We are who we *say* we are. We *are* the stories we tell about ourselves.[1]

13
Does God Have the Right to Destroy the Universe?

GALEN A. FORESMAN

Chuck is a likable character during the Apocalypse. He is clearly on the side of good, the side of the Winchesters. There isn't really any reason to suspect he's the architect of those end times. Fans of the show willingly suspend their disbelief on many things, so another character, like Chuck, whose writings predict the future is easily dismissed as a prophet rather than the creator of all things. Instead, Chuck is just another fan of the brothers, like everyone else—a bystander, expectantly awaiting salvation from an impending doom.

Although the extent of Chuck's power was implied by his supernatural departure during "Swan Song's" (Season Five, Episode 22) denouement, his role as God isn't fully confirmed until the episode aptly titled, "Don't Call Me Shurley." (Season Eleven, Episode 20)—at which point, his past transgressions are easily overlooked or overshadowed by the release of his sister, Amara.

By series end, Chuck is a villain—the monster at the end of his book, so to speak. Sam and Dean refuse to play their respective parts in Chuck's tale, and a frustrated God brings everything to an end, including countless universes of a multiverse obliterated. A once sympathetic and likeable character, even described by Metatron as "nebbish," transformed into an almighty narcissistic asshole, wiping the slate clean because the Winchesters won't capitulate to his will. It's a return of the God whom Metatron fondly reveres as "a total badass."

From humanity's perspective, the role reversal casts Chuck, the simple novelist, as God's better self. After all, a Chuck that resurrects Castiel and roots for the Winchesters is a god who at least cares about *some* people. In retrospect, Chuck's little apocalypse in Season Five pales by comparison to systematically wiping out all of humanity and most of existence simply because the Winchesters rebelled. Not even Lucifer elicited such an extreme response, and he was Chuck's favorite, prior to the creation of humankind.

It's safe to say that Chuck's shift to villainy is complicated, much like his favorite son Lucifer. And much like Lucifer, Chuck probably has a perfectly consistent—perhaps convoluted—rationale for his actions, and so for the sake of argument, I'll grant he could spin a sympathetic yarn transforming his chosen folly into unavoidable tragedy. However, whether Chuck is a mere victim of the Winchesters' rebellion or an unjust tyrant and bully depends largely on whether he is morally permitted to destroy the universe. If he isn't, then it doesn't matter why he's doing it. The Winchesters need to stop him.

Rights, Wrongs, and God

The term "right" has thus far been used rather loosely to mean morally permissible and free from outside interference. These are two distinct meanings of the term, but taken together, they are often referred to as a "negative right," because it protects the exercise of a freedom by establishing that others have no authority to *stop, prohibit,* or *prevent* the exercise of that freedom. A positive right, on the other hand, entitles a person to support, and obligates others to assist in preserving that right.

For this discussion, *a right to destroy something* should be understood as a negative right. I may, for example, burn some logs to heat my home, thereby destroying the wood. My right to do this is a freedom from anyone else's interference in my doing it. As a negative right, this does not entitle me to wood, a fireplace, or anything else needed to carry through with it. But, if I already possess the means— if the wood and fire already belong to me—then I am free to use them in this way.

Talking about God in terms of rights is unusual. Normally, we discuss humans as having rights that are God-given, natural, or both, but we don't bother discussing whether God has any rights. Some people certainly speak as though God has rights, because there's no shortage of talk about the ways in which humanity has fallen from grace and will always fail to be good enough to deserve a heavenly afterlife. Religions often presume God has a right to our love, admiration, and worship, but these are typically entitlements—positive rights.

When it comes to negative rights, there isn't ordinarily any reason to conceive of these for God, because there aren't any conceivable occasions for God to need to assert them. There is nothing that could potentially limit God's liberty and freedom to do as God pleases, except for God. Likewise, if there were prohibitions on what God could do, there certainly aren't any means for enforcing them, unless God wishes to enforce them on himself. Because the Winchesters clearly interfere with and rebel against Chuck's plans, *Supernatural* provides a unique opportunity to discuss God's otherwise unspoken rights and liberties.

For some, the notion that God has a right to destroy the universe is an indisputable and fundamental truth of reality, even despite the incomprehensible loss. Again, it isn't common to articulate this right of God's, but nevertheless, many God-fearing humans believe that God will someday bring everything to a close without considering whether God has a right to do so. For those that accept this, it means that it's perfectly acceptable and morally unobjectionable for Chuck to destroy everyone and everything. It also means the Winchesters are morally prohibited from interfering in Chuck's plan.

While Sam and Dean are far from perfect, I think most fans will agree that they did nothing wrong in stopping the destruction of their universe. And so, there is a significant point of disagreement between those who believe God is permitted to bring about the destruction of the multiverse, and those who think Sam and Dean are heroes for stopping it. Since it's generally just assumed God has a right to do this, we should consider why this would be the case.

No doubt, there are multiple ways we might come to conclude that *God has a right to destroy the universe,* but some are better than others. For example, it would follow that *God has a right to destroy the universe* if you believed the broad, blanket assumption that *God always has a right to do whatever God wants*. By virtue of being God, Chuck has a right to do whatever Chuck wants, so it follows that if Chuck wants to destroy the universe, Chuck has a right to do so. Unfortunately, such simple, clever reasoning begs the question against Winchester fans who would deny Chuck has a right to destroy everything, and so, also deny that God has a right to do whatever God wants.

There is, of course, no real harm in a disagreement such as this, but it creates an unhelpful impasse leaving nothing more to discuss. If, on the one hand, Chuck fans believe God can do whatever God wants, while Winchester fans deny God can do whatever God wants, then what grounds can be given to adjudicate the impasse? Presumably, an argument should be built upon reasonably acceptable assumptions and so we should favor the argument supported by assumptions that are reasonable to accept based on the evidence. In this case, the blanket assumption that *God is permitted to do whatever God wants* is difficult to accept without some evidence for why this would be the case.

Power, Property, Religion, and Rights

Whether we accept the claim that *Chuck has a right to destroy the universe* depends largely on our view of his authority. Neither Chuck's power nor his ability to wield it is in question. Instead, our concern is whether Chuck has the legitimate authority to wield his vast power to destroy everything. If he does, then Sam and Dean infringed upon Chuck's rights when they prevented him from cleaning the slate.

Rather than arguing that Chuck has a right to destroy the universe from the fact that God has a right to do whatever God wants, which we've seen is problematic, we might reason that Chuck has a right to destroy everything, largely because he created everything. It's natural to think that it would be permissible for me to create scrambled eggs for breakfast in the morning and promptly destroy them in my mouth for sustenance. Presumably, this and cases like it demonstrate that there are some occasions where the destruction of something is perfectly permissible, but was it the making of scrambled eggs that gave me the right to eat them?

Suppose my sister eats the scrambled eggs before I can. Of course, I get angry with her for destroying what I created, but she reminds me that the raw eggs belonged to her when I created breakfast with them. If the raw eggs weren't mine to begin with, my claim to the scrambled eggs quickly evaporates. Because the eggs were my sister's property initially, I had no right to create with them without her permission. And, although my sister didn't create the eggs, they were her property. As a result, the eggs belonged to her and so it was permissible for her to eat them. In fact, I destroyed my sister's raw eggs to create scrambled eggs, so initially, I infringed on her property rights. Similarly, if Chuck has a right to destroy everything, it isn't simply because he created everything. It must also be that he stands in a certain relationship to everything such that it belongs to him, like property. The eggs belong to my sister as her property, so she may destroy them.

Although this example appears to show that my sister's property rights permit her to eat the scrambled eggs I made, it's still unclear from this example alone whether ownership grants us boundless license to the use of property. It's possible that a person may amass enough power and wealth to legally and legitimately acquire possession of all the greatest works of art ever produced by humankind, but it's debatable that ownership of these works would entail unlimited license to do whatever that person pleases with those works of art. If it's discovered that my land is the only place in the world that can grow a plant that cures all forms of cancer, do I have a right to prohibit the use of my land for that purpose? Isn't the survival of others a good reason to restrict my property rights? In other words, even if we grant—for the moment—that the universe belongs to Chuck, it's still an open question as to whether those property rights give him absolute authority to destroy it.

Limited Property Rights for a Limitless Universe

It has thus far been assumed that Chuck has a right to destroy the universe because it belongs to him and not because he created it. This is based on the assumption that property rights give someone absolute authority to destroy anything that is their property. My sister can eat the scrambled eggs I made, because they belong to her, not me. In order to have a right to eat the eggs, I would have needed permission of the property owner, so it seems that being the property owner gives my sister some authority over what is done to the eggs and by whom. This does not yet, however, explain what gave my sister the right to completely destroy the scrambled eggs.

Yes, they belong to her, so she gets to decide *whether* they are used and by whom, but this does not tell us whether there is a limit to her authority over *how* they are used. Basically, we haven't explained why something being your property gives you a right to destroy it. Clearly in some cases it does, like eating scrambled eggs. But we have already briefly considered two examples where property rights appear limited. In one case, the cultural, historic, and/or artistic value seems to limit the use of the property. In another case, a person's right to live seems more important than an individual's absolute right to life-saving property.

The philosopher and statesman John Locke (1632–1704) famously argued that people have a right to life, liberty, and property. Like the Winchesters, Locke was familiar with tyrants, rebellion, and revolution. During the 1640s, Locke's father fought in the English Civil Wars on the side of Parliament led by Oliver Cromwell against King Charles I and his son Charles II. Locke spent time in exile during the 1680s after a failed attempt to stop the Catholic Duke of York from ascending the throne to become King James II.

After the Glorious Revolution of 1688 and 1689, which gave Parliament more power in relation to the monarchy, Locke was able to return to England, where he published his *Two Treatises of Government* (1689). In that work, Locke adamantly opposed the Divine Right of Kings and argued that government must be established by the consent of the governed, by the people and for the people. Locke's own words heavily influenced Thomas Jefferson, and were later used in Jefferson's writing of the Declaration of Independence (1776). Published a little over 330 years ago, Locke's *Two Treatises of Government* is the perfect tool for justifying the Winchesters' rebellion against a tyrannical God's complete destruction of all property.

Most of the time we take our property rights for granted, because we live in a society oriented to protect and maintain property. Most of us know how to get it, use it, and lose it. We would know how to do all of this even if government didn't exist and we were in what Locke and others called a state of nature. According to Locke, property manifests through our labor when we mix it with things in nature that are unowned by anyone else. Borrowing from one of his examples, picking an apple from an unowned apple tree makes the apple my property. Because I own my labor and no one owns the apple, mixing what I own with something unowned makes the apple mine. In his own words:

> every man has a property in his own person: this no body has any right to but himself. The labour of his body, and the work of his hands, we may say, are properly his. Whatsoever then he removes out of the state that nature hath provided, and left it in, he hath mixed his labour with, and joined to it something that is his own, and thereby makes it his property. (Section 27 of the Second Treatise)

Much as an animal doesn't need permission to use items from nature for its survival, humans don't need permission to remove items from nature for our survival. So long as the object I mix my labor with isn't the property of someone else, I can make it my own. Once something is mine, I can do as I please with it within some natural limits.

For Locke, "all men are naturally in . . . a state of perfect freedom to order their actions, and dispose of their possessions and persons, as they think fit, within the bounds of the law of nature" (Chapter 2, Section 4). And, "though man in that state have an uncontroulable liberty to dispose of his person or possessions, yet he has not liberty to destroy himself, or so much as any creature in his possession, but where some nobler use than its bare preservation" (Chapter 2, Section 6). This means that without government, the default position allows us to do whatever we want with our property, except destroy ourselves or any other creature we own, unless the destruction of the creature is for some greater good. Presumably, eating scrambled eggs counts as a nobler use than the bare preservation of the scrambled or raw eggs, which thereby makes their destruction permissible.

In a way, Chuck is always in a state of nature, because there is no authority over him. He can create and maintain property just like we do. He can also destroy or dispose of his property as he thinks fit. As we have just learned, however, even within the state of nature there are reasonable limitations on property rights. Unfortunately, the limitations articulated here by Locke are limitations to humanly use of God's property. For Locke, humans can't destroy themselves, because we are God's property, and only God gets to decide when we begin and end. Similarly, creatures and other things in our possession can only be disposed of if some greater good comes from it.

Locke also thought that we did not have a right to possess as much as we wanted of something, even if we had the means to obtain it. He believed there were limits to how much property a person could rightfully own to the extent that one should not own more than one can possibly use for their own enjoyment. This leaves open how much that is, but it does introduce the idea that one should not have an excess that spoils from lack of use. In other words, a person does not have a right to property beyond what they can use, because that would effectively prevent the use of property available to others.

If Chuck destroyed the universe, then he would certainly be preventing others from using it for their own enjoyment. Even if Chuck can claim to have created everything, he readily admits that he gets bored with one story and simply makes another. In other words, there's no need for him to destroy any universe. The very fact that Chuck is God means he can always make more, so he's really never in need of existing property. If he were, he could make it, as opposed to taking or breaking property that already existed.

Tyrants and a Right to Rebel

Applying Locke's theory of property and legitimate government to Chuck is tricky because Locke just assumed everything belonged to God and that God had a right to do with it whatever he pleased. For Locke, this was fine, because God was good and had given the world to mankind for our enjoyment. But what we find by the end of *Supernatural* is that

Chuck is not Locke's God. Instead, Chuck is a tyrant, which Locke described as "making use of the power any one has in his hands, not for the good of those who are under it, but for his own private separate advantage . . . and his commands and actions are not directed to the preservation of the properties of his people, but the satisfaction of his own ambition, revenge, covetousness, or any other irregular passion" (Chapter XVIII, "Of Tyranny," Section 199).

While he may have created every universe in the multiverse, and while they may all belong to him, he never needs to destroy any of them to create more. Chuck was likeable as a storyteller because he was creating universes for people to enjoy. By the series's end, he's destroying universes unnecessarily, because he has no interest in them or he's embarrassed by them. Either way, as Locke said, "whenever the legislators endeavour to take away, and destroy the property of the people, or to reduce them to slavery under arbitrary power, they put themselves into a state of war with the people, who are thereupon absolved from any farther obedience, and are left to the common refuge . . . against force and violence" (Chap. XIX. "Of the Dissolution of Government," Section 222).

So when Sam and Dean say enough is enough, and rebel against Chuck, we can rest assured that he had it coming. Creator of the universe or not, he has no right to destroy anything unnecessarily.

14
Baby's Identity

DARCI DOLL

In 75 B.C.E. Plutarch wrote about Theseus, the legendary king and hero of Athens. Plutarch outlines the origins of Theseus's birth, adolescence, and rise to fame and power. And Plutarch records:

> The ship wherein Theseus and the youth of Athens returned had thirty oars, and was preserved by the Athenians down even to the time of Demetrius Phalereus, for they took away the old planks as they decayed, putting in new and stronger timber in their place, insomuch that this ship became a standing example among the philosophers, for the logical question of things that grow; one side holding that the ship remained the same, and the other contending that it was not the same.

Is the ship the same once planks have been replaced? Are these differences significant enough to render the ship a new ship? Does the ship remain the same so long as a certain threshold of sameness is maintained? Does the ship remain the same even if *all* the planks have been replaced? At the crux of this puzzle is the question what, if any, parts are essential to a thing's identity. And we can extend this to a person's identity. Do you remain the same person if more and more bits of you are replaced?

Plutarch does not proceed to attempt to solve this puzzle, now known as Theseus's paradox or the Ship of Theseus. This question, however, has bothered philosophers ever since. To this day, philosophers can't agree on whether this puzzle challenges or illustrates a conception of metaphysical identity.

Regarding the ship, the fundamental question is whether the ship remains the same if any planks or pieces are replaced. This thought experiment is puzzling because it challenges our basic way of thinking about what makes a thing—or a person—the same, identical thing or person.

The Most Important Object in the Universe

One of the strongest personalities in *Supernatural* belongs not to a human, Hunter, demon, angel, or other living being. No, one of the most important and iconic personalities belongs to Baby, the Winchesters' 1967 Impala.

Though at face value Baby is just a car, to the Winchesters, and to *Supernatural* fans, she's so much more. In "Swan Song" (Season Five), Chuck Shurley narrates Baby's backstory whilst the showdown between Castiel, Dean, Sam and Lucifer (with Lucifer using Sam as a vessel) is going on. Baby was produced days after the millionth car rolled off the assembly line.

Chuck says, "No one gave two craps about her. But they should have." Baby would "turn out to be the most important object in pretty much the whole universe." Chuck describes the ways in which Baby is different from other regular vehicles; the army men in the ashtray, the Legos in the vent, the carved initials in the floorboard. While these artifacts remain part of Baby, the true value, Chuck explains, is the life that Sam and Dean shared in the car.

Dean says just as much in "Mamma Mia" (Season Twelve) when he mentions that when John disappeared, the only thing the brothers had beyond the car, was each other. Baby's role as a member of the Winchester family is obvious from the earliest seasons. When the Impala is totaled in a collision with a Semi in "Devil's Trap" (Season One), the form of Baby as we know her is gone. The frame is bent, the entire passenger side is crashed in, the glass is broken, dents cover her body.

When Sam and Bobby look at Baby after her accident in "In My Time of Dying" (Season Two), Bobby says that the car isn't worth being towed. He suggests they "empty the trunk and sell the rest for scrap." Sam replies, "No, Dean would kill me if I did that. When he gets better, he's going to want to fix this." At the beginning of this episode, Dean is lying in the hospital due to his injures from the crash. Bobby, still unconvinced tells Sam there is "nothing *to* fix. The frame's a pretzel, The engine's ruined. There's barely any parts worth salvaging." Sam, resolute in his decision replies, "If there's only one working part, that's enough. We're not just going to give up on it."

The Impala of Theseus

This is the first substantial time that we see Theseus's paradox unquestionably apply to Baby. After this accident, the form of Baby has changed dramatically. She's no longer recognizable, no longer functions. As Bobby puts it, she's barely more than a big paperweight. The original parts are damaged beyond repair. Baby's identity is called into question. Do we think of her at this point as a damaged version of the original car? Or do we say that Baby has changed *so* significantly that she's no longer "Baby" but something new entirely?

One interpretation, based on Sam's response, is that as long as there is one original working part the criterion for the Impala remaining to be "Baby" has been met. Perhaps this is satisfactory. The original parts are still there (minus some broken glass and other pieces that broke off in the accident) albeit damaged. The damage may have transformed the original shape and form, but the original identity persists sufficiently enough. If we feel that's enough, we're about to be disappointed. In the next episode, "Everybody Loves a Clown," we see a montage of Dean rebuilding Baby in Bobby's junkyard. The car has been stripped to the frame, parts removed, and in the scenes we don't see, the parts are replaced and Baby is rebuilt—or is she?

How do we feel about this now? The majority of Baby's body has been removed and replaced; not just one bit of a time like the planks in Theseus's ship but large chunks at one time. Yet, the *form* remains the same. This leads us to one potential solution offered by Aristotle.

Aristotle's Impala

Within Aristotle's metaphysics he addresses the four "causes." These four "causes" each play a role in an object's or a person's existence. These are what Aristotle refers to as "it's why" in the *Physics*. To understand a person's, or object's, or Impala's, identity or existence we must, according to Aristotle, understand the correlating four causes.

We can understand these causes through the example of a statue. The first cause is the "material cause," or that out of which the thing is composed. In the case of a statue, the "material cause" would be the bronze used to make the statue. The material is that out of which something is constructed. The "formal cause" would be the shape of the statue. This second cause is the literal form of the object. The "efficient cause" would be the artisanal or artistic process that allows the statue to be created. This third cause is what makes the thing possible. The fourth cause, the "final cause," is the end or goal of the thing, "that for which it is done." The final cause of the statue may be art, representation, historical representation. While all four causes are important for Aristotle, the one that may be contrary to the way we naturally think is the final cause. For Aristotle, all things, living and inanimate, have a final cause or an "end." The end of a seed is to become a plant; health may be the end, or final cause, of seeing a doctor.

What does this mean for Baby? First, the parts, seats, interior coverings, and metal create Baby's material cause. Second, her shape, the model type, are her formal cause. The workmanship at the Janesville auto manufacturing plant would be the efficient cause. The likely final cause would be to be used as an object of transportation.

That may not satisfy the *Supernatural* fans, though. Baby, to them, is more than a mode of transportation. For fans, the final cause may be to provide a home for the Winchesters. To be an aid in Hunting. To be part of the family. The options are likely more than I can imagine. The exact final cause, for now, is not important to this discussion. We have an idea of the initial final cause (transportation) and some ideas of extended final causes as perceived by fans. These four causes are integral to Baby's existence and identity and help us understand what type of object she is. That should make us feel comfortable in knowing where Baby starts and ends. However, while this gives us a starting point, it does not help us with respect to the Theseus paradox. We don't know how *essential* each of these causes are, what, if any, room there is for change or modification.

We know that the parts make up Baby's material cause. However, what happens to Baby if there is a change to that material? Does Baby stop being Baby if she gets some rust, chips some paint, gets some minor scratches? The likely immediate intuition is no, these changes are too minute to constitute a significant change. Thinking in terms of personal identity, for example, I wouldn't say I'm a new person when I get a haircut. It's a change of the material form, but it seems to be an insignificant one. But at the beginning of Season Two, we see nearly all of the material replaced. With little of the original materials present, we can say that Baby is *materially* a different object with a different identity. The efficient cause helps us understand how Baby was created, but it doesn't help us understand changes in identity. Workmanship built her at the plant, Dean's work followed the essence of the artisanry that created her as did the parts used to rebuild her.

It's likely that Dean used Chevy manufacturer parts that are made especially for the 1967 Impala. It's even possible Dean used stock paint. Consideration of this does, however, raise another question about identity. Do knockoff parts have the same type of identity as the stock parts? Or are the knockoffs in some way inferior? For example, would Baby be less of herself if she were made of fabricated "fake" parts? Is her identity influenced by the quality or origin of the materials?

While it was different people carrying out the "art" the spirit is still the same so it does not tell us whether the identity changes at all. Finally, we can examine the formal cause. When disassembled, we can say that the form of Baby has changed so significantly that she has a different form and thus is a different object. Yet, once Dean painstakingly rebuilds her (making sure to include all of the Winchester specific details that document their journey), her form has resumed. Thanks to Sam's saving Baby from salvage and Dean's meticulous attention to detail, Baby after repair has the same exact form (with different material causes) as she did before the accident.

Aristotle's solution to this paradox is to look at the formal cause. This is not what you might expect, because you would likely assume that the final cause would be more important to Aristotle than the formal cause. The reason for focusing on the formal cause instead of the final, I think, is because there are multiple things that have the same final cause. For instance, acorns all have the final cause to become trees, but each acorn is distinct. For Aristotle, the object (or person) retains their identity so long as the form remains the same. With this approach, Baby would become Baby again after being rebuilt, when her formal cause is restored.

Does this really resolve the problem though? If we apply this line of thinking to people instead of objects, focusing on the formal cause is problematic. The day I was born I was twenty-two inches long and was smaller in all aspects of my form. As I grew, the form grew. Once I reached adulthood the form stopped changing so much. Perhaps *that's* when I "became" myself, but then how do I account for the previous "versions" of myself? The forms are different so the identities are different, according to Aristotle's rule. Likewise, if I lost a limb most people would stay that while my form has changed, I'm still the same person.

A second problem with emphasizing form is how to resolve identity of different objects or people that have the same form. We would not say that identical twins are the same person because they have the same form. We also wouldn't say that all 1967 Impalas are the same because they follow the same mold and blueprints, yet we think of them as distinct cars, and *Supernatural* fans think of Baby as being especially unique amongst Impalas.

Perhaps it's a matter of a combination of the material and formal causes? It's not just the form by itself. What sets Baby apart is the unique material combined with the form of the Impala. Yet this does not solve the problem of Theseus's ship (or in this case Aristotle's Impala). As I grow, my physical composition changes. Cells rejuvenate and are replaced; my form changes. This would imply that there is no consistent self that persists over time. Ultimately, while Aristotle's four causes help us identify an objects composition and function, it does not help us determine the extent and limitations of an object's essential identity.

Baby, Interrupted

Perhaps one of the reasons for the failure of Aristotle's attempt to explain how identity can persist through time despite changes is that it fails to take into consideration a fourth dimension, time. If we take a "four dimensional" view, we can think of an object as extending backwards into the past or forwards into the future, then we can think of it as persisting through space and time independently of the presence of any particular features.

An example given by Theodore Sider is that of a fingernail. If I examine my fingernails, I can see that each nail is composed of different parts and areas. If I use fingernail clippers to trim my nails, I can recognize that the part trimmed off was previously temporarily part of the nail, but is no longer spatially or temporarily part of the nail. Despite this missing piece, the nail maintains the same identity, notwithstanding some changes. It does not cause puzzlement or paradox to say that the discarded piece of nail was once part of the fingernail but no longer is. It still retains some of the identity, however, as it is a *piece* of the fingernail (or, to be more accurate, a former piece). There is something that remains that allows the fingernail to have one persistent ~~identity; the existence of an enduring place in time.~~ The changes are mere subsections in the history of the object through time.

With the four dimensional view, Baby is an object whose identity does not cease with changes. Rather, Baby exists throughout the time of her beginning and end because of her relationship to time. There is a continuity of existence through time that connects each "version" with the previous and future ones. Because we're seeing Baby as an existing thing that may change over time with temporal connections between the changes, we can maintain that Baby, in all of her instantiations, is still *the* one and only Baby. There are just different chapters of her life: Baby pre-production; Baby post-production; Baby as owned by Sal Moriarty; Baby as owned by John Winchester: Baby as owned by Dean and

Sam (but mostly Dean) Winchester; Baby totaled; Baby re-assembled, and so on.

To borrow another of Sider's examples, I change spatially when I go from sitting down to standing up. Though there has been spatial change, I am still the same person because I'm essentially the same object through time. This view may be attractive as it draws the connection of the personal identity through a historical connection through time. It may not be compelling to everyone, though, because in the case of Baby, there will exist a time where there is little to no temporal connection to the original Baby and the final Baby. This is especially true since Baby is totaled once again in "The Man Who Knew Too Much" (Season Six) with Dean rebuilding her once again. With these multiple rebuilds, it may be that it's difficult to identify a temporal thread that holds the identity together. What this view seems to require is a sense of eternalism; where something exists within a temporal time frame permanently. However, this "eternalist" view seems difficult to justify.

As with the original discussion of the paradox, it remains unresolved why something existing in the same temporal space has a continuity of identity that somehow begins and ends and endures in those time parameters. While it's easy to say that my fingernail is the same despite being trimmed, the fact of the matter is that the fingernail I have now is materially and formally different from my fingernail ten years ago. An additional worry is that things may exist in an overlapping temporal space and not be part of the same identity, object, or person.

The Born-Again Identity

Baby provides a good example of the problem of Theseus and the limitations of the attempts to solve the paradox. In *Supernatural,* however, the problem goes beyond just inanimate (albeit special) objects like Baby. In "The Spear" (Season Fourteen) Jack mentions the sleeplessness he had been experiencing since coming back to life. Castiel responds, "We've all been through it. It's a rite of passage around here." And in typical Castiel fashion, this is said without hyperbole. The Winchester boys have died, and returned many times. Dean was brought back from Hell by Castiel in "Lazarus Rising" (Season Four). In this resurrection, Dean is entirely a new Dean when it comes to the material cause as his body was previously destroyed in a Hunters' funeral. Dean dies innumerable times in "Mystery Spot" (Season Three).

Sam also has his chance to be resurrected, including a return without a soul. Castiel explodes after engaging with an archangel and also virtually explodes when overcome by Leviathans. Rowena dies more times than we know and comes back with the aid of witchcraft. (We can presume that Rowena has died many times that we haven't seen in the episodes.) Mary dies in Season One and is resurrected thirty-plus years later by Amara. Dying and resurrecting is second nature to the Winchesters and their fellow Hunters. The additional wrinkle in the paradox is the people from the Alternate Universe. For example, "Alternative" Charlie has the same form as "our" Charlie, the same material cause. The same is true of the other "Alternative" Hunters and our world Hunters.

According to Aristotle's account, the only potential difference would be the final cause; however, some of the "Alternative" individuals, such as Bobby Singer, have the same final goal as our world versions. For Aristotle, then, these clearly different people would be identical to their "Alternative" versions. Theodore Sider's four dimensional theory has the advantage of being able to separate our world from Alternative Universe persons. However, the problems with continuity through time still remain. The Alternative Universe individuals have both different spatial and temporal spaces which makes them distinct from our versions. While these views help us articulate the problem and some potential solutions, there is an approach within the *Supernatural* universe that may be able to give us a more satisfying answer.

Defending Your Life

In the discussion thus far, we have been neglecting something that exists in the *Supernatural* universe. A solution for our problem comes in the form of "souls." In the universes Chuck created, humans and angels have souls while demons are those whose souls have been corrupted. When we try to find a thread of continuity to explain persistence of identity over time, we can merely say that it is the presence of a soul that will explain how Dean can die, lose his body, go to Hell, be brought back months later and still be the *same* Dean despite all of the changes. The same will be true of all of the others who have died and came back, with one caveat. When Sam returns without his soul, we could say he's not the same Sam. He has properties that make us think he's the same man, but until he regains his soul, he's a different person. This view also helps us distinguish the Alternative Universe people from our people. They have different souls so despite their similarities we can say that so long as they have distinct souls they are different people.

This solution to the problem will not be accepted by people who disbelieve in the existence of souls. But it's part of the *Supernatural* universe that there are souls, so in that universe you just have to accept the existence of souls. The solution may work within that universe, but may or may not work for the real world.

There's No Place Like Home

What, then, can we conclude about Baby? As an inanimate object, Baby (as far as we know) does not have a soul, even within the universe of *Supernatural*. Without the soul persisting through the individual's existence, how can we say that the Baby in "Pilot" (Season One, episode 1) is the same as the Baby in the show's final episode, "Carry On" (Season Fifteen, episode 20)?

Without the presence of a soul, this last theory does not help us resolve the problem of Baby's identity. It may boil down to something relatively clichéd: Baby is special because we see her that way. There's a subjective, or relativistic, value placed on her. She means so much to us because she means so much to the Winchesters. For them, all that has to remain is a single working part. For them, no matter how she transforms she's still *the* Baby. What really matters is the home she created for the Winchesters, the *spirit* or idea of Baby is sufficient. Even without a soul, Baby carried on with her wayward sons. For that she will always be the most important non-sentient object in the universe.

One other question this raises is how we classify the Baby in Heaven. The car still exists on Earth, but the car is only truly meaningful to Dean if he understands it to be *the* Baby. This discussion also comes up when fans of the show see Baby at conventions; fans debate whether the Baby they see is *the* Baby (despite the fact that there are several Impalas used in making the show). Even in the universe of *Supernatural*, the metaphysical question of identity won't go away.

15
God Is Good (Chuck Not So Much)

JOSEPH L. GRAVES, JR.

Carry on, my wayward son.
There'll be peace when you are done.

—Kansas, "Carry on, My Wayward Son"

The script-writers of *Supernatural* did not utilize any concept or issue within the series that didn't originate within the cultural traditions of the world's religions. The series relies heavily on the Judeo-Christian concept of God.

In the fifth season we're left with clues as to the identity of the God character in the series. We're introduced to Chuck Shurley as a prophet of the Lord. He's the author of the *Winchester Gospels*. During the introduction of "Swan Song" Chuck is writing a portion of what might be a continuation of the *Winchester Gospels*. This episode was projected to be the last of the series, until fan acclaim led to the show being extended for more seasons (eventually amounting to fifteen, making it the longest running horror-fantasy series in the history of American television). At the end of "Swan Song," Chuck Shurley vanished into thin air, implying that Chuck was something more than just a prophet.

In "Don't Call Me Shurley," Season Eleven, we learn that Chuck definitely is God. He reveals this to Metatron. At this point in the story, Metatron had failed in his own plan to be God. He cast the other angels out of Heaven, causing them to lose their wings and be bound to Earth. Eventually, Castiel and the Winchesters defeat Metatron causing him to lose his angelic grace. When Chuck finds Metatron he is human and is dumpster-diving to find the sustenance to survive. In this episode we also learn that since "Swan Song," God had been traveling the Earth, experiencing life as much as possible, as humans live it.

Chuck did not experience human life, as the God of Christianity did according to the Christian scriptures. In the Christian narrative Jesus, the son of God, was made man. According to Caird and Hurd, *New Testament Theology*, the Christian view of the Trinity is that God, Jesus, and the Holy Spirit are one entity. As Jesus experienced human life, so did God. Jesus grew from birth through childhood and began a ministry preaching the gospel throughout Roman-occupied Judea. He came into conflict with the structures of social oppression in the forms of both the Jewish Sanhedrin and the Roman Empire. He was put to death by crucifixion, a punishment reserved only for those whom the Roman state deemed dangerous enemies of the social order.

Nor did Chuck met the standard of the Jewish conception of God, as illustrated by the actions of Yahweh in Psalm 82. In this verse Yahweh speaks in the council of the Canaanite God El. He calls for the weak and the orphan to have justice, that there must be fairness to the weak and the destitute, and that the weak and needy must be rescued from the wicked.

Psalm 82 was most likely written by a musician Asaph some time during the reign of King David 1010–970 B.C.E. In the New International Translation of the Bible, reference to El is removed and the council is described as the "great assembly." In the New American Standard translation this is called "his own congregation." The identity of this assembly as that of the Canaanite God El is discussed in Armstrong's *A History of God*.

Chuck spent his time amongst humans having carnal relations with both men and women, and appreciating the beauty of musical art forms such as the blues. Chuck spent no time working against the grave injustices of human society. This lack of concern by the Chuck character is notable given that Season Eleven aired in 2015 after the high-profile racially-motivated killings of Eric Garner and Tamir Rice. There could be no starker difference in the vision of God coming to know the human condition presented by the Christian gospels and Jewish traditions compared to that used in the television series *Supernatural.*

Chuck's return to the *Supernatural* plot was predicated upon the release of his sister Amara (The Darkness) at the end of Season Ten. Amara is the antithesis of Chuck and her goal is to destroy all that he created as revenge for his locking her away for untold thousands of years. In the creation of "the Darkness" as God's sister it is hard to know whether the writers of the series are relying on the notion of the gender duality of God. In the ancient religions of the Levant, creation was considered divine. The Canaanites were polytheists and El was their most powerful God. His wife was Asherah and she was the mother of all the other Gods. It has been argued that the God of Abraham was in fact, El, not Yahweh. The deity that established a covenant with Abraham introduced himself as El Shaddai, or El of the mountain (*A History of God*, p. 14). By this logic, if Abraham's God was El, he still had a wife Asherah. Originally, the two were worshiped as co-deities; one no more important than the other. This conception, however, is thought to have changed between 800 and 200 B.C.E.

Prior to this period, the veneration of goddesses in this region reflected the veneration of females. The decline of female status, however, was associated with the rise of the new cities, that valued male-associated traits such as skill at warfare and physical strength. By the time the "J and E" writers of the Hebrew Bible began their chronicles, patriarchy was well established in the societies of the Middle East (p. 30). This can be evidenced in part from the fact that King Solomon had at least seven hundred wives and three hundred concubines.

The "J" writer is called this by scholars because this writer always referred to God as "Jehovah" or "Yahweh"; and the "E" writer always referred to God as "Elohim." According to Richard Elliott Friedman, in *Who Wrote the Bible?*, the J writer lived in Judea, while the E writer lived in the kingdom of Israel. Both El and Yahweh (the God of Israel) were male and patriarchal (p. 35). Some scholars like Diana Edelman have argued that Zechariah 5:5–11 is a story of how Yahweh killed his wife Asherah. Zechariah was writing during the sixth century B.C.E. after the fall of Jerusalem and the exile of many Hebrews.

These verses refer to a vision in which angels reveal to the prophet a woman sitting in a measuring basket. The woman is supposed to represent the iniquity of the people. It could be argued that the choice of a woman to represent iniquity could have occurred simply by chance alone, but it is entirely consistent with the patriarchy that now dominated Jewish religious discourse. So, in this way, we see Amara also portrayed in *Supernatural* as an evil entity. Thus, in "Oh Brother Where Art Thou?" (Season Eleven), a fully grown and powered up Amara slaughtered preachers in a park and church in an attempt to get her brother's attention. From their acts throughout the series, we can begin to question both Chuck's and Amara's goodness.

The Theodicy of Chuck

]Theodicy is the intellectual project that involves the defense of God's goodness and omnipotence in view of the existence of evil. To understand how this project might work, one first has to have a definition of what is good. For the Greek philosopher Plato, his conception of the "Good" was derived from his theory of forms. Indeed, for Plato the knowledge of the subsidiary good things, such as beauty, was dependent upon the super form of the Good. The Good was an eternal, essential, and ultimately mystical category. For later Christian theology, Plato's good and God were really interchangeable. He further held that knowledge of the Good would result in the individual becoming good. Those who were bad, did so because of ignorance of the Good.

This position is in stark opposition of the Judeo-Christian narrative of free will. In this system, individuals can choose to rebel or sin against the good (God). The war in Heaven narrative is prefaced on Lucifer's rebellion against God. This was a willful act on his part, resulting from his resentment of God for placing humans on one of the empty thrones in Heaven. Thus, evil comes into the universe by one of the sons of God rebelling against God. Lucifer then turns to corrupt humans as treasured components of God's creation.

194

In Season Nine's "Holy Terror" we learn that the incompetence of the angel Gadreel, resulted in the success of Lucifer's plan to corrupt human kind. This event immediately calls into question either God's omniscience, omnipotence, or concern for humanity (or all of these things). Chuck's omniscience should have warned him of Lucifer's plan, his omnipotence should have prevented it, and even if it did happen, a truly concerned and loving God would have forgiven Adam and Eve for their sin. Instead, in the Genesis narrative sickness and death result from the curse that God places on Adam and Eve for disobeying the commandment against eating the fruit from the tree of knowledge. In Genesis 16, woman's pain in child bearing is increased and woman are made subservient to men. In Genesis 17, humans are cursed to have to work for sustenance and eventually to death.

This text immediately calls into question God's goodness. An omniscient and caring entity could clearly have foreseen the agony that generations of humans would suffer from these curses. How would the naive children of God's creation be expected to resist the cunning of the archangel Lucifer? Why should the curse be passed on to the unborn children of Adam and Eve? Couldn't an omnipotent creator, simply erase the existence of creation and start over again. In this second iteration, wouldn't the best strategy have been to create archangels without free will? In this way they wouldn't have been capable of being jealous of God's power.

The *Supernatural* universe presents us with an interesting scenario that could account for the creation of archangels (although not ones with free will). The rationale for this would be Amara (The Darkness). If Amara, an equal entity, refused to allow Chuck to undergo his acts of creation, then his creation of powerful assistants, would make sense to defeat his sister. This still does not explain the ongoing punishment of humans after Amara was safely locked away.

In our universe, this punishment is manifested in aging, famine, disease, injustice, and war. Given the means by which our species evolved, these conditions of human life were unavoidable. The theologian, John Haught presents the challenge of unifying theology with the fact of the evolution of life:

> Evolutionary biology not only allows theology to enlarge its sense of
> God's creativity by extending it over measureless eons of time, but
> also gives comparable magnitude to our sense of divine participation
> in life's long and often tormented journey. (*God After Darwin*, p. 50)

We know that the writers of *Supernatural* had Chuck creating humans via evolution by means of natural selection in "The Man Who Would Be King" (Season Six). I have to admit that if I were a supreme being I would not have employed evolution to bring into existence sapient living beings (especially those that I wanted to keep my commandments).

The theodicy of attempting to prove the beneficence of God by examining the works of nature has utterly failed. The failure resulted from measuring the beneficence of God against the immense suffering experienced by humans. The argument that disease and death entered the world as the result of divine curse is still argued by some special creationists <http://creation.com/why-is-there-death-and-suffering>.

William Paley made the argument in his *Natural Theology* that we ought to find our position in the world secure because of the careful planning that God put into every aspect of nature's design. *The Bridgewater Treatises* (1833–1840), by multiple authors, attempted to use nature as proof positive of both the omnipotence and beneficence of God. This argument focused on the wonderful and beautiful aspects of nature, such as the intricacy that could be found in the construction of a butterfly wing, but failed to address the existence of epidemics such as yellow fever, malaria, typhus, bubonic plague and a host of other diseases that ended the lives of untold millions of people in great agony. The theological responses to the existence of pandemics across history included themes of divine punishment or protection, culpability placed on individual or community actions deemed sinful or immoral, blame or scapegoating placed onto those deemed a theological, racial, or national other. Throughout history, the responses by faith communities have either informed or stifled the development of scientific inquiry, at times theology changed with and in view of scientific knowledge and medical practice, and some religious communities articulated rejection of science or projected scientific explanations or recommendations as an affront to the ideas and practices of their faith (Camat et al., *Pandemic Theology*).

War, slavery, and colonialism have claimed the lives of untold millions of humans. The victims of these atrocities are disproportionately women and children. Add to this that in Chuck's universe he also allowed the existence of monsters (such as shape shifters, werewolves, and vampires), which added to the untold misery of humanity.

Amara (the Darkness), freed from her imprisonment, wanted to dismantle Chuck's creation. As a co-equal deity, she had every right to do so; especially since she never agreed to creation to begin with, and due to her resistance to Chuck, she was betrayed and imprisoned against her will. From the argument of theodicy, we can evaluate her "goodness" in attempting to carrying out the act of undoing creation. In "Oh Brother Where Art Thou?" Amara explains to Dean what will happen to all the souls of people now living after she unwinds creation. She says that they would become part of her (as would he) and it would be as if they had never lived. It is hard to argue against the "good" of that action, even if you might argue with the way she was attempting to carry it out, given the widespread misery that dominates our world.

In my quasi-autobiographical *Voice in the Wilderness* I ask God why I was sent to this planet to suffer under the yoke of structural racism. This question is similar to the theme of Phillip José Farmer's novel "Venus on the Half-Shell." The story revolves around the sole survivor of planet's Earth's destruction who travels the galaxy to find an answer to the ultimate question: "Why did God create so many beings to suffer and die?" Another example of this theme is provided by the Titan Thanos from the Marvel universe. He explains to Captain America, Thor, and Iron Man in *Avengers: Endgame*; his grand scheme. Using the Infinity Stones he also wanted to unwind creation, but this time creating new life that would only understand the gift that it had been given, not the misery of what it had lost. Similarly, Amara's goal, even if self-serving, would have eliminated the suffering of humanity by erasing their creation.

God and the Good of Humanity

Ancient Judaism is based on the premise that God acted in history for the good of humanity. The stories of God's good activities were remembered and studied. These stories were written down in the documents known as the Hebrew Bible (*Tanakh*, meaning laws, prophets, and writings). The Hebrew Bible is a sacred document to Christians as well (referred to as the Old Testament). The earliest historical events of the Hebrew Bible are thought to have taken place between 2000 and 1400 B.C.E. This narrative hinges on the covenant between God and Abraham/Sarah.

However, from the perspective of the final seasons of *Supernatural* understanding earlier portions of the book of Genesis are crucial. In Genesis 6:1 we learn that the "sons of God" (who are likely either sons of Adam and Eve's third son Seth or sons of fallen angels) saw that the daughters of men were beautiful, and that they took human wives for themselves. The children of these matings were called "Nephilim." The chapter describes these children as "mighty men of old." The third century C.E. church father Julius Africanus argued that the proliferation of Nephilim was part of the rationale for God's conclusion that humans were hopelessly wicked and thus deciding to destroy all flesh including the Nephilim (except for the progeny of Noah) in the great flood (Bosman and Poorthuis, "Nephilim").

Once again, we're left with a moral dilemma concerning God's judgment about humanity (and also of women). It's hard to imagine that celestial beings would not have been attractive to poor nomadic women. It certainly wasn't these women who searched out angels for husbands, but the angels who searched out human women and took them as wives. Thus, it would seem that the correct action here would have been to act against the angels who transgressed against God's law, not the women and their children. However, there is some suggestion in the Bible (Numbers 13, Luke 10:18, 2 Peter, and Jude 6) that Nephilim (or their descendants) survived the great flood (p. 5). In *Supernatural*, several episodes revolve around the idea that the practice of angels fathering Nephilim continued throughout human history (Season Twelve, "Lily Sunder Has Some Regrets").

The core theme of the final four seasons flows from the birth of Jack at the end of Season Twelve ("All Along the Watchtower"). Castiel and the Winchesters begin their campaign against Jack's birth by assuming that Nephilim are inherently evil, and that specifically a Nephilim fathered by Lucifer might be the ultimate evil. In doing so, they are committing an elementary logical error, that of division. Here one thinks that something that is true of a group collectively must be true of each of its members. Thus, if Nephilim tend to be evil, then all Nephilim must be evil. Furthermore, they are also committing the fallacy of thinking that Jack's moral character will be inherited from his father (nature versus nurture). From what we know of human complex behavior, there is no evidence to suggest that moral character is inherited as a complex trait.

Chapter 9 of my book (co-authored with Alan Goodman) *Racism, Not Race* explains what modern genome-wide association studies have revealed about the inheritance of personality. There is a weak genetic component to the inheritance of personality, and in all cases environmental influences are either more or equally important. However, there are some extreme examples of defects in the capacity for moral behavior that have modest heritability, such as in the case of psychopathy/sociopathy (Dhanani et al., "A Systematic Review"). The prevalence of true psychopathy/sociopathy in humans is less than one percent. However, throughout the series no one argues that Lucifer was suffering from either of these conditions. If he were, he would have inherited them from Chuck. Aside from that, there is no reason to suppose that supernatural creation and genetic inheritance of traits in humans works the same way.

Kelly Kline's heroism in Season Twelve is not to be understated. Despite the fact that she was misled by Lucifer into a pregnancy she did not want; targeted for death by Castiel, the Winchesters, the British Men of Letters (a.k.a. "dicks") and angels; kidnapped by Dagon; and aware that Jack's birth would mean her death, she never gave up on Jack. In Season Thirteen's finale, "All Along the Watchtower," she records a video for her son telling him that his parentage and the expectations of others would not determine whom he was going to become. She felt his good, and baby Jack communicated that good to Castiel. Throughout the final seasons, Jack's real parent was Castiel, his uncles were Sam and Dean Winchester, and his grandmother was Mary Winchester. It seems that in his case that nurture definitely trumped nature.

Chuck as Pathological Narcissist

The core theme of the entire *Supernatural* series is the chaos created on Earth and in Heaven due to Chuck's hiatus and then return. During the early seasons we witness a world in which Hunters (including the Winchesters) are consistently fighting demons and monsters, yet have never encountered an angel. When angels appear in the series at the beginning of Season Four ("Lazarus Rising") their mission is not the protection of humanity, but in fact to help usher in the apocalyptic showdown between Lucifer and Michael (which will result in a great loss of human life).

When Sam and Dean are killed (Season Five, "Dark Side of the Moon"), tour Heaven, and speak to Joshua they are told that God doesn't feel that the apocalypse is his "problem." We are finally exposed to the deep psychological dysfunction of Chuck during Metatron's conversation with him in "Don't Call Me Shurley," Season Eleven). Here we learn that Chuck's greatest concern is his authoring of the lives of his creation (particularly that of the Winchesters) as great literature. Chuck's behavior gets increasing worse as the series continues. In "Moriah," Season Fourteen, God plans to kill Jack, is angered when Dean doesn't accomplish the task, and decides to turn the world into darkness by unleashing the souls of Hell in retribution for Sam and Dean's disobedience. Believe it or not, things get worse from there. In "Atomic Monsters," Season Fifteen, God begins to undo creation (just as his sister Amara had once wanted to do).

This portrayal of God is in direct opposition to the premises of the Hebrew scriptures (on which Christianity is also based). The character Chuck, the original creator of the universe, displayed behavior that can only be expected of someone with classical narcissist personality disorder (Caligor et al., "Narcissistic Personality Disorder"). Individuals with this disorder can be grandiose or self-loathing; extraverted or socially-isolated; captains of industry or unable to maintain steady employment; and finally model citizens or unable to maintain steady employment.

All of these conditions could have described Chuck at various points of the *Supernatural* series. They result from the core psychological problems underlying the condition: vulnerable self-esteem, feelings of inferiority, emptiness, boredom, affective reactivity, and distress. These characteristics could explain Chuck's decision to enter into the act of creation to satisfy his own vanity, his abandonment of creation when he was bored with it, and his decision to destroy it as an act of affective reaction. This raises the question of whether Lucifer's evil can be thought of as resulting from an inherited mental illness derived from his father Chuck, or simply a learned behavior resulting from observing his father.

We can contrast Chuck's deterioration with the developmental improvement of the demon Crowley across the series. Crowley was always consistent and fair in his decisions, carried out the missions that he was assigned (cross roads demon and King of Hell), and in the end was capable of sacrificing himself to save the lives of people he had come to love over the course of the series (Sam and Dean). There were also monsters who displayed moral actions and witches (such as Garth's werewolf family and Crowley's mother Rowena) who move from bad to good. This all illustrates that even supernatural entities can change. For example, Chuck from good to evil, the Darkness from vengeful to forgiving sister, and Jack from newborn to new God. Thus, the series overturns the idea that we can judge individuals by the characteristics of the groups to which they belong.

It's hard to know whether the decision to write Chuck's character as narcissistic despot had anything to do with the events in world society in the years 2016–2020. Certainly there were parallels in our world, particularly the rise of two particularly dangerous world leaders, Donald Trump and Vladimir Putin. It has been argued by Anton Ashcroft that Trump clearly fits into the profile of someone suffering from narcissistic personality disorder. If that is true, then Putin also certainly should be considered in that category. Human history has several examples of despotic leaders at the head of world economic and military powers, such as Adolf Hitler and Joseph Stalin in the 1940s. Just as Trump admires Putin, Stalin admired Hitler; and trusted him up until the point when Nazi tanks were rolling into the Soviet Union.

The real mystery is why people follow such despotic narcissistic leaders. Unfortunately, *Supernatural* provides us with no answers to that question. The angels followed Chuck because they had to (lacking free will), the ancients followed

Chuck because they thought his actions were to their benefit, and the Winchesters relied on God when the burden of their mission was beyond their capacity. It was only in the end that allegiance to Chuck was revealed to be a mistake. Let's hope that Jack does better.[1]

---

[1] My discussion of the plot of *Supernatural* Seasons One through Five draws upon my earlier essay, "Naturalizing *Supernatural*."

The Lore

Anonymous. 1985. *Tanakh: A New Translation of the Holy Scriptures*.
  Jewish Publication Society.
Armstrong, Karen. 1993. *A History of God: The 4,000-Year Quest of
  Judaism, Christianity, and Islam*. Knopf.
Ashcroft, Anton. 2016. Donald Trump: Narcissist, Psychopath or Rep-
  resentative of the People? *Psychotherapy and
  Politics International* 14:3
  <https://doi.org/10.1002/ppi.1395>.
Atwood, Margaret. 2017 [1986]. *The Handmaid's Tale*. Penguin.
Bosman, F.G., and M. Poorthuis. 2015. Nephilim: The Children of
  Lilith. *Online Heidelberg Journal for Religions* 7.
Brace, Patricia L. 2013. Mothers, Lovers, and Other Monsters. In
  Foresman 2013.
Brock, W.H. 1966. The Selection of the Authors of the Bridgewater
  Treatises. *The Royal Society Journal of the History of Science*
  <https://doi.org/10.1098/rsnr.1966.0016>.
Brown, Nathan Robert. 2011. *The Mythology of Supernatural: The
  Signs and Symbols behind the Popular TV Show*. Berkley.
Burgess, Molly. 2021. Biostasis Research Institute to Create "Human
  Organ Banks" through Cryogenic Storage. *Gasworld* (April 22nd)
  <www.gasworld.com/biostasis-research-institute-to-create-
  human-organ-banks-through-cryogenic-storage/2020797.article>.
Caird, G.B., and L.D. Hurst. 1994. *New Testament Theology*. Clarendon.
Caligor Eve, Kenneth N. Levy, Frank E. Yeomans. 2015. Narcissistic
  Personality Disorder: Diagnostic and Clinical Challenges. *Ameri-
  can Journal of Psychiatry* 172:5.
Camat, Jamela, Jonathan Wiebe, Paul Dansereau, Lucas
  Tombrowski, Austin Mardon, and Catherine Mardon. 2020. *Pan-
  demic Theology*. Golden Meteorite.
Campbell, Joseph. 1949. *The Hero with a Thousand Faces*. Princeton
  University Press.

Cave, Stephen. 2017 [2012]. *Immortality: The Quest to Live Forever and How It Drives Civilization*. Skyhorse.

Cooper, Laurence D. 2008. *Eros in Plato, Rousseau, and Nietzsche: The Politics of Infinity*. Pennsylvania State University Press.

Crossan, John Dominic. 2012. *The Power of Parable: How Stories by Jesus Became Stories about Jesus*. HarperCollins.

Davis, John K. 2018. *New Methuselahs: The Ethics of Life Extension*. MIT Press.

Dhanani, S., V. Kumari, B.K. Puri, I. Treasaden, S. Young, and P. Sen. 2018. A Systematic Review of the Heritability of Specific Psychopathic Traits Using Hare's Two-Factor Model of Psychopathy. *CNS Spectrums* 23:1.

Dostoevsky, Fyodor. 2007. *The Karamazov Brothers*. Wordsworth Classics.

Edelman, Diana. 2003. Proving Yahweh Killed His Wife (Zechariah 5: 5–11), *Biblical Interpretation* 11:3.

Farmer, Phillip José [Kilgore Trout]. 2013 [1975]. *Venus on the Half-Shell*. Dell.

Fischer, John Martin, ed. 1993. *The Metaphysics of Death*. Stanford University Press.

———, ed. 2019. *Death, Immortality, and Meaning in Life*. Oxford University Press.

Foresman, Galen, ed. 2013. *Supernatural and Philosophy: Metaphysics and Morals for Idjits*. Blackwell.

French, Peter. 1997. *Cowboy Metaphysics: Ethics and Death in the Western*. Rowman and Littlefield.

Friedman, Richard Elliott. 2019 [1987]. *Who Wrote the Bible?* Simon and Schuster.

Giannini, Erin. 2021. *Supernatural: A History of Television's Unearthly Road Trip*. Rowman and Littlefield.

Graves, Joseph L. 2013. Naturalizing *Supernatural*. In Foresman 2013.

———. 2022. *Voice in the Wilderness: How Evolution Can Help Us Solve Our Biggest Problems*. Basic Books.

Graves, Joseph L., and Alan H. Goodman. 2021. *Racism, Not Race: Answers to Frequently Asked Questions*. Columbia University Press.

Grey, Aubrey de, and Michael Rae. 2007. *Ending Aging: The Rejuvenation Breakthrough that Could Reverse Human Aging in Our Lifetime*. St. Martin's.

Haught, John F. 2008. *God After Darwin: A Theology of Evolution*. Westview.

Houlgate, Stephen. 2012. *Hegel's* Phenomenology of Spirit: *A Reader's Guide*. Bloomsbury.

Hutcheon, Linda, and Mario J. Valdés. 2000. Irony, Nostalgia, and the Postmodern: A Dialogue. *Poligrafías* 3 <http://revistas.unam.mx/index.php/poligrafias/article/viewFile/3 1312/28976>.

Jung, Carl G. 1980. *The Archetypes and the Collective Unconscious.* Princeton University Press.

Kerouac, Jack. 1985. *On the Road.* Penguin.

Kierkegaard, Søren. 2012. *The Sickness unto Death: A Christian Psychological Exposition of Edification and Awakening by Anti-Climacus.* Bloomsbury Academic.

King, Stephen. 1988. *The Dark Tower: The Gunslinger.* Plume.

Locke, John. 1980. *Second Treatise of Government.* Hackett.

———. 1988. *Two Treatises of Government.* Cambridge University Press.

Meade, Michael. 2016. *The Genius Myth.* Greenfire.

Millbank, John. 2006 [1990]. *Theology and Social Theory: Beyond Secular Reason.* Blackwell.

Milton, John. 2008. *The Major Works: Including* Paradise Lost. Oxford University Press.

Mitchell, Stephen. 1987, *The Book of Job.* North Point Press.

Naylor, Mark. 2017. Nose Bite Victim Says He 'Doesn't Feel Human' After Attack in Grimsby Pub. *Grimsby Telegraph* (June 16th) <www.grimsbytelegraph.co.uk/news/grimsby-news/nose-bite-victim-says-left-116054>.

Neiman, Susan. 2001. What Is the Problem of Evil? In Maria Pia Lara, ed., *Rethinking Evil: Contemporary Perspectives.* Berkeley: University of California Press.

———. 2015 [2002]. *Evil in Modern Thought: An Alternative History of Philosophy.* Princeton University Press.

Nietzsche, Friedrich. 1977. *The Portable Nietzsche.* Penguin.

———. 1990. *The Twilight of the Idols and The Antichrist: Or How to Philosophize with a Hammer.* Penguin.

———. 1994. *Human, All Too Human.* Penguin.

———. 2003. *Beyond Good and Evil: Prelude to a Philosophy of the Future.* Penguin/

———. 2009. *Thus Spoke Zarathustra. A Book for Everyone and Nobody.* Oxford University Press.

———. 2017. *The Will to Power.* Penguin.

———. 2018. *The Joyous Science.* Penguin.

———. 2021. *God Is Dead. God Remains Dead. And We Have Killed Him.* Penguin.

Nystrom, Bradley P., and David P. Nystrom. 2004. *The History of Christianity: An Introduction.* McGraw-Hill.

Paley, William. 2008 [1829]. *Natural Theology or Evidences of the Existence and Attributes of the Deity, Collected from the Appearance of Nature.* Oxford University Press.

Palmer D. 2006. *Looking at Philosophy: The Unbearable Heaviness of Philosophy Made Lighter.* McGraw Hill.

Plato. 1997. Plato: Complete Works. Hackett.

Plutarch. 1960. *The Rise and Fall of Athens: Nine Greek Lives.* Penguin.

Prudhom, Laura. 2014. 'Supernatural' at 200: The Road So Far, an Oral History. Variety.com. <https://variety.com/2014/tv/spotlight/supernatural-oral-history-200-episodes-ackles-padalecki-kripke-1201352537>.

Raglan, Fitzroy. 2003 [1936]. *The Hero: A Study in Tradition, Myth and Drama*. Dover.

Rousseau, Jean-Jacques. 2019. *On the Social Contract*. Hackett.

Sartre, Jean-Paul. 1989. *No Exit and Three Other Plays*. Vintage.

———. 2020 [1943]. *Being and Nothingness: A Phenomenological Essay on Ontology*. Simon and Schuster.

Sider, Theodore. 1997. Four Dimensionalism. *Philosophical Review* 106.

Sides, Hampton. 2004. *Americana: Dispatches from the New Frontier*. Doubleday.

Spinoza, Benedict de. 2018. *Ethics: Proved in Geometrical Order*. Cambridge University Press.

Vernon, Mark. 2011. Carl Jung, Part 4: Do Archetypes Exist? markvernon.com <https://www.markvernon.com/carl-jung-part-4-do-archetypes-exist>.

Williams, Bernard. 1973a. *Problems of the Self*. Cambridge University Press.

———. 1973b. The Makropulos Case: Reflections on the Tedium of Immortality. In Williams 1973a

Team Free Will

PATRICIA L. BRACE is a Professor of Art History and Humanities at Southwest Minnesota State University, in Marshall, Minnesota. Her research and writing are focused on aesthetics and popular culture. Her studio work is in jewelry design, creating versions of historical style work with semi-precious gems. She did cry at the end of "Lebanon," but it might have been more because they had to smash that really big, beautiful pearl than because John was sent back to 2003 . . .

GERALD BROWNING teaches English, Literature, and Self-Defense for Grand Valley State University and Muskegon Community College. When he's not salting his office or pestering crossroads demons to cure his sinus problems, he contributes to Pop Culture and Philosophy books, and writes horror fiction. His first novel, *Demon in My Head*, solidified him as a horror hound. He cross trains in multiple martial arts and is an all-around idjit.

MICHELLE DEVRIES holds a dual Bachelor of Arts in both Philosophy and English with an emphasis on creative writing from Weber State University, an achievement that relied heavily on her affinity for Eighties rock music and varieties of pie. When she's not thinking up fun loopholes for crossroads demons to pepper into their contracts, she works as a managing editor for an education publishing company. While she would like to say she is as cool as Dean, as clever as Sam, and as quirky as Charlie, the truth is that she is as awkward as Castiel trying to come up with an insult for Lucifer.

DARCI DOLL is a philosophy professor at Delta College in Michigan. In her free time she follows the family business of examining the ethics of Hunting the supernatural. Darci has presented and published on pop culture and philosophy topics, including *Twin Peaks*, *Black Mirror*, and *The Handmaid's Tale*. While she wants to have pride in her accomplishments, she knows that only through Chuck's will are such things possible.

GALEN A. FORESMAN is a Professor of Philosophy at North Carolina Agricultural and Technical State University. He lives happily with his loving and supportive wife, two daughters, two cats, and an adorable monster, Frankie, who haunts their home. He also has an amazing son who has long been his best Hunting companion. Select, enjoyable publications include *Supernatural and Philosophy: Metaphysics and Monsters . . . for Idjits* (2013), *The Critical Thinking Toolkit* (2016), and "Why Batman Is Better than Superman" (in *Batman and Philosophy*, 2008).

JOSEPH L. GRAVES JR. is Professor of Biological Sciences at North Carolina A&T State University. He is the author of three books on biological and social conceptions of race, including *Racism, Not Race* (with Alan Goodman), 2021. His current project is designed to expose the Thule Society's secret plans to resurrect dead Nazis in their attempt to improve the leadership of modern white supremacist organizations.

HEINRIK HELLWIG is Visiting Assistant Professor of Philosophy at the University of Alabama at Birmingham. He understands the Winchesters' burden of being stuck with Hell, but only because it's the first syllable of his surname.

A.G. HOLDIER is a big, beautiful, lumbering pile of flannel doing graduate work in philosophy and public policy at the University of Arkansas. When not researching social and political epistemology or philosophy of language, he will always volunteer to interrogate the cat.

CHERISE HUNTINGFORD has always had a thing for old school monsters and Led Zeppelin. So it was perfect, cosmic serendipity that the twain should meet in a *Supernatural* multiverse with a pair of gunslinging dudes to kick ass and carry the tunes. Cherise has written for both a London film magazine, and rock magazine, too—mostly along the lines of creature-features, and songs about anything vaguely paranormal. She has also contributed chapters to *American Horror Story and Philosophy*, *Twin Peaks and Philosophy*, and *Stranger Things and Philosophy*. A Bachelor of Arts degree in psychology grants her delicious insight into real-world demons—although her favorite demon will forever be Sammy Winchester.

TRIP MCCROSSIN teaches in the Philosophy Department at Rutgers University where he works on the nature, history, and legacy of the Enlightenment in philosophy and popular culture. For better or for worse, promising that he can write a conventional syllabus is a bit like Lucifer promising he can make angels.

NUR BANU SIMSEK tries to steer clear of cities the Winchesters seem to frequent. That's why after getting her BA from the University of Chicago, she moved to the east coast to pursue her MA at the CUNY Graduate Center. When she isn't busy crying over a fallen angel who sacrificed himself for humanity, she can be found reading Plato, Aristotle, or a curated selection of works on AO3.

EMMA STEELE is Concertmaster with the Orchestra of the Danish Royal Theater in Copenhagen, Denmark. When she was born, a menacing yellow-eyed demon was hanging around, but her father kept reading aloud from *The Logic of Scientific Discovery*, and Old Yellow Eyes evidently got the wind up and skedaddled.

ANDREA ZANIN has a Law degree plus an Honors degree in English Literature (cum laude), and has contributed a bunch of chapters to previous Pop Culture and Philosophy titles—all tangential to the amount of time she spends reliving her childhood (OurFiresideStories.com) in an attempt to prove that Dean and Sam Winchester infiltrated suburban South Africa in the mid-nineties and soul-snatched her younger brothers, who were living their best lives: setting booby-traps, eating hamburgers, listening to metal and pounding one another. Andrea may have been skeptical of their potential at the time but is proud that "the boys" have gone on to save the world, more than once.

Index

Abadeen, 159
"Abandon All Hope" (episode),
    15, 86, 143
Abel, 159
Abraham, 12, 80, 155, 161, 193,
    198
Ackles, Jensen, 60
Adam, 8, 26, 157, 195, 198
Aerosmith, 44
Aeschylus, 83
Africanus, Julius, 198
"After School Special" (episode), 78
Alex; *see* Jones, Annie
"All Along the Watchtower"
    (episode), 92, 198–99
"All Hell Breaks Loose Part 1"
    (episode), 121
"All Hell Breaks Loose Part 2"
    (episode), 31, 61
Alzheimer's, 72
Amara, 49, 87–88, 93–94, 114,
    160, 169, 187, 193–95, 197,
    200
America, 23, 38, 42–43, 90
the Angel Tablet, 159
Apocalypse World, 94–95, 161
Aristotle, 124–25, 131–32,
    181–82, 184–85, 187;
    Nicomachean Ethics, 124,
    131
Armstrong, Karen: *A History of
    God*, 192, 193

Ashcroft, Anton, 201
Asherah, 193
Athena, 36
Athens, 179
"Atomic Monsters" (episode),
    200
Atwood, Margaret: *The
    Handmaid's Tale*, 151, 156;
    The Testaments, 156
Avengers: Endgame, 28, 197
Azazel, 40, 86, 87, 90–91, 119,
    121

Baby, 88, 92, 179–189
Back to the Future, 139
"Bad Boys" (episode), 30
Bad Boys (movie), 22–23
Bartholomew, 128
Bastian, Adolf, 39
Batman v Superman, 151
Bay, Michael, 22
Beat Generation, 43–44
"The Benders" (episode), 109
Benton, Doc, 55–63, 65–69, 73
Beowulf, 52
Berkeley, California, 73
Bevell, Lady, 90
Bible Belt, 48
Bildad, 153
Billie, 90, 129, 133
Biostasis Research Institute, 73

Blade Runner, 156
"Bloodlust" (episode), 105
Blue Öyster Cult, 78
Bon Jovi: "Wanted Dead or
   Alive," 24, 36
Book of Job, 153
Book of the Damned, 97
Boone, Josh, 151
"Born Under a Bad Sign"
   (episode), 57
Bradbury, Charlie, 97, 187
Brace, Patricia L.: "Mothers,
   Lovers, and Other Monsters,"
   86
Braeden, Ben, 29, 165
Braeden, Lisa, 29, 157, 165
The Bridgewater Treatises, 196
"Bring 'Em Back Alive" (episode),
   97
British Men of Letters, 80, 88,
   90, 91, 96, 161, 199
Buckmaster, Briana, 89
Burnett, Marcus, 23
Butters, Mrs., 93, 95–97

Cain, 80, 159, 160
Caird, G.B.: *New Testament
   Theology*, 192
Camat, Jamela: *Pandemic
   Theology*, 196
Campbell, Joseph, 48, 51; *The
   Hero with a Thousand Faces*,
   39, 45
Campbell, Mary; *see* Winchester,
   Mary
Canaanites, 193
Čapek, Karel: *The Makropulos
   Affair*, 63
Captain America, 197
"Captives" (episode), 88
"Carry On" (episode), 7, 9, 33,
   188
Carver, Jeremy, 157
Cas; *see* Castiel
Casey, 149
Cas; *see* Castiel
Castiel, 6, 9, 16, 27, 40, 43, 47,
   95, 113–14, 120, 121–134,

138, 141, 150, 161, 167, 170,
   180, 187, 191, 198–99
Cave, Steven: *Immortality*, 57
Cavell, Benjamin, 151
"Celebrating the Life of Asa Fox"
   (episode), 90, 120
Celia, 93
Charles I, King, 174
Charles II, King, 174
Chevy Impala, 40, 50, 88, 183;
   see also Baby
Chuck, 3–5, 6–9, 12–14, 17–18,
   20, 27–29, 36, 43, 47–49,
   88, 93–95, 114–16, 131–33,
   160–67, 169–177, 180, 187,
   191–202; *see also* God;
   Jahweh; Shurley, Edlund
"Citizen Fang" (episode), 29
the Colt, 22, 40, 56, 137
Connecticut Inn, 142
COVID-19, 72
"Croatoan" (episode), 137
Cromwell, Oliver, 174
"Crossroad Blues" (episode), 137,
   143
Crowley, 12, 17, 40, 49, 89,
   93–95, 113, 126, 130,
   157–59, 201

Dabb, Andrew, 160
"Dark Side of the Moon"
   (episode), 87, 150, 153, 200
the Darkness, 4, 22, 49, 57, 93,
   129, 160, 193, 195, 197
David, King, 192
Davis, John K., 70, 73
New Methuselahs (Davis), 70, 73
Detective Comics (DC), 11
de Grey, Aubrey, 72–73
Ending Aging, 73
"Dead Men Don't Wear Plaid"
   (episode), 89
Deckard, Rick, 156
Declaration of Independence,
   174
Def Leppard, 43
"Defending Your Life" (episode),
   86, 187

Demon Tablet, 159
Devil, 8
"Devil's Trap" (episode), 137,
    180
Dexter, 156
"Do You Believe in Miracles?"
    (episode), 49
Dodge, 49
"Don't Call Me Shurley"
    (episode), 27, 43
"Don't You Forget about Me"
    (episode), 89
Dostoevsky, Fyodor
    Mikhailovich, 23–29, 31–32;
    The Karamazov Brothers,
    23–24, 27–28, 30–31
Duke of York, 174

Earth, 6, 21–22, 24, 49, 61, 83,
    97, 107, 114, 116, 133, 153,
    156–57, 159, 166, 189,
    191–92, 197, 200
Edelman, Diana, 193
Edlund, Carver, 160
El Shaddai, 193
El, Canaanite God, 192–93
Eliphaz, 152
EM; *see* Makropulos, Elina
Emerson, Ralph Waldo, 44
the Empty, 165
English Civil War, 174
Erie, Pennsylvania, 56
Europe, 4, 96
Eve, 93, 195
"Everybody Loves a Clown"
    (episode), 181
Evil in Modern Thought
    (Neiman), 151

Farmer, Phillip José: *Venus on
    the Half-Shell*, 197
Fergus; *see* Crowley
Fischer, John Martin: *Death, Im-
    mortality, and Meaning in
    Life*, 57, 62
Fox, Asa, 120
Frankenstein, 24, 97, 151

French, Peter: *Cowboy
    Metaphysics*, 38
"Fresh Blood" (episode), 108, 139
Friedman, Richard Elliott: *Who
    Wrote the Bible?*, 193
"Funeralia" (episode), 94

Gabriel 9, 40, 128
Gadreel 97, 128, 195
Gamble, Sera, 157
Garner, Eric, 192
Garth, 201
Gautama, Siddhartha, 38
Genesis 17, 195
Genesis 6:1, 198
Geneva, 19
Ghostbusters, 75
Ghostfacers, 77
Ghostpocalypse, 162, 163
God, 3–8, 11–14, 17–18, 20,
    23–28, 32, 40, 48–49, 50, 57,
    80, 83, 86–87, 93, 94, 104,
    112, 115–17, 122, 138, 141,
    149–150, 152–161, 163–66,
    169, 170–72, 174, 176–77,
    191–98, 200–02
God after Darwin (Haught), 196
God of Israel, 193
Golem, 96
The Good Place, 62
Goodman, Alan, and Graves,
    Joseph L. Jr.: *Racism, Not
    Race*, 199
Gospel of John, 154
Goyer, David, 151
Grand Architect, 36
Graves, Joseph L., Jr.:
    "Naturalizing *Supernatural*,"
    202; *Voice in the Wilderness*
    197
Great Depression, 76
Gregory, Father, 149
Grim Reaper, 8
Grimsby, 71
Groundhog Day, 139

Hades, 40

Haine, Sam, 122
"Hammer of the Gods" (episode), 9
Hand of God, 160
Hannah, 128
Hanscum, Donna, 88–89
Harbin, China, 63
The Hardy Boys, 128
Harris, Thomas, 151
Harvelle, Ellen, 21, 22, 85–86, 88, 97, 143
Harvelle, Jo, 85, 86, 88, 143
Harvelle's Roadhouse, 85
Haught, John F., 195; *God after Darwin*, 196
"Heart" (episode), 86, 103
Heaven, 7, 17–18, 20, 27, 34, 40–41, 61, 93, 115–16, 123, 141, 154–55, 157–59, 160, 164, 189, 191, 194, 200
The Heavenly Host, 8
Hebrew Bible (*Tanakh*), 198
Hebrews, 194
Hegel, Georg, 44–48, 51
Hell, 7, 17–18, 21–22, 27, 40, 45, 55–56, 58–59, 60–61, 63, 65, 77, 83, 86, 94–95, 107, 115–16, 122, 130, 133, 137–38, 141–42, 144, 150, 154, 156–57, 159, 187–88, 201
Hell Gate, 21, 22
Hell Hounds, 150
"Hell House" (episode), 75, 79–80, 83
HellHoundsLair (website), 76–82
Hess, Dr., 90, 91
Hitler, Adolf, 201
Hogwarts, 90
Holy Spirit, 192
"Holy Terror" (episode), 195
"Home" (episode), 86, 89, 104, 137, 188
Homer: *Odyssey*, 42, 58, 83
"Hook Man" (episode), 78
Horus, 52
"Houses of the Holy" (episode), 24–25, 33, 149

Hutcheon, Linda, 42

Ice and Snow Festival, 63
"In My Time of Dying" (episode), 19, 137, 180
"In the Beginning" (episode), 87
"Inherit the Earth" (episode), 5, 6, 28, 48
Internet Movie Database, 142
Iron Man, 197
Isaac 12, 161

Jack, 6–9, 40, 50, 92, 93, 96, 113, 116, 121, 130, 131, 133–34, 161–63, 165–67, 186–202
Jack (character in *He Never Died*), 58
James II, King, 174
Janácek, Leoš, 63
Janesville, 182
Jefferson, Thomas, 174
Jehovah, 193
Jerusalem, 194
Jesus, 38, 154, 192
Jewish Sanhedrin, 192
Job, 150, 152, 155
Jones, Annie, 89
Joshua, 150, 153, 200
Journey: "Wheel in the Sky" 38
Jude 6, 198
Jung, Carl G., 37, 39–40, 49–51

Kansas: "Carry on Wayward Son," 47, 191
Kant, Immanuel, 87, 143, 150, 163
Karamazov, Alyosha, 24–27, 31, 32–33
The Karamazov Brothers/The Brothers Karamazov; *see* Dostoevsky
Karamazov, Dmitri, 24–26, 31–33
Karamazov, Fyodor, 24, 32
Karamazov, Ivan, 24–26, 31–33
Karamazov, Sofya, 25

Keel, Dana, 78, 80, 82
Kerouac, Jack: *On the Road*, 43
Ketch, Arthur, 91, 97
Kierkegaard, Søren 46, 51; *The Sickness unto Death*, 46
King, Stephen, 41, 151; *The Stand*, 151
Kline, Kelly, 92–93, 161, 199
Knight of Hell Abaddon, 95
Knights of Hell, 159
Krawczyk, Jason: *He Never Died*, 58
Kripke, Eric, 4, 23, 27, 29, 43, 85, 160, 163–64
Kripke's Hollow, Ohio, 4

Lance of Michael, 130
Lawrence, Kansas, 91
Lazarus of Bethany, 154–55
"Lazarus Rising" (episode), 27, 121, 149, 187, 200
Leahy, Eileen, 95
"Lebanon" (episode), 92
Lebanon, Kansas, 40, 88
Lecter, Hannibal, 151
Led Zeppelin, 43; "Ramble On," 42
Leibniz, Gottfried, 150
Leone, Sergio, 39
"Let It Bleed" (episode), 29
Levant, 193
Leviathans, 88, 97, 158, 187
Lilith, 87, 156
"Lily Sunder Has Some Regrets" (episode), 198
Locke, John, 174, 175, 176, 177; "Of the Dissolution of Government," 177; "Of Tyranny," 177; *Two Treatises of Government*, 174, 175
Loki, 14, 26
the Lone Ranger, 41, 44, 46
the Lord, 12, 27, 121–22, 124, 128, 158, 191
Love, Liam, 71, 72
Lowrey, Mike, 23
Lucifer, 8, 11–12, 15–17, 27, 80, 86, 88, 92, 94, 96, 115, 123–25, 129, 130, 138, 152, 156–57, 160–61, 164, 170, 180, 194–95, 199, 200
Luke 10:18, 198
Luke, Saint, 154
Lynyrd Skynyrd: "Simple Man," 49

Ma'lak Box, 120
MacLeod, Gavin, 94
MacLeod, Rowena, 17, 93–95, 97, 130, 187, 201
Madison, 103, 105
Makropulos, Elina, 63
The Makropulos Affair/The Makropolos Case, 63
"Malleus Maleficarum" (episode), 108, 139
"Mamma Mia" (episode), 180
"The Man Who Knew Too Much" (episode), 186
"The Man Who Would Be King" (episode), 196
Mark of Cain, 44, 94, 97, 159
Martha, 154
Marvel, 11, 197
Massachusetts General Hospital, 73
Masters, Meg, 57
The Matrix, 116
Meade, Michael: *The Genius Myth*, 36
Meg, 40, 57, 157
Metallica: "Some Kind of Monster," 35
Metatron, 3, 4, 8, 12, 128, 159–160, 162, 166, 169, 191–92, 200
Michael, Archangel, 4, 11, 12, 88, 95, 120, 157
Middleton, Celeste, 96
Milbank, John, 143
Miller, George, 151
Mills, Jody, 88–91, 97
Mills, Owen, 89
Milton, Anna 16, 123
Milton, John: *Paradise Lost*, 48

Mitchell, Stephen: *The Book of Job*, 152
"The Monster at the End of This Book" (episode), 3, 13
Moore, Jessica, 29, 40, 91
Moriarty, Sal, 185
Moseley, Missouri, 89
Mulder, Fox, 41, 45
Murdoch, Mordechai, 76–78, 69, 80–82
Murdock, Martin, 77–79

Nadia Codex, 97
Naomi, 159
Neiman, Susan, 150
Nephilim, 161, 198–99
New American Standard (Bible), 192
New Blood, 156
New Testament, 154
Nietzsche, Friedrich, 4–5, 7–9, 16–19, 117; *The Antichrist*, 17; *Beyond Good and Evil*, 17; *Ecce Homo*, 7; *The Gay Science*, 4–5, 7; *Thus Spake Zarathustra*, 7; *The Will to Power*, 17
"No Rest for the Wicked" (episode), 22, 24, 33
Noah, 198
Novak, Claire, 89, 123, 129
Novak, Jimmy, 123
Numbers 13, 198

Odysseus, 39, 42, 52, 58
"Oh Brother Where Art Thou?" (episode), 194, 197
Old Testament, 14, 150, 198
Osiris, 86
Oskar, 94
"Our Father Who Aren't in Heaven" (episode), 95

Paley, William: *Natural Theology*, 196
Paradise, 48, 116

Parliament, 174
Pepsi, 48
Perdition, 121
Peter 2, 198
Phalereus, Demetrius, 179
the Phoenix, 113
"Pilot" (episode), 86, 188
Plant, Robert, 44
Plato, 58, 81, 194; *Apology*, 58; *Republic*, 81, 83
"Playthings" (episode), 142
Plutarch, 179
"Point of No Return" (episode), 16
The Prindle Post, 9
"Prophet and Loss" (episode), 120
Propp, Vladimir, 39
Psalm 82, 192
Purgatory, 116, 158–59
"The Purge" (episode), 31
Putin, Vladimir, 201

Queen of Moondoor, 97

Raglan, Lord: *The Hero: A Study in Tradition, Myth, and Drama*, 37
Raphael, Archangel, 157
"The Rapture" (episode), 123
"The Rupture" (episode), 95
"Remember the Titans" (episode), 36
Revolution of 1688–1689, 174
Rice, Tamir, 192
Richard Roman Enterprises, 97
Richardson, Amelia, 29
Richardson, Texas, 75
Ridgway, Gary, 59
"Roadkill" (episode), 78
Rollins, Henry, 57
Roman Empire, 192
Rooney, Jefferson, 161
Rose, Axel, 44
Rousseau, Jean-Jacques, 19–20; *The Social Contract*, 19
Route 66, 42

Rowena; *see* MacLeod, Rowena
Ruby, 40, 104, 108

Salustius, 35
San Francisco, 77, 103
Sartre, Jean-Paul, 45–47
Satan, 4
Scooby Doo, 22
the Scribe of God, 3, 8
Scully, Dana, 41
SENS (Sensibly Engineered
   Negligible Senescence
   Research Foundation), 72
Shelley, Mary, 151
Ship of Theseus, 179
Shurley, Chuck, 3–6, 8–9, 12–14,
   17, 20, 27, 29, 36, 43, 47–49,
   88, 93–95, 114–16, 129, 131,
   133, 160, 161–67, 169,
   170–73, 176–77, 180, 187,
   191–92, 193, 195–97,
   199–202
Sider, Theodore, 185–87
Sides, Hampton, 42
"Simon Said" (episode), 106–07
"Sin City" (episode), 149
Singer, Bobby, 21–22, 28, 34, 40,
   61, 86, 88–89, 120–21, 126,
   140, 149, 150–52, 180, 181,
   187
Singer, Robert, 156
Sioux Falls, South Dakota, 88, 91
Sisyphus, 58
"Skin" (episode), 136
Skinner, Daniel, 71
Smerdyakov, Pavel Fyodorovich
   (character in *The Karamazov
   Brothers*), 24, 26, 31–32
the Smoking Man, 45
Snyder, Zack, 151
Socrates, 58, 81, 83
Solomon, King, 193
"The Song Remains the Same"
   (episode), 11, 12, 87
Sonny, 30
Soviet Union, 201
"The Spear" (episode), 186
Spengler, Harry, 77–81

Spinoza, Benedict, 14; *Ethics*, 14
Stalin, Joseph, 201
Star Trek, 85
Star Wars, 156
Stark, Tony, 28
Stetson, 48
Stillwater, Minnesota, 88
Styx, 39
Styx (band), 43
Supernatural and Philosophy
   (Foresman), 86, 202
"Swan Song" (episode), 47, 180,
   191–92

Talley, Jake, 138
"Taxi Driver" (episode), 61
Team Free Will, 6, 11, 27, 94,
   124, 127
Teddy, 142, 143
The Terminator, 66
Terrio, Chris, 151
Tessa, 19
Thanos, 197
"There's Something about Mary"
   (episode), 91
Theseus, 179, 181, 183, 184, 186
Thor, 197
Thule Society, 96, 161
Thurston, Craig, 76, 78, 80, 82
"Time Is on My Side" (episode),
   56, 73
"Torn and Frayed" (episode), 29
Tran, Kevin, 88, 144
Tran, Linda, 88, 144–45
the Trinity, 192
Trump, Donald J., 201
Turner, Patience, 89
Twin Peaks, 156
Twin Peaks: The Return, 156
Tyrell, Rachael, 156

Übermensch, 7
Union Jack, 68
University of Minnesota, 7

Variety, 85

Vernon, Mark, 38

Walker, Gordon, 105, 106, 108, 139
the Wendigo, 50
"What Is, and What Should Never Be" (episode), 47, 87
"What's Up, Tiger Mommy?" (episode), 88, 144
"When the Levee Breaks" (episode), 87
the White Knight, 52
"Who We Are" (episode), 33, 91
Williams, Bernard, 61, 62, 63, 64, 65, 68, 69, 71; *The Makropulos Case*, 63
Winchester Brothers, 3–6, 8–9, 12–13, 17, 20, 23, 26, 30, 35, 50, 86, 88–89, 92–97, 101, 103, 106–07, 110–13, 115–17, 119–122, 124, 126–133, 135, 136–37, 139–140, 141, 143, 169–171, 174, 180, 186–87, 191, 198–99, 200, 202
The Winchester Gospels, 191
Winchester, Dean, 4–9, 11–13, 15–16, 18, 20–33, 36–37, 40–41, 43, 44–48, 50–52, 55–62, 65–67, 69, 71, 72, 75–83, 86–97, 101–114, 116, 119–144, 149, 150–53, 155–167, 169, 171–72, 177, 180–81, 183, 185–89, 197, 199, 200–01
Winchester, John, 21, 25–26, 29, 40, 56, 61–62, 86–87, 90, 92, 119–120, 124, 136–37, 140, 143, 145, 154, 180, 185

Winchester, Mary, 22, 25, 29, 32–33, 86–93, 97, 113, 119, 129, 131, 138, 140, 154, 160–61, 187, 199
Winchester, Sam, 4, 6–9, 11, 13, 15, 18, 20–33, 36–37, 40–41, 43–46, 48, 50–51, 55–56, 58–60, 69, 75–76, 77–83, 86–91, 93–97, 101–114, 119–121, 123, 125–26, 128, 130–32, 135–144, 149–150, 153, 155–57, 159–165, 167, 169, 171–72, 177, 180–81, 183, 186–88, 199–201
"Wishful Thinking" (episode), 142
the Wizard of Oz, 97
Woman in White, 50
the Word of God, 159
World War II, 96

The X-Files, 41, 45, 149

Yahweh, 13, 192, 193
"Yellow Fever" (episode), 44
Yellow-Eyed Demon, 11, 21, 22, 32, 86, 106, 137–38, 140

Zachariah, 14–15, 87
Zechariah 5:5–11, 193
Zeddmore, Ed, 77–81
Zeus, 36
Zophar, 153
Zossima, Father (character in *The Karamazov Brothers*), 28, 30, 33–34

DAVE CHAPPELLE
AND PHILOSOPHY
WHEN KEEPING IT WRONG
GETS REAL

Edited by Mark Ralkowski

This book has not been prepared, authorized,
or endorsed by *Dave Chappelle.*

Dave Chappelle and Philosophy

When Keeping It Wrong Gets Real

VOLUME 1 IN THE OPEN UNIVERSE SERIES,
POP CULTURE AND PHILOSOPHY®

Edited by Mark Ralkowski

"Dave Chappelle. Truth-teller or out of touch? Progressive or retrograde? Timeless or tired? Feminist or misogynist? Ally or apologist? Iconic or infamous? The philosophers gathered here confront these questions and more, offering readers a deeper appreciation of Chappelle's art and a better understanding of Chappelle as an artist."

—SHEILA LINTOTT, Professor of Philosophy, Bucknell University

"Hunkered down in our various ideological bunkers, we live certain in our knowledge of who's on our side and who's the enemy. Dave Chappelle is unique in his ability to make us laugh while scrambling the lines, making everyone uncomfortable. This is also what good philosophy does. Put the two together and the result is this volume."

—STEVEN GIMBEL, author of *Isn't That Clever: A Philosophical Account of Humor and Comedy* (2020)

"This wonderful collection approaches Chappelle as 'the most talented comedian in the world' and humor as 'one of the most valuable things in life'. Explaining why we're drawn to Chappelle's comedy despite its flaws, this remarkable study of the value of comedy, its relationship with truth, and its ties with freedom succeeds in unraveling the unique job of comedy through a close and engaging analysis of a controversial phenomenon in contemporary culture."

—LYDIA AMIR, Tufts University, author of *The Legacy of Nietzsche's Philosophy of Laughter* (2021)

MARK RALKOWSKI is the editor of *Louis C.K. and Philosophy: You Don't Get to Be Bored* (2016) and *Curb Your Enthusiasm and Philosophy: Awaken the Social Assassin Within* (2012). He is the author of *Plato's Trial of Athens* (2018) and *Heidegger's Platonism* (2009).

ISBN 978-1-63770-002-0 (paperback)

ISBN 978-1-63779-003-7 (ebook)

For more information on Open Universe books, go to

www.carusbooks.com